Japanese
Social
Organization

Japanese Social Organization

Edited by
Takie Sugiyama Lebra

UNIVERSITY OF HAWAII PRESS
HONOLULU

93 94 95 96 97   5 4 3 2

Library of Congress Cataloging-in-Publication Data

Japanese social organization / edited by Takie Sugiyama Lebra.
    p.   cm.
Includes bibliographical references and index.
ISBN 0-8248-1386-3. — ISBN 0-8248-1420-7 (pbk.)
    1. Japan—Social conditions—1945-   2. Social structure—Japan
—History.   I. Lebra, Takie Sugiyama, 1930-
HN723.5.J3693   1992
306'.0951—dc20   92-3835
                                                    CIP

Designed by Janet Heavenridge

Contents

ACKNOWLEDGMENTS   vii
A NOTE ON JAPANESE NAMES   viii
FOREWORD
    Robert J. Smith   ix

Introduction
    Takie Sugiyama Lebra   1

Chapter 1
    CONFLICT, LEGITIMACY, AND TRADITION IN A
    TOKYO NEIGHBORHOOD
    Theodore C. Bestor   23

Chapter 2
    THE SPATIAL LAYOUT OF HIERARCHY:
    RESIDENTIAL STYLE OF THE MODERN JAPANESE
    NOBILITY
    Takie Sugiyama Lebra   49

Chapter 3
    CHRISTMAS CAKES AND WEDDING CAKES:
    THE SOCIAL ORGANIZATION OF JAPANESE WOMEN'S
    LIFE COURSE
    Mary C. Brinton   79

Chapter 4
    LIFE ON OBASUTEYAMA, OR, INSIDE A JAPANESE
    INSTITUTION FOR THE ELDERLY
    Diana Lynn Bethel   109

Chapter 5
    UNDER THE SILK BANNER: THE JAPANESE COMPANY
    AND ITS OVERSEAS MANAGERS
    Tomoko Hamada   135

Chapter 6
  DOING AND UNDOING "FEMALE" AND "MALE"
  IN JAPAN: THE TAKARAZUKA REVUE
  Jennifer Robertson   165

Chapter 7
  DEATH BY DEFEATISM AND OTHER FABLES: THE
  SOCIAL DYNAMICS OF THE RENGŌ SEKIGUN PURGE
  Patricia G. Steinhoff   195

CONTRIBUTORS   225
INDEX   227

Acknowledgments

Every publication owes thanks to many people, either known or unknown by the author, for their collaboration and support, and this anthology is no exception. Critiques on earlier drafts by reviewers were enormously helpful. I am in special debt to Professor Joseph Tobin for his thorough reading and for giving me incisive and yet kind comments. I am also grateful to the contributing authors for complying with requests for revisions and patiently waiting for the final product, and to Professor Robert J. Smith for managing the time to write the foreword.

Editorial work was partially funded by a Faculty Research Award from the University of Hawaii Japan Studies Endowment. James Roberson was more than an assistant in expediting the final stage of editing with his professional judgment, perfectionism, and bilingual expertise. Finally, I wish to express my gratitude to the highly motivated and competent staff of the University of Hawaii Press.

Takie Sugiyama Lebra

A Note on Japanese Names

According to established convention, Japanese names appear with family names first. Where a cited author has published in English, the name is given in Western order, surname last.

Foreword

ROBERT J. SMITH

People say that if you engage in an enterprise long enough, you may be lucky enough to gain some perspective on it. They are also inclined to observe that in all probability the gain in perspective will be offset in part by failing eyesight. I would counter with my own observation that, however dim, it is a perspective nonetheless, and the invitation to write a foreword to this volume affords me a rare chance to share some thoughts on edited collections of papers dealing primarily with Japanese society.

Although this collection of extraordinary papers is by no means the first to offer divergent views of that society, there can be no denying that its coverage is unprecedented. If memory serves —a risky assumption, given my opening lines—the first such volume appeared in 1946. It was edited by Douglas G. Haring, an anthropologist, and published by the Harvard University Press. Looking at the table of contents of *Japan's Prospect* today, one can only marvel at all that has happened in the intervening years to alter the intellectual landscape. Only a few of the papers are directly concerned with Japanese society; none of the contributions is by a Japanese. The reasons for these circumstances are not far to seek. The handful of American sociologists and anthropologists who were to become the first postwar generation of Japan specialists for the most part were just beginning their graduate studies, and so soon after the end of the war there was not the slightest likelihood that a Japanese scholar would be asked to contribute to such a volume.

Many other collections have been published in the intervening forty-five years, each differing more or less dramatically from its predecessors in conception and execution. Let me mention only four of them, chosen because they afford some perspective on the development of Japan Studies and the changing composition of its practitioners. In 1963, fifteen years after the publication of Haring's volume, Richard K. Beardsley and I edited a collection of papers originally presented at the Tenth

Pacific Science Congress in Honolulu. Published by the Wenner-Gren Foundation for Anthropological Research, it was entitled *Japanese Culture: Its Development and Characteristics*. The eighteen papers are grouped under four headings: archeological and linguistic origins, social structure, village organization, culture and personality. The congress sessions on Japanese society and culture were designed by Beardsley, who thought Honolulu the perfect place to bring together colleagues from Japan and the United States in order to give wider currency to the results of postwar research than they had enjoyed up to that time. Almost half the authors are Japanese. The coverage given to each topic, by American and Japanese participants alike, is highly normative, for we were concerned to offer information about the what, how, and why of things Japanese. The immediate postwar scholarship in Japan was overwhelmingly normative in its orientation simply because there was so little of it.

A decade later, in 1971, a wide-eyed collection of previously published material was edited by George K. Yamamoto and Tsuyoshi Ishida. Of the twenty papers in *Selected Readings on Modern Japanese Society*, published by McCutchan, one-third were written by Japanese scholars. Once again, the impulse was normative, and the editors explicitly state that the papers were chosen with a view to providing an overview of Japanese society.

Three years later, in 1974, Takie Sugiyama Lebra and William P. Lebra brought out an edited volume called *Japanese Culture and Behavior: Selected Readings*. Published by the University of Hawaii Press, it is, I think, the only book of readings on Japan ever to go into a second edition, which appeared in 1986. In both editions, Japanese authors account for about one-third of the twenty-three papers. In the first, the American authors' contributions by and large lay out the normative dimensions of various aspects of Japanese society and culture. Significantly, the bulk of the papers by Japanese scholars tend to deal with stress, deviancy, and corrective behavioral therapy. It is as though at this period of the development of the study of Japan such topics remained largely the purview of members of the society for whom the normative was simply a given. It is in the second edition, however, that one of the most significant developments in Japan Studies in the past twenty years is thrown into high relief. The editors have included seven papers by women, three of them Japanese. And now, we have the collection at hand, whose editor and all but one of whose contributors are women. Two are Japanese-born scholars who have made their careers in the United States.

I have gone into the issues of nationality and gender of authors not because I think that either characteristic necessarily dictates choice of research topic or the style of analysis of their papers. On the contrary, I think it obvious that the papers collected here demonstrate definitively that if such dictation was true in the infancy of Japan Studies, it no longer is the case. The research reported is of a dizzying variety, some touching on familiar topics presented in a startling new light. Most, however, is on topics so little explored until recently that they are not even mentioned in the earlier collections I have referred to. I can think of few readers in or out of Japan Studies who will fail to be instructed as they are introduced to the urban neighborhood newly understood, the members of the old peerage, the lives of women and the very elderly, the overseas company-manager, the all-female theatrical troupe, and the Japanese Red Army in the throes of self-destruction. Through these multiple lenses, the authors allow us to view a society of considerable complexity, variety, conflict, and dynamism. It is a characterization that cannot be made too often or too forcefully, and it is the signal contribution of this volume that its readers can never again fall into the error of thinking of contemporary Japan as invariant, homogeneous, and unchanging.

Introduction
Takie Sugiyama Lebra

It is widely known that a key to Japan's economic success lies in its human resources. I would go further to argue that the human capital of Japan is not inherent in individual qualities such as "workaholism," perseverance, talent, loyalty, or "group-mindedness." Rather, I claim that Japan's human capital is a product of the social arrangement of people that releases or inhibits their motivations, energy, and capacities. In other words, Japan's *human* capital is distinctly *social* capital. Scholars, as represented by Ronald Dore, have reminded the Western audience that Japan presents a viable alternative to the Western model of free economy guided by the price-competitive market. The Japanese market for goods and labor alike has been characterized by social terms such as "relational," "obligatory," "benevolent," "organization-oriented" (Dore 1973; 1987). To "the invisible hand," Dore (1983, 479) counterposes "the invisible handshake," a phrase he quotes from an economist.

This volume is intended to contribute to further understanding of Japan by focusing on its social-organizational features which, unlike its economy, are elusive to or hidden from outsiders and therefore call for analytical unraveling. Taken as a whole, the essays in this collection address how social organizations are constructed, reproduced, managed, disrupted, or transformed. Individuals are looked at primarily as involved in organizational activities, goals, and problems. They are seen as creative, manipulative, or constitutive of, as well as constrained by, various organizations.

This social focus also makes linguistic sense in view of the difficulty of translating the widely circulated terms that are considered to epitomize Japanese behavior or feeling, terms like *on, giri, enryo, amae.* Translation is difficult because these are socially contingent terms, irreducible to discrete attributes such as benevolence, obligation, reserve, and dependence. Amae, for example, signifies not simply dependency of one individual upon another but one's attitude of seeking or accepting dependence contingent upon another's presumed or signaled indulgence.

Cultural Symbols and Social Relations

The orientation toward social focus in this volume is two-fold. On the one hand, we look at a social organization from the standpoint of a system of symbols that are circulated by its constituents, through which they communicate with one another, and without which there could be no organization. Symbols, whether verbal utterances or other forms of representation, are not only to be interpreted in terms of their presumed or intended meanings, obvious or hidden, literal or metaphorical, but also to be produced and reproduced for communication. Social actors cannot avoid engaging in receiving and sending messages, decoding and encoding, or in a dramaturgical analogy, taking turns in the roles of audience and performer in a social theater. Symbols, whether subjectively interpreted or performatively produced, can create a world of their own, removed from or in opposition to other aspects of reality, as implied by the theater trope. Culture as a storehouse of such symbols is tapped to embellish, simplify, metaphorize, distort, or otherwise transform social reality. Through such cultural intervention, social organizations are strengthened or weakened, stabilized or disrupted, created or destroyed. The contributors to this volume pay much attention to the interrelationship between culture and social organization in this sense. The reader will see how Japanese, like any other people, tend to confuse symbol with reality, turn rhetoric into truth, manipulate metaphors as literal representations, either for the good or ill of collective life. To this extent we acknowledge having been inspired by symbolic anthropology associated with notable names like Clifford Geertz, Victor Turner, and Mary Douglas.

It would go against the purpose of this book, however, to accept symbologist, culturalist, or semiotic reductionism. Here we consider the second point of our orientation. Social reality, after all, includes an aggregate of human beings, with their bodies occupying physical space, exchanging energy with the environment, charged with emotions, vulnerable to sickness, and bound to die. The term *social organization* has been used to refer to such people's contacting and interacting with one another and forming relationships and networks. These relationships and interactions are defined and regulated by culture, to be sure, but they are not synonymous with or reducible to culture. I argue that the sense of social reality that keeps us from making such reduction complements the cultural apparatus and that the two together make up the whole of social organization. This balance between social reality and cultural apparatus is what keeps us, I believe, from temptations to overinterpret or overdramatize a symbol beyond a reasonable degree. It is my wish to restore the sociological perspective that has been abandoned by symbolic purists, without being trapped into a functionalist model.

The anticulturalist viewpoint is often taken by those who see reality in political economy, power, hegemonic structure, exploitation, and the like. Keesing states, "Where feminists and Marxists find oppression, symbolists find meaning" (1987, 166) and joins critics of Geertz's (1980) Negara in pointing out the absurdity of looking at nineteenth-century Bali as a theater state in disregard of its power structure. It should be acknowledged that, given the level of sophistication in contemporary social science as well as the intellectual climate sensitizing all of us to problematics of representation, one cannot simply dichotomize culturalists and realists, symbologists and political/economic structuralists, idealists and materialists. Nevertheless, debate goes on about which position should take precedence over another in terms of relevance, significance, causality, or commitment. For us, social reality is much broader than political economy, and it assimilates culture as an indispensable part of it. Our focus on social organization requires an integration of culture and power, symbolic representation and political reality. In my view, cultural capital and political/economic capital both flow through, and in turn build up or reproduce, social capital. I argue that reductionism in either direction, whether symbolic or political, ideational or economic, unreasonably dissociates us from the complexity of reality.[1] This book therefore aims at capturing *social* relations embodied by *human* beings whose existence and action inevitably depend on *symbol* processing.

The fact that Japan is a postindustrial, information-intensive, rapidly changing and diversifying society rules out the possibility of formulating a single structural model from which to generalize or singling out a "typical" organization. It would also be ridiculous to try to cover the whole spectrum of variation. As a compromise, this collection presents a number of diverse organizational units. It follows that this book is far from supporting the stereotypic image of Japanese society as a "harmonious," "orderly," "homogenous," "unitary" family, the image often attributed to the so-called *nihonjinron* (treatises on the Japanese as unique). It was my wish that each author present a conclusion on the subject on which I knew s/he had been working for years. Without hampering the authors' creativity by an imposed single editorial proposition, I only asked them to be innovative by presenting entirely new sets of data or new interpretations or looking into how an old and familiar organization is recast in a new one. With confidence I can say that every author has come up with an impressively or excitingly innovative essay.

In an innovative attempt, stereotypes that distort our sense of reality must be challenged, and the epistemological fallibility shared by every one of us must be acknowledged. But the main purpose of this collection is to present Japanese society from the vantage point of selected organizations in order to complement earlier studies by filling gaps rather than to dismantle them.[2] The reader will discern the volume's indebtedness to and connections with its predecessors. In other words, conventional views of Japan reenter anticonventional ones and harmony is interlaced with conflict, hierarchy with equality, order with disorder, collectivism with egocentrism. How such crisscrossing takes place is the main point of inquiry. We are not trapped in the rationalistic Western logic that places these contrasts into mutually exclusive categories of opposition.

The subjects range from a more representative unit like an urban neighborhood to an extreme case like a tiny revolutionary group; from the vanishing aristocracy to the current economic vanguard like a multinational company or to an institutional home for the elderly as a good sign of the rapid graying of Japan. While most chapters deal with social groups, one chapter focuses on the woman's life course as an organizational nexus. Another shift occurs when a stage of popular culture, an all-female theater, takes the reader's attention from workaday realms of life.

Space/Time Boundaries

To avoid redundancy, I refrain from summarizing chapters and rather let each chapter speak for itself. However, precisely because chapter topics are so varied, it is necessary to pull them together by some conceptual threads. In doing so, I cite selections from chapters for illustrations. I look for such threads in the pancultural basis of social organization, particularly space and time as regulators of social actors. There would be no organization without distributing and coordinating people and their actions over social terrains and schedules. Basic to social organization is "time-space zoning" (Giddens 1987), located by a common map and synchronized by a common calendar. Social organization presupposes requiring or prohibiting a simultaneous occupancy of certain spaces by certain categories of people in certain frequencies, intervals, or durations. It should be also noted that all ethnographic studies are conditioned by particular zones—specific sites, fields, or settings, with a historical time span with a beginning and ending.

This universal requirement of zoning adds a local color when applied to Japan. Actually, this concept of zoning is quite pertinent to a characterization of Japanese social organization where the idea of *boundary* stands out. The saliency of *"ba"* (place or situation) in Japanese social life has been recognized by many scholars, notably Nakane (1967b). More recently, Linhart (1986)[3] gave an interesting analysis of *sakari*ba amusement quarters where overworked commuters stop on their way home from work for a temporary "evaporation." "Ba" is characteristically well-bounded in space and/or time, as suggested by the English translation of Nakane's "ba" as "frame" (1970). If the Western way of thinking and acting presumes the structural opposition of mind and body, subject and object, transcendental and mundane, true and false, it appears that Japanese are more guided by the social binary of *uchi* (inside) and *soto* (outside) or *ura* (rear) and *omote* (front). The social boundary gives rise not only to insiders and outsiders, but to core and peripheral members and to marginals or liminals who are neither insiders nor outsiders or are both.

The spatial boundary is contingent upon the temporal one, making it difficult to distinguish the two, but it will be noted that there is differential emphasis among the authors. I begin with the spatial dimension, then shift to the time dimension, and end where the two dimensions merge into one.

In Chapter 1, Theodore Bestor describes a densely populated neighborhood in Tokyo that he calls Miyamoto-chō in association with its symbolic center, the local shrine *(miya)*, with spatial boundaries from adjacent neighborhoods. The spatially bounded division of neighborhoods *(chō)* is a basic social unit that is integrated into larger and higher-order units of organization. Miyamoto-chō is part of Shinagawa ward *(ku)*, which in turn is among the twenty-three special ku of Tokyo-*to*, the capital prefecture. While ku and to are administrative, coercive units headed by their respective governments, chō is not. Thus Miyamoto-chō, or its association, called *chōkai*, is in ambivalent relationship with the ku (or higher) government and its agencies: the former is dependent upon the latter which for its part uses the chōkai as a liaison between the government and citizens, but at the same time the chōkai strongly and successfully resists the government's tampering with its unofficial boundary.

In wider space, Miyamoto-chō places itself in *shitamachi* (downtown), because it is characterized by the densely packed streets of small, family-owned shops-cum-residences, not because its history goes back to the Tokugawa period when the new shogunal capital, then called Edo, was divided between a narrow strip of reclaimed bay area allocated for the merchant/artisan class and a vast uptown area, *yamanote,* reserved for the warrior class. (For the yamanote-shitamachi opposition, see also Dore 1958; Seidensticker 1983; Wagatsuma and DeVos 1984; Kondo 1990; Chapter 2, this volume). In today's Tokyo, the shitamachi-yamanote boundary is, geographically speaking, fuzzy or almost nonexistent, but it survives symbolically because it carries the historical meaning of class boundary, the samurai having been replaced by modern white-collar commuters and professionals. It is interesting to note that social classes are thus translated into spatial terms, an identification indicative of the common Japanese practice of using spatial tropes to designate persons and their statuses.

Spatial representation of hierarchy is the central topic of Chapter 2, where the residential lifestyle of the modern aristocracy, called *kazoku,* is portrayed. A product of imperial Japan, this group, abolished under the postwar constitution, is surviving only in the fading memory of descendants and in cryptic, shrinking existence. My chapter focuses on the spatial arrangement of the residential domain, as recalled by surviving informants. Kazoku decidedly belonged, and still largely do, to the choice areas of Tokyo's yamanote, and thus complement the shitamachi-like feature of Miyamoto-chō residents. Neighborhood hardly entered the aristocratic way of life in any significant way. These contrasts notwithstanding, one can find some duplication, particularly where Bestor lays out the spatial hierarchy of the meeting hall to determine seating arrangement for the formal gathering of residents— the very point I elaborate in the aristocratic version. The crux of the second chapter lies in the design of the domestic space as symbolic of the intrahousehold hierarchy.

Three spatial oppositions emerge: above versus below, front versus rear, and interior versus exterior. Residents of a household (the family and retinue) and guests were assigned to quarters differentiated by various permutations of these oppositions, according to their ranks, roles and functions, and very importantly, gender. The chapter looks into the interrelationships among those who occupy different spaces.

Diana Bethel, the author of Chapter 4, lived as a participant-observer for fifteen months with residents of a municipal home for the elderly in Hokkaido. The chapter begins with the legendary space called Obasuteyama, the mountain where the economically burdensome aged parents were abandoned to die. How this horrible association, initially held by the home entrants, is managed through various symbolic resources is the focal theme of this chapter. Contiguity, distance, and boundary are created spatially and architecturally within the home or in the home's relation to the world outside. These matters enter the mental construction of social units and subunits ranging from the entire home community to smaller mini-neighborhoods down to room-sharing "families." To be noted is the keen sense held by the residents of the spatial demarcations between inside and outside, or private and public realms. Nonetheless, there is no real private space or true "interior" here for individual residents hidden from public surveillance.

The home residents try to build a family out of strangers. The "family" here has nothing to do with the tradition of the *ie*, the stem-family household (which will be discussed at the end of

this introduction), since intergenerational separation and discontinuity are essential features of institutionalized aging. It is a loose,
joint family more in the sense of constant copresence of residents.
Closer correspondence is found between this "home" and Bestor's
neighborhood: both involve lateral more than lineal relationships
without, however, precluding a hierarchy. Similarity goes further:
a family/community is forged out of strangers in the home, while a
"traditional" neighborhood is created out of a new one in Miyamoto-chō. Both organizations are created through symbolic manipulation.

Chapter 5 extends our spatial scope to and beyond the
national boundary. Today, internationalization is a catchword,
foreigners are employed, international schools are thriving, home-
stay and other exchange programs are under way, multinational
conferences are mushrooming, interracial marriage is no longer
an anomaly, legal and illegal immigration is taking place. Japanese and non-Japanese are sharing more and more of the same
space-time zones so that it is no longer possible for a Japanese to
avoid encounters with foreigners entirely. The situation confounds
most Japanese, whether they are generous hosts for foreign guests
and/or avid consumers of foreign products or, conversely, defend-
ers of the national boundary and/or racial "purity." This latter
attitude escalates the foreigners' perceptions of Japan as a racist
country. It seems that the uchi-soto boundary is sharpest here at
this national level. Against this background, Tomoko Hamada
brings the multinational business organization to light, coming
closest to what is one of the most urgent issues today in international relations—trade barriers.

Japanese businesses are expanding their operations on a
global scale to their multifarious advantage by setting up overseas
subsidiaries, with a sharp surge in the amount and directness of
investment in the 1980s. Hamada locates such transplanted overseas companies in the intercorporate grouping called *keiretsu,* a
term that has gained notoriety in the international business community. The keiretsu organization, to put it in spatial terms, combines horizontal and vertical space so that the centrifugal spread
from the inner core (head company) to outer peripheries (subsidiaries and *their* subsidiaries) corresponds to the multilayered hierarchy, even though member companies are legally independent of
one another. In this system the overseas assignee may become

marginalized; his hope of being recalled to the head office dimin-
ishes; eventually, he may be forgotten and "dumped" in the foreign land.

Thus far I have applied spatial zoning as a common
thread to pull together four chapters. I have suggested how the
notion of spatial boundary is stressed, elaborated, or sharpened as
a basis for defining, building, stabilizing, or expanding social
organization. This tendency to spatialize human relations may be,
conversely, the result of a tendency to see human existence in
terms of social relationships. In this respect I should refer to a Japanese philosophical tradition represented by Watsuji Tetsurō
which, according to Yuasa (1977), recognizes the importance of
space for Japanese as a corollary of their notion of the human
being *(ningen)* as "being between persons" *(aidagara)*. Aidagara
posits space between persons. Yuasa extends Watsuji's idea of
space to explain the importance of the body for the Japanese self in
opposition to the Cartesian dualism of mind and body in which
the mind, with its transcendental status, is equated with the self.
The spatial focus in Japanese philosophy is opposed to the Cartesian emphasis upon "time," the flow of which is essential to the
operation of the autonomous mind. The primacy of space over
time, in Yuasa's interpretation, implies the recognized significance of the body, or the indivisibility of body and mind. While
the mind itself can be conceptualized through time, the body-
mind must be situated in space.

My only reservation with Yuasa's argument is that space
and time are difficult to separate in Japanese social organization.
And I contend this difficulty has much to do with the notion of
time itself, which imitates the spatial model. Like space, time *(toki)*
is conceptualized, when applied to social organization, in terms of
boundaries or frames, rather than in terms of infinite continuity,
whereas time for the autonomous mind may be devoid of such
boundaries.

This philosophical footnote prompts us to move from
space to time for organizational zoning, however difficult it is to
separate one from the other. Various time spans, cycles, historical
periods, or daily schedules are dealt with by every author. But
Mary Brinton, above all, takes the time boundary, particularly the
life course, as the central organizing frame. Inseparable from any
perspective of life span is age which, like gender, is a universally

recognizable factor that enters social organizations. Japan, more than most other industrialized countries, is known as a society in which age is important as a determinant of one's social status and identity. Age grading does not necessarily mean social stability or gerontocracy. A sharp sense of generation gaps, accompanied by the keenly felt age-peer identity, prevails among Japanese today. Bestor shows how age and generational divisions are played up in forming conflicting subgroups in the neighborhood community. All this demonstrates the perception of age as determining where one belongs. It makes much sense, then, to look at Japanese social organizations from the viewpoint of age, generation, and life stages.

Brinton, in Chapter 3, focuses on women's life course in Japan and the United States under the implicit assumption that the female life course is mirrored by the male. She takes three time-relevant key concepts to characterize life transitions that involve entering or leaving social institutions such as education, family, marriage, the labor market. These concepts are "spread" (the span of time taken by a portion of a population to make a transition), "reversibility" (the option to reverse entry and exit from institutional positions), and "age-congruity" (the simultaneous holding of multiple roles or statuses). Through several graphic representations of demographic data, we learn that Japanese and American women are quite different in these three dimensions of the life course. Brinton's analysis gives new insight, for instance, into the familiar M-shaped distribution of Japanese women's labor force by age.

Inseparable from the Japanese life course is a set of "stakeholders," that is, those who have a stake in pulling or pushing others in and out of social positions, in regulating their life transitions in terms of timing and directions. Among critical stakeholders are parents, teachers, employers, and the like. If parents are such stakeholders, the children in turn constrain their parents' life courses. In other words, time enters social organization in coordinating the life schedules of two or more generations. This is an important point connecting Brinton's chapter to Hamada's. Given an overseas assignment (even a domestic relocation), the transferee often goes as *tanshin funin* (the employee alone, unaccompanied by his family), a situation that makes such an appointment all the more stressful. The commonly given reason for the wife's refusal to join him is that a child's education is at a critical juncture and must not be disrupted by school transfer.

These two chapters also pose a suggestive contrast in career predictability as another aspect of the time frame. While Brinton describes the Japanese woman's life course as very structured by comparison with the American counterpart, Hamada (Chapter 5) portrays the man's career, subject to the authority of the top level of the keiretsu, as demoralizingly unpredictable, even though transfers are almost certain, even unavoidable in the Japanese career track. The difference derives partly from the different stages of life focused on and partly from the different categories of people studied (overseas male employees versus the domestic sample of women). In addition, I want to emphasize two different camera angles in looking at career predictability or unpredictability. Brinton looks at it objectively and externally using impersonal, quantitative, and cross-cultural data, while Hamada goes into the subjective data that comes directly from her informants.

This methodological difference throws light upon another important difference in career patterns. Americans are supposed to build and execute their own career plans, whereas for Japanese the career plan is constructed by and embedded in the social organization. Careers or life courses can thus be predictable or unpredictable in both societies but for opposite reasons: a career may be haphazard for an American because it is supposed to be an individual matter beyond organizational planning, whereas a Japanese may find his/her career unpredictable because it is beyond individual control and subject to organizational decisions (see Plath 1983; Noguchi 1990).[4]

One life stage or another is touched upon in other chapters as well in conjunction with spatial boundaries. Sexual maturation is particularly significant in this respect. In Chapter 6, Jennifer Robertson discusses the Takarazuka Revue, an all-female theater often regarded as the female counterpart of the all-male Kabuki, with special attention to the gender boundary. Sex segregation is enforced not only upon students of the Takarazuka Academy, who are subject to the Spartan discipline of the spatially bounded dormitory life with its strict curfew, but also upon its graduates and performers in full adulthood. In other words, Takarazuka women as a whole, regardless of their chronological age, are categorized as *shōjo,* "heterosexually inexperienced females between puberty and marriage." Only after retirement can they become heterosexually involved, and they are expected to marry. The reader will learn from Robertson's discourse analysis how this extreme control of the sexual, premarital life schedule is counteracted by actors and fans asserting their sexuality and forming lesbian alliances. Central in this process is the contradictory double role of the idolized "male" actor who goes through the spatially defined role switch between her on-stage male "gender" as a cultural construct and her off-stage female "sex" as a natural attribute.

Pre- and postpubescent segregation is also discussed in Chapter 2 as it was imposed upon boys beginning at age seven (in old counting) and lasting until their marriage. The interior-exterior demarcation of the domestic space symbolized a sexual barrier between young, unmarried sons and maids; in some cases this demarcation involved a daily cycle of shifting between the two regions.

The life course issue today cannot bypass the extraordinary lengthening of life expectancy in Japan, an increase that has given rise to new problems of aging likely to alter the life course pattern characterized in Chapter 3. Bethel highlights old age as a natural step forward from where Brinton has left off. Life in the home goes on over well-marked space and time zones shared by its inhabitants. The residents are not only grouped into one single category of elderly as distinguished from the younger population outside but are internally graded, we are told, by age and seniority. Here, too, a strict schedule governs the daily cycle. The resident sooner or later must face the last phase of life in the home, nursing home, or hospital. Ironically, death reunites some residents with their original families: the corpse returns where it properly belongs to be buried in the family grave and enshrined at the family altar. For other residents, the home provides its own grave and altar. This world and the next world, or predecessors and contemporaries, are connected through the Buddhist altar, with survivors reclaiming the tradition of ancestor cult, however unsatisfactorily. We are reminded that transcendental time for Japanese is bound to connections with the dead and ancestors, a point to reappear below when the ie is discussed.

The last chapter, by Patricia Steinhoff, presents the most dramatic amalgam of space and time, location and tempo, isolation and momentum. Chapter 7 is her latest research outcome on the Rengō Sekigun (the United Red Army) wherein she reconstructs the group's organizational process and shows how it leads toward the astonishing climax of the group's self-destruction. The author attributes this incident to manifold interactions between pan-human social psychology and group dynamics, the particular collective and individual histories, and Japanese culture. What happened to the Sekigun reminds us of many other group phenomena that have drawn attention elsewhere as well as in Japan: brain washing, consciousness raising, programming in cults, some psychotherapies, other forms of resocialization. When contextualized in the cultural background of Japan, the general group dynamic is given, it seems, an additional spurt.

Spatial seclusion of the group was essential to ensure immunity from external intervention. That the mountain camp was not only an isolated system but one without an exit made the collective oppression deadly. In time, this micro space was divided into two spaces: inside and outside the cabin, the latter for victims of interrogation. What makes this chapter breathtaking is the momentum of group dynamics in which each brutal action against a singled-out individual unleashes another more atrocious example of the tyranny of group power.[5]

In closing this section, I interject my opinions about the time dimension as dealt with in the following chapters. The time span varies from a single dramatic event, as in Steinhoff's chapter on the Sekigun, to longer spans. The authors pay attention to the history of the time before their research. Beginning with the Meiji Restoration (1868), several critical events have marked transitions in Japanese history. The event probably most often mentioned by contemporary Japanese is the end of World War II (1945), which marked the transition between prewar *(senzen)* and postwar *(sengo)*. My chapter refers to the aristocratic lifestyle as it was recalled to have existed in prewar times, and Robertson emphasizes the prewar Takarazuka history along with its postwar legacy and change. The other chapters focus primarily on the late postwar era down to 1990 while connecting it to historical antecedents or transitions. Bestor describes the current features of the neighborhood that came into existence only after the 1923 earthquake that shook the Kanto region—another event still recalled by older Japanese as something that altered "everything" in Japan overnight. Further, we might add that modern Japanese frame their generational identities and discrepancies by the names of imperial reigns— Meiji (1868–1912), Taishō (1912–1926), Shōwa (1926–1989), and now Heisei (1989–)—since their birth years as well as common calendars are dated by these reign names.

Change is to be taken for granted, but it is not to be confused with a linear progression toward "convergence" with the Western model. Brinton's comparative data defies the convergence hypothesis. Against the popular idea, held by many Japanese and by many Americans as well, that Japanese women are becoming more and more like their American sisters, the two groups of women are found to have been more alike decades before the 1980s, when Brinton's work was done. Note the comparative trends in the woman's age at first childbirth, divorce rates, proportion of married students, career continuity. The speed and amplitude of change among Americans is striking, while Japanese have not changed as much or have changed in a reverse direction.

But the cultural inertia theory should not be overstated. Bestor, for example, argues that the continuity of "tradition" was not a historical fact of Miyamoto-chō but a rhetoric used to legitimize one vested interest against another. He thus differentiates tradition from "traditionalism." I subscribe to the viewpoint that culture does not survive so much in inertia as in renewal for new purposes and in a new format.

Further, it may be that traditionalism serves not only the vested *interest* of some quarters of society but the individual's *identity* at a more existential level of selfhood. When the world around is perceived as unpredictably changing, it is only natural for a person to compensate by connecting him/herself to something immutable, something beyond here and now. The ie, which used to provide a base for a sense of transgenerational perpetuity, is no longer a viable institution, as we have seen through the home for the elderly, which disconnects one generation from the next. Meanwhile, the information-centered technological revolution is cresting, and waves of internationalization are surging, swallowing young and old, rich and poor alike. Although at a much more tardy pace, the feminist tide is also threatening the old order based on male supremacy and role division by gender. In reaction, there are signs that some Japanese are coping by rediscovering, renewing, or reconstructing things old, traditional, or "ancient"; these are often conveniently integrated into tourist programs, whether an old village community, a Tokugawa-period merchant's house, a feudal castle, or a shrine. Popular historical dramas on television continue to depict the old gender hierarchy in a nostalgically idyllic form. It seems that communal or national ancestors are displacing ie ancestors in a general effort to counterbalance change and discontinuity. National ancestry for Japanese is inseparable from the imperial house and lineage. Here the simplistic dichotomy between prewar and postwar Japan breaks down, and the content of each chapter will be found to extend beyond its primary time span backward or forward, into the prewar or postwar period.

Japanese are handling this complicated situation in a usual way, by marking a spatial and/or temporal boundary between old and new, change and durability. Symbolic of such management was the double funeral ceremony for the Shōwa emperor and the double enthronement of the Heisei emperor. One part of the ceremony in both cases consisted of Shintō-fashioned, "ancient" court rituals defined as a private, inner affair of the imperial family but which at the same time symbolized the prewar empire of Japan. The other part was presented as a public, outer event of the state consisting of secularized rituals in accordance with the postwar constitution mandating the separation of the state and religion.

The Ie Revisited

No discussion of Japanese social organization would be complete without some reference to the ie. We have a rich legacy of ethnographic literature in both English and Japanese on the Japanese family. This being the case, it was not deemed necessary to devote a chapter of this volume specifically to the subject. Nevertheless, for those unfamiliar with the literature, I will conclude this introduction with a few remarks on this important social institution.

Like many other prewar institutions, the ie was abolished as a legal unit by enactment of the post–World War II civil code formulated under the Allied Occupation's "democratizing" policy. Nevertheless, the ie still survives as a cultural unit, and does so even as a definite social entity among some parts of the population (see Hamabata's [1990] elite business family for example). It would be difficult to find a single academic study on Japanese social structure that does not mention the ie. Some scholars— including Kawashima (1949); Nakane (1967a); Murakami, Kumon, and Sato (1979)—have gone as far as to characterize Japan itself as an ie-society in the sense that the ie is the most basic unit and penetrates Japanese society or is replicated in many other organizations. In this introductory chapter alone, I could not help mentioning ie several times. Here I reformulate the ie in terms of space and time.

The ie as a household with a residential locus is spatially bounded in terms of uchi and soto, and in fact the term *ie* is oftentimes used interchangeably with uchi. The spatial boundary, which, if taken alone, may be more or less transcultural, is made more culturally loaded when it is locked with the time frame. Indeed, it is our ethnographic legacy (notably Befu 1962, Nakane 1969, Pelzel 1970) to characterize the ie as an indivisible corporate entity to be perpetuated independently of its human composition (i.e., the family, or kinship, here and now). In this view, the ie has its own identity and goal, whether as a political, economic, occupational, social, or religious organization. Bachnik (1983) goes further in this direction when she replaces the kinship model with that of "positional succession," a term borrowed from Kitaoji (1971), in which the indiscriminate practice of successor adoption in Japan makes perfect sense. Succession is to ensure the ie's perpetuation over future generations, but its transcendental rationale comes from the past, from generations of ancestors. The ie is thus grounded in the cult of ancestors and the dead, reproduced through ancestor rites, and embodied by such ancestor symbols as tablets, household shrines, and graves (see Smith 1974 for a detailed study of ancestor worship).

Successional continuity of the ie is in a single line, represented by one successor couple (or one househead) per generation, a practice that rules out the ideal of joint family as in traditional China. This unigenitural rule, however, does not preclude the formation of *dōzoku*, a group of ie composed of the *honke* or *sōke* (main, original house) and its *bunke* (branch, satellite houses) established by the honke head's nonsuccessor son (or adopted son) and hierarchically organized and tied together in mutual obligations. A dōzoku may be as small as the honke plus a few bunke but is expandable over time into a large multilayered organization topped by the superhonke commanding many branches and sub-branches. The importance of dōzoku in understanding Japanese society, particularly its ie and village organizations, can be marked by the large number of publications on this subject from various points of view (to mention a few: Ariga 1966; Befu 1963; Brown 1966, 1988; Cornell 1964; Johnson 1976; Kitano 1962; Nakano 1964). Far from being outmoded, a loose version of dōzoku can form the core of a present-day business corporation, often called a *dōzoku-g/kaisha*. The ie perpetuation comes under additional pressures if it is surrounded by dōzoku, and especially if it is the honke.

The dōzoku may be regarded as a prototype or model for many other organizations, among which stands out the organization of the *iemoto,* schools of traditional arts and crafts (tea ceremony, flower arrangement, dance, music, calligraphy, ceramics, etc.). The iemoto school, headed by its grand master, a putative descendant of the original founder (also called iemoto), is expected not only to continue over time through succession but to expand spatially through certified students setting up branch schools. It can form a huge pyramid combining educational and commercial purposes.[6] The lineage-like structure of iemoto, in which Francis L. K. Hsu (1975) saw the "heart" of Japan, is replicated by a variety of contemporary social organizations including religious cults, academic or political factions, the corporate organization of keiretsu (the subject of Chapter 5). In short, the ie and its extensions—dōzoku and iemoto—constitute a cultural set of models available to or encumbering social organizers. Social organizations described in this volume may be understood in the context of or in opposition to these models.

Notes

1. It is ironic that David Schneider, as one of such purists, was a Parsonian, considering that Parsons' systemic sociology would preclude any sort of reductionism including Schneider's (1968, 1969) cultural reductionism.

2. To pursue the same point, I might add that stereotyping is to be blamed not only on those ill-informed, simplistic, biased observers

appealing to popular audiences who look for a sweeping answer to a complicated question, but on those critics as well who specialize in discrediting earlier serious studies by stereotyping them to the point of absurdity. I would argue that along with nihonjinron there should be *nihonjinron-ron* (treatises on nihonjinron) on agenda.

3. Linhart's is one of the papers focused on space and time that appeared in Hendry and Webber 1986.

4. Debates on Japanese culture and society—such as harmony versus conflict, groupism versus individualism, homogeneity versus heterogeneity—may be in part reducible to methodological differences such as distance between observer and observed, units of analysis (micro versus macro), comparative references (cross-cultural, historical), and so on.

5. The Red Army also had a sexual agenda to deal with because it was a heterosexual group, including a woman coleader. Even though men and women were sleeping next to each other, sexual abstinence was enjoined, and sexual "crime" was exposed. All this brings sexual prohibition versus freedom, and heterosexuality versus homosexuality—the issues raised by Robertson—into another perspective. It may be that feminism is allied with heterosexuality in two opposite directions: on the one hand, advocacy of free love and free sex against sexual segregation, arranged marriage, or monogamous rule, and on the other, immunity from erotic impulse itself. One viewpoint sees heterosexual access as an expression of woman's freedom, and the other takes heterosexual involvement as detrimental to the feminist cause. In view of this polarization, Robertson's argument on lesbianism may be taken as a third alternative that combines sexual freedom and rejection of heterosexual dependency.

6. For insightful information on the iemoto I owe a debt to Christine Yano's (1990) paper, in which she spells out how two criteria, achievement and ascription, converge and negotiate with each other in various dimensions of the iemoto organization.

References

Ariga Kizaemon. 1966. "Nippon kazoku seido to kosaku seido" (The Japanese family system and tenancy). In *Ariga Kizaemon chosa-kushū* (Collected works of Ariga Kizaemon). Vols. 1 and 2. Tokyo: Miraisha.

Bachnik, Jane. 1983. "Recruitment Strategies for Household Succession: Rethinking Japanese Household Organization." *Man* 18:160–182.

Befu, Harumi. 1962. "Corporate Emphasis and Patterns of Descent in the Japanese Family." In *Japanese Culture: Its Development and Characteristics*, edited by R. J. Smith and R. K. Beardsley. Chicago: Aldine Publishing Co.

————. 1963. "Patrilineal Descent and Personal Kindred in Japan." *American Anthropologist* 65:1328–1341.

Brown, Keith. 1966. "Dōzoku and the Ideology of Descent in Rural Japan." *American Anthropologist* 68:1129–1151.

————. 1988. "The Stem-Family: Consanguinity and Descent Redefined." Paper presented at the annual meeting of the Association for Asian Studies, March 25–27, San Francisco.

Cornell, John B. 1964. "Dōzoku: An Example of Evolution and Transition in Japanese Village Society." *Comparative Studies in Society and History* 6:449–480.

Dore, Ronald. 1958. *City Life in Japan: A Study of a Tokyo Ward*. Berkeley: University of California Press.

————. 1973. *British Factory, Japanese Factory: The Origins of National Diversity in Industrial Relations*. Berkeley and Los Angeles: University of California Press.

————. 1983. "Goodwill and the Spirit of Market Capitalism." *British Journal of Sociology* 34:459–482.

————. 1987. *Taking Japan Seriously: A Confucian Perspective on Leading Economic Issues*. Stanford, Calif.: Stanford University Press.

Geertz, Clifford. 1980. *Negara: The Theatre State in Nineteenth-Century Bali*. Princeton, N.J.: Princeton University Press.

Giddens, Anthony. 1987. *Social Theory and Modern Sociology*. Stanford, Calif.: Stanford University Press.

Hamabata, Matthews Masayuki. 1990. *Crested Kimono: Power and Love in the Japanese Business Family*. Ithaca, N.Y., and London: Cornell University Press.

Hendry, Joy, and Jonathan Webber, eds. 1986. *Interpreting Japanese Society: Anthropological Approaches*. JASO (Journal of the Anthropological Society of Oxford) Occasional Papers, no. 5. Oxford.

Hsu, Francis L. K. 1975. *Iemoto: The Heart of Japan*. Cambridge, Mass.: Schenkman.

Johnson, Erwin. 1976. *Nagura Mura: An Ethnohistorical Analysis*. Cornell University East Asia Papers, no. 7. China-Japan Program, Cornell University.

Kawashima Takeyoshi. 1949. *Nippon shakai no kazoku-teki kōsei* (The family-modeled construction of Japanese society). Tokyo: Gakuseishobō

Keesing, Roger. 1987. "Anthropology as Interpretive Quest." *Current Anthropology* 28:161–169.

Kitano, Seiichi. 1962. "*Dozoku* and *Ie* in Japan: The Meaning of Family Genealogical Relationships." In *Japanese Culture: Its Development and Characteristics*, edited by R. J. Smith and R. K. Beardsley. Chicago: Aldine.

Kitaoji, Hironobu. 1971. "The Structure of the Japanese Family." *American Anthropologist* 73:1036–1057.

Kondo, Dorinne K. 1990. *Crafting Selves: Power, Gender, and Discourses of Identity in a Japanese Workplace*. Chicago: University of Chicago Press.

Linhart, Sepp. 1986. "*Sakariba:* Zone of 'Evaporation' between Work and Home." In *Interpreting Japanese Society: Anthropological Approaches*, edited by J. Hendry and J. Webber. JASO (Journal of the Anthropological Society of Oxford) Occasional Papers, no. 5. Oxford.

Murakami Yasusuke, Kumon Shumpei, and Satō Seizaburō. 1979. *Bunmei to shite no ie shakai* (The ie society as a civilization). Tokyo: Chūōkōronsha.

Nakane, Chie. 1967a. *Kinship and Economic Organization in Rural Japan*. London: Athlone Press.

———. 1967b. *Tateshakai no ningen kankei* (Human relations in a vertical society). Tokyo: Kodansha.

———. 1969. *Kazoku no kōzō: shakai jinruigaku-teki bunseki* (The family structure: A social-anthropological analysis). Tokyo: Tokyo Daigaku Tōyō Bunka Kenkyūjo.

———. 1970. *Japanese Society*. Berkeley and London: University of California Press.

Nakano Takashi. 1964. *Shōka dōzokudan no kenkyū* (The merchant-dōzoku). Tokyo: Miraisha.

Noguchi, Paul H. 1990. *Delayed Departures, Overdue Arrivals: Industrial Familism and the Japanese National Railways*. Honolulu: University of Hawaii Press.

Pelzel, John C. 1970. "Japanese Kinship: A Comparison." In *Family and Kinship in Chinese Society*, edited by M. Freedman. Stanford, Calif.: Stanford University Press.

Plath, David W., ed. 1983. *Work and Lifecourse in Japan*. Albany: State University of New York Press.

Schneider, David M. 1968. *American Kinship: A Cultural Account*. Englewood Cliffs, N.J.: Prentice-Hall.

———. 1969. "Kinship, Nationality and Religion in American Culture: Toward a Definition of Kinship." In *Forms of Symbolic Action*, edited by V. Turner. Proceedings of the 1969 Annual Spring Meeting of the American Ethnological Society. Seattle and London: American Ethnological Society; distributed by the University of Washington Press.

Seidensticker, Edward. 1983. *Low City, High City: Tokyo from Edo to the Earthquake.* New York: Alfred A. Knopf.

Smith, Robert J. 1974. *Ancestor Worship in Contemporary Japan.* Stanford, Calif.: Stanford University Press.

Wagatsuma, Hiroshi, and George A. DeVos. 1984. *Heritage of Endurance: Family Patterns and Delinquency Formation in Urban Japan.* Berkeley, Los Angeles, and London: University of California Press.

Yano, Christine R. 1990. "The Iemoto System: Convergence of Achievement and Ascription." Manuscript.

Yuasa Yasuo. 1977. *Shintai: Tōyōteki shinshinron no kokoromi* (The body: an Asian view of mind and body). Tokyo: Sōbunsha.

CHAPTER I

Conflict, Legitimacy, and Tradition in a Tokyo Neighborhood

Theodore C. Bestor

Traditions are generally regarded as unproblematic artifacts of social life, the comforting residue of the past carried gently into the present. Particularly in a society such as Japan, where the contrast between tradition and modernity has been drawn so forcefully and repeatedly by both foreign observers and Japanese commentators alike, traditions have a reassuring ring of historical authenticity about them.

My research has focused on old-fashioned, seemingly traditional patterns of community organization in Tokyo, on patterns of social organization that are frequently thought to be historical survivals from preindustrial life. Over the past decade I have conducted research in a neighborhood I call Miyamoto-chō,[1] an area of Tokyo that conforms to Japanese stereotypes of the "urban village"—a place where myriad organizations intertwine to form a highly cohesive, localized social structure that directly affects many residents across a very wide spectrum of their lives and livelihoods; a place where strong and enduring informal ties create for many residents a face-to-face community; a place where communal identity and cohesion—including symbolic and ritual expressions of community—continue to be stressed, reproducing the community in each succeeding generation.

In many ways, Miyamoto-chō epitomizes an old-fashioned Tokyo neighborhood where the weight of historical tradition appears to sustain community social structure and values of communal identity, cohesion, and autonomy. The story could end there, and for many Japanese observers it does. But on closer inspection, Miyamoto-chō's apparent retention of traditional patterns of community is at best a historical illusion, for the neighborhood is heir neither to a preindustrial hamlet nor to the preindustrial city of Edo (as Tokyo was known before 1868). The neighborhood simply did not exist before 1923, and much of the content of local tradition is developed anew every few years. Miyamoto-chō's traditions (and the image of the neighborhood as being traditional that many residents subscribe to) are thus present-day social constructions that owe little to local historical antecedent but owe much to the interplay of contemporary political, economic, social, and cultural forces. This creation or representation of Miyamoto-chō as a seemingly traditional community reflects a process I call traditionalism, and I use the term *traditionalistic* to underscore distinctions between historical antecedents and contemporary constructions.

In this essay I am specifically concerned with how the neighborhood's traditions are formed and shaped in response to ongoing social conflicts within Miyamoto-chō. I focus on the ways in which symbols of "traditionalism" are created and modified in events such as the neighborhood's annual festival. And I examine how different groups within the neighborhood put forward their own interpretations or versions of local tradition in order to control events, establish their own claims to social status, and maintain or overturn Miyamoto-chō's established social order.

As Bernard Cohn notes in his study of the British Raj, "authority once achieved must have a secure and usable past" (1983, 167, quoting J. H. Plumb). Tradition provides just such a secure and usable past, and it is tradition that so frequently becomes the focus of struggles within Miyamoto-chō to assert, maintain, or extend the authority of a variety of actors and interest groups. Claims that Miyamoto-chō's present reflects a venerable tradition, of course, add luster to the image, the standing, and the legitimacy of the community as a whole. But within the encompassing aura of community tradition, competing factions emphasize or legitimate their own authority over Miyamoto-chō through their control of that tradition, selectively invoking and interpreting elements of tradition—or, when necessary, creating them on the spot—to justify their specific interests or positions.

In particular, competition for legitimacy waged in the name of tradition proceeds on several levels, external and internal. Externally, Miyamoto-chō competes with nearby neighborhoods for political power, for economic position, and for ritual standing. In this latter instance, Miyamoto-chō's case is bolstered by its position as home to the local shrine and hence primus inter pares among the seven neighborhoods of the shrine's parish. Miyamoto-chō is also continually skirmishing with the municipal government over the government's efforts to redefine boundaries and to undermine the legitimacy of "traditional" community institutions.

On internal levels, within the neighborhood different groups assert their control over the content of local tradition to advance their own interests. Conflicts exist among members of the community over their standing and legitimacy based on cleavages of age, gender, length of residence, occupation, and socioeconomic class. Among insiders, leadership factions divided along generational lines squabble over the control of community events. Similarly, struggles break out between "respectable" and "marginal" members of the community, with the "marginals" trying to wrap themselves in tradition to ensure their social recognition. And finally, conflicts over the meaning of traditions and the kind of community social structure they engender take place in the context of much broader—though rarely overt or explicit—antipathies between members of the so-called old middle class and the new, that is, between self-employed merchants and artisans on the one hand and white-collar salaried businesspeople and bureaucrats on the other.

Before outlining in more detail how these competitions work themselves out, let me turn to a brief description of the neighborhood itself.

Miyamoto-chō is about twenty minutes by commuter train from Tokyo station in what is now considered an older section of the city. Until the early decades of this century the area was a farming hamlet; after the 1923 Kantō earthquake destroyed central Tokyo, this hamlet was engulfed by Tokyo's outward expansion and was fully urbanized within a decade. The neighborhood therefore is a recent creation, largely populated and formed in the 1920s and 1930s, with institutional antecedents neither in the rural past nor in preindustrial urban life, although both are frequently cited to explain the neighborhood's present. Now asserted to be "natural" communities, neighborhoods like Miyamoto-chō were created throughout Tokyo in the 1920s and 1930s by national, prefectural, and municipal agencies as administrative expedients, and their boundaries were drawn and redrawn throughout the 1930s up to the eve of World War II.

The neighborhood is less than a tenth of a square kilometer in area, with about 1,900 residents in 750 households. Miyamoto-chō is a densely packed, mixed residential and commercial area centered around a bustling shopping street that runs near a small Shintō shrine, from which the neighborhood derives its name. Miyamoto-chō's jumbled homes and apartment buildings are interspersed with about 100 small stores and 40 tiny workshops, almost all of which are owned and operated as household enterprises. The neighborhood is a middle- or lower-middle-class community, dominated socially, politically, and commercially by the self-employed merchants and manufacturers for whom Miyamoto-chō is both home and workplace.

Miyamoto-chō is an ordinary place similar to hundreds of other neighborhoods that stretch in a wide arc to the north, east, and south of central Tokyo. No visible signs of social, economic, or cultural distinctiveness set Miyamoto-chō apart from its surroundings. Yet there is no question in the minds of those who live and work there, or on the part of those outsiders such as government officials who regularly deal with the neighborhood, that Miyamoto-chō exists as a distinguishable entity.

Structurally, Miyamoto-chō has a full complement of interlocking social groups and interpersonal ties of the sorts that typify a traditionalistic urban neighborhood like those found in *shitamachi*, the classic merchant quarter of central Tokyo. Local groups include a quasi-administrative neighborhood association, or *chōkai*, as well as its women's auxiliary and old people's club; a shopkeepers' guild; several PTAs and school alumni clubs; a festival committee and several shrine organizations; a political club; and many recreational or hobby groups. Networks of personal ties run throughout the neighborhood and are relied on by residents in most of the transactions of daily life. Residents are linked to one another by elementary school friendships carried over into adult life; by organized hobbies such as flower arrangement, tea ceremony, or travel; by economic and political self-interest; and by joint participation in the many local associations and groups mentioned above. Through these organizations and through these individual social, political, and economic networks, interaction among residents is frequent; for many people the neighborhood *is* a face-to-face community.

The chōkai is unquestionably the neighborhood's most important and visible organization. It acts as a semiofficial local government, providing services to residents both at local initiative and on the orders of the municipal authorities. It transmits demands, requests, and information that flow from municipal agencies and higher levels of government to the neighborhood, and vice versa. The chōkai distributes information on government programs and regulations and assists the government in record keeping, census taking, and conducting other surveys of local conditions. It lobbies the municipal government on behalf of residents on issues ranging from building a traffic bypass to limiting noise from a local daycare center.

Local groups sponsor a wide range of mutual aid, public safety, public health, and recreational activities. They help at funerals; they aid residents whose homes have been destroyed by fire; they organize earthquake drills; they sponsor traffic safety campaigns; they patrol the neighborhood against fire and crime; they maintain street lights; they spray the neighborhood with pesticides throughout the summer; they run recycling programs; and they sponsor festivals, folk dances, and trips to hot springs.

Informal ties among residents form a base without which many aspects of the formal organizations' activities could not function. Without them consensual decision making would be impossible, mutual aid and social control would fail, and the chōkai and other groups would lack the means to mobilize residents to contribute time, labor, and money to neighborhood activities.

On another level, the neighborhood is an important sphere of economic activity, and the local shopping street's sixty-odd businesses provide a wide spectrum of goods and services for a primarily local clientele; almost all households do the bulk of their shopping for day-to-day needs within a couple of blocks of home. Most shopkeepers, craftspeople, factory owners, and even professionals, such as doctors, dentists, or accountants, conduct business in small shops, workshops, or offices attached to their homes. Family members are often involved in all aspects of the household enterprise. Ties between customers or clients and the merchant or professional are often close; shops and offices frequently become neighborhood social centers as residents stop to chat over a cup of tea. Local tradespeople and professionals, therefore, play an important role in community life not simply because of the links they establish or maintain among other residents.

Socially, if not numerically, Miyamoto-chō is dominated by the households of small merchants and other petty entrepreneurs, who set the tone for neighborhood interaction and local social life. In the central role assumed by entrepreneurs and in the plethora of institutions and associations that loom so large in Miyamoto-chō, the neighborhood resembles shitamachi, the older mercantile and artisanal districts of central Tokyo. The distinction between shitamachi and its opposite—*yamanote,* the nonmerchant areas of Tokyo dominated by white-collar employees and their more "modern" lifestyles—is one of the most fundamental social, subcultural, and geographic demarcations in contemporary Tokyo. This dichotomy is not only applied to Tokyo as a whole, but also is projected upon the social life of even so small a unit as Miyamoto-chō.

In the minds of most Japanese, class standing and involvement in neighborhood affairs are inextricably linked. Neighborhood social life is seen as an aspect of the lifestyle of the so-called old middle class, a lifestyle that persists because of the cultural conservatism thought to be inherent in shitamachi. Although Miyamoto-chō itself has no direct historical ties to the classic merchant quarter, and few if any of its merchant households go back in the neighborhood more than two generations, many residents of Miyamoto-chō self-consciously identify themselves, their community, and the neighborhood's style of social life with that of shitamachi.

Although no one is formally excluded from participating in the social life of Miyamoto-chō, members of the new middle class—*sarariiman,* salaried employees of large corporations and government bureaucrats—are excluded de facto, by their lack of time to assume leadership roles, by their involvement in other kinds of social institutions, and by their general social values; that is, they tend to look down on community involvement as parochial, feudal, and undemocratic. In this they share the standard outlook of yamanote Tokyo, the Tokyo of the new middle-class elite.

But the·neighborhood is defined not only through its

internal institutions and interactions, nor only through the attitudes of its residents. Rather, the neighborhood and especially the neighborhood association—the chōkai—are also defined through their interactions with the municipal government of the ward in which Miyamoto-chō is located.

The Neighborhood and the Government

Although the chōkai is nominally a nongovernmental body, it is in close and constant contact with a wide range of municipal agencies, particularly the branch office of the ward government.[2] This office handles various official transactions for individual residents and acts as a liaison between the ward government and ten contiguous neighborhoods, including Miyamoto-chō. Municipal authorities regard chōkai as little more than semi-official agencies of the government itself, and the branch office considers these ten chōkai to be under its jurisdiction. Neighborhood leaders dispute this interpretation of their organizations' roles and complain about the responsibilities they feel they are forced to shoulder by the municipal, metropolitan, and at times even national governments in pursuit of the government's rather than the neighborhood's goals.

Beyond coordinating administrative functions, in recent years the branch office has become the focal point for the ward's increasingly active policy of *machi-zukuri*, or "community-creation." Machi-zukuri policies stem from a belief—widely held by scholars and officials—that existing patterns and institutions of neighborhood life as exemplified by chōkai are outmoded and inappropriate in contemporary society; the municipal government therefore feels it must step in and create institutions that will foster a sense of community and citizenship appropriate to a modern, democratic society (see Nakamura 1980). Ironically, in its attempts to do so, the ward government takes the existing neighborhoods and their activities not only as the instruments but also as the models for creating new senses of community awareness. Thus, these efforts do little to lessen mistrust between neighborhoods and the municipal government. This mistrust in part reflects lingering memories of the government's wartime role in regimenting local neighborhood institutions as part of the general war mobilization. And contemporary efforts by the municipal and metropolitan governments to promote machi-zukuri are seen as simply another effort to supplant chōkai both as institutions and as focal points of residents' sentiments of identity.

One conflict arose in the 1960s when the government attempted to merge local chōkai into larger, allegedly more rational units of administration. To an outsider nothing differentiates the neighborhoods that were to be affected by this plan, but their residents loudly and, in the end, successfully fought the ward government to a standstill.

In Miyamoto-chō this opposition took a seemingly curious form. On the face of things, residents of Miyamoto-chō and the adjacent neighborhood with which it was to be merged have political and economic interests that would not have been served by a merger. Each neighborhood has routinely been able to elect a member to the ward assembly, so there was political turf to protect.[3] Similarly, merchants' groups in each neighborhood strive to maintain and increase their share of local trade in the face of competition not only from other neighborhoods, but also from the large shopping district surrounding a nearby railway station.

Undoubtedly, such factors played a part in mobilizing resistance to the merger; but these are not the reasons mentioned by residents. Instead, they explain resistance as an effort to preserve the "distinct" traditions of the neigborhoods involved. Neither neighborhood was willing to alter practices they felt best suited their own needs and their own sense of autonomous tradition and identity. These sentiments, in Miyamoto-chō at least, revolved in part around the neighborhood hall. The issue was not simply a question of sharing ownership of an old and dilapidated building; it also involved symbolism central to the neighborhood's self-definition. Miyamoto-chō's hall had been built by residents out of the rubble of homes and shops destroyed during World War II. It was thus an important symbol (at least for older residents) of their communal survival through adversity. And this they were unwilling to share with other neighborhoods. The hall became an important rallying point for their opposition to the neighborhood merger, and ultimately this opposition prevailed.

To be sure, in 1967 the ward government went ahead and redrew the boundaries, and now the two neighborhoods appear on maps as a single unit. But today that larger unit is used for almost nothing but numbering houses. The chōkai and other local groups do not recognize the larger unit, nor in fact does the ward office. Since the ward office depends on the chōkai to carry out many of its tasks, it is forced to work within the frameworks that chōkai acknowledge.

Today, the government's branch office also plans and sponsors a variety of traditionalistic activities that often duplicate events put on by individual neighborhoods themselves. Events sponsored by the ward government frequently involve many of the trappings common to the activities of chōkai, and neighborhood leaders grumble about being upstaged by the larger, more lavish events the ward government can afford to put on. One example is the extremely elaborate Kumin Matsuri (Ward Residents' Festival), modeled on customary Bon Odori folk-dance festivals held in midsummer throughout Japan. The ward government first sponsored the Kumin Matsuri in 1979, and it included a specially commissioned ward residents' folk song and a folk dance, both of which conform to the conventions of contemporary, commercialized "traditional" folk song and dance genres.[4] The ostentatiousness of this first annual festival aroused so much ill will among chōkai leaders that the following year each of the ward government's eleven branch offices was forced to hold separate scaled-down versions. But the ward festival continues to be more elaborate than the corresponding efforts of the chōkai, and neighborhood leaders continue to complain about the "cooperation" they feel forced to give the branch office in its planning of this event.

By the summer of 1984, the Kumin Matsuri had become routinized to such an extent that leaders in Miyamoto-chō and adjacent neighborhoods had discontinued their own independent summer folk-dance festivals. In part, however, the decision to abandon the summer folk dances to the government was related to Miyamoto-chō's autumn festival, which over the past five years had grown increasingly elaborate; increasingly had drawn the neighborhood's time and money; and increasingly had become the focus of internal neighborhood dispute.

The Festival

The annual autumn festival, or *aki-matsuri,* for the tutelary deity of the Shintō shrine from which Miyamoto-chō derives its name, is one of Miyamoto-chō's most vivid community events.[5] In contrast to the municipal government's Kumin Matsuri, which loosely appropriates the Shintō term for festival *(matsuri),* the annual autumn festival in Miyamoto-chō is at its core an authentic Shintō ritual that involves both the local shrine and its parishioners. The focus of activity for many residents is not the shrine itself, but the observances held separately in each of the seven neighborhoods, including Miyamoto-chō, that make up the shrine's parish. During the matsuri the enshrined tutelary deity descends from its normal abode in the shrine's inner sanctum and is carried in *mikoshi* (portable shrines) through the streets of each neighborhood to bestow its blessings and ensure that all is well in the area under its sway. Whether for these theological reasons or for other, social ones, each neighborhood's observances are largely distinct from those at the shrine, and for many residents the neighborhoods' festivals—not the shrine's—are the centers of attention.

The two-day matsuri is a dramatic symbol of communal identity, and the community celebrations draw wide participation. It is, of course, a Shintō rite (and given the postwar separation of church and state the ward government has to keep its hands off).[6] But despite the festival's clear Shintō character, for most who participate it is a largely secular ritual of obscure religious significance, although full of social meaning. Even those whose beliefs are incompatible with Shintō sometimes play a part. One local leader, himself a Baptist, once explained to me that he felt no compunctions against playing a leading role in the festival since he saw it not as a religious observance but as a community event.

The matsuri is organized by a committee (known as the *sairei-iin*) convened each summer by the chōkai but whose members are drawn from the full range of local associations and include residents who otherwise take no active part in neighborhood affairs throughout the rest of the year. Each August the committee's leaders draw up an elaborate organizational table of festival assignments. Two or three weeks before the festival a delegation of leaders pays a formal call on the 150 or so households that have been assigned tasks related to putting on the festival. Each household is presented a printed copy of the list of positions on festival subcommittees, a small cotton hand towel *(tenugui)* decorated with the year's festival motif, and a pair of straw sandals to be worn during the festival. Each job—for example, serving on the subcommittee charged with overseeing the musicians' cart, or leading the dancing troupe from the women's auxiliary, or supervising the children's mikoshi—is ranked in prestige, and festival participants gradually work themselves up from position to position and from subcommittee to subcommittee over the years.

In part, these positions and people's status within the festival are related to the monetary contributions they make. Households with no position on the festival committee usually give two thousand or three thousand yen, if they contribute at all. Leaders are expected to contribute at least ten thousand and perhaps as much as thirty thousand yen. Donations are tricky, however, and reflect or correspond to one's standing both in the community and in the festival organization. One can easily err in either direction; too small a donation, of course, marks one as stingy, but too large betrays arrogance and ambition, rather than open-hearted generosity.

Through the matsuri, several important but sometimes contradictory social themes are expressed. Social stratification and ranking within Miyamoto-chō are expressed and enforced through assignments of positions on the festival committee. Public posting of residents' contributions confirms one's standing or holds one's pretensions up to public view. Distinctions are underscored between newcomers and residents of long standing and between those who work in the neighborhood and those who work elsewhere. The management of the festival, even the spatial and temporal distribution of activities during the matsuri, reflects rigid divisions of labor along gender and generational lines.

In even the most seemingly trivial fashions, the festival symbolizes distinctions of status among residents. At banquets and other formal meetings, for example, seating arrangements clearly reflect hierarchies of status and power. At the *hachiarai,* the banquet marking the completion of the year's festival, held in the old chōkai hall, men sit arranged along the "inner"[7] wall with older and more prestigious but less powerful men seated at the "top" of the room; the younger, active, more powerful leaders sit in the middle; and the youngest leaders-to-be, hangers-on, and other anomalies (like the anthropologist) occupy the "bottom." Women sit along the "outer" wall facing the men, but as power and authority are less differentiated among women, they array themselves from "top" to "bottom" with less self-conscious attention.

This spatial representation of hierarchy first struck me when my wife and I attended the hachiarai after the 1979 festival, only a few months after I began fieldwork. Of course, we violated one rule simply by attending the event together. We compounded our error by *sitting together* in what I judged to be an innocuous location well down the "outer" wall, in the midst of a group of women we knew. Consternation reigned. Men tugged at my sleeve. Women whispered to my wife. Our stupidity got worse— we resisted our hosts' entreaties and simply stayed put! As I watched with gradually dawning comprehension and growing horror, the formal banquet shifted around us. We stayed in place as geography was rearranged. Men moved so that my seat became the end of the male chain of hierarchy now wrapped around both sides of the room, and women scrunched together to assure that my wife, although by my side, was clearly seated within women's territory!

But despite the social differentiation that plays so visible a role throughout the festival, an overt spirit of egalitarianism and community solidarity is publicly presented as the matsuri's dominant motif.

This ideology of communal solidarity is manifested in many ways, some of them quite concrete. One important example is the mikoshi, the portable shrine, a small replica of a shrine building a meter square and equally tall, placed on a framework of horizontal poles that if laid on the ground would occupy the area of a small automobile. The mikoshi, mounted on this latticework of poles, is carried on the shoulders of twenty or thirty people, customarily men.

When the priest sanctifies the mikoshi and installs the deity into temporary residence within it, the mikoshi is said to be under the control of the deity rather than the bearers. The mikoshi indeed seems to take on a life of its own and becomes a bucking, pitching, careening force beyond the control or influence of any individual among its bearers, who are themselves often more than a little under the influence of sake. Accompanied by almost deafening, hypnotic, rhythmic chants and drum beats punctuated by a rapid counterpoint of whistle blasts, the mikoshi is steered, if that is the correct term, by two or three men who clear away bystanders and try (not always successfully) to prevent damage to property. These several men continually shove against the mikoshi bearers to try to turn the direction of the mikoshi, to slow its speed, or to calm its gyrations.

The link between the mikoshi and communal ideology becomes evident in several ways. For example, a common opinion during 1979–1981 was that Miyamoto-chō's two mikoshi were too small and really should only be carried by children. Both were thought to be light enough that one person among the bearers could influence their course and behavior; ideally, many people told me, a mikoshi should be so heavy that no single person's actions could affect or even be noticeable in its movements. Lacking a larger, more substantial mikoshi, the adults of Miyamoto-chō continued to carry the larger of the two small mikoshi in the processions, but sentiment clearly favored replacing it with an impressively massive mikoshi.

In another way, as well, the mikoshi and the processions that carry them serve as compelling markers of the community's boundaries and identity. In each of its major circuits of the neighborhood, the mikoshi is carried (or perhaps directs itself) to the borders of the neighborhood—and no farther. Where the neighborhood's definition of its boundaries disagrees with the borders drawn by the ward government, the mikoshi observes the neighborhood's. The mikoshi is careful to pass through all corners of the neighborhood, and the processions trace Miyamoto-chō's boundaries as closely as they can. When the route of a mikoshi unavoidably must pass through the territory of an adjacent neighborhood —as when roads or alleys linking parts of one neighborhood run through another—the festival committees from the neighborhoods involved negotiate the route beforehand. When a mikoshi, or a women's dance troupe, takes an unnegotiated detour through another neighborhood, leaders from the invaded neighborhood grumble and expect an apology from the festival committee of the offending neighborhood.

In short, on its annual round of inspection, the tutelary deity offers powerful symbolic support for the legitimacy of Miyamoto-chō's borders, reaffirms the solidarity of those who live within them, and provides a rationale for maintaining the integrity of those boundaries and the unit they surround in the face of pressures from the ward to reconstitute the neighborhood.

Finally, although the matsuri nominally promotes cooperation and identification among the seven neighborhoods of the shrine's parish, the mikoshi and their processions provide a venue for interneighborhood competition. In the late 1970s the neighborhood adjacent to Miyamoto-chō triumphed with an impressive new mikoshi, hand built by local young men. But during 1979–1981 Miyamoto-chō countered with the as-yet-unsurpassed spectacle of a foreign anthropologist and his exotic, red-haired, folk-dancing wife featured prominently in its processions.

But in the longer run, other strategies were required to uphold the neighborhood's standing, and after the 1980 festival the debate about whether and how to raise the money to build a new mikoshi was beginning to be waged publicly in Miyamoto-chō. At the banquet following the 1980 festival, one of the young leaders of the neighborhood unexpectedly rose during the final formal speeches and proposed that the neighborhood dedicate itself to obtaining a new mikoshi.

The Festival and Internal Conflict

Thus far, my account of Miyamoto-chō's festival has focused primarily on ways in which traditions of community—vividly symbolized through the festival and its paraphernalia—emphasize the internal solidarity of Miyamoto-chō at the same time that internal cohesion plays a role in the neighborhood's "foreign relations," highlighted in conflicts with the ward government and paraded in competitions with Miyamoto-chō's immediate neighbors. But with the drive to build a new mikoshi, Miyamoto-chō's festival became an arena for the expression and enactment of intense institutional and personal rivalries *within* the neighborhood.

The speaker who proposed the new mikoshi drive represented a faction of "younger" leaders: men in their forties and fifties who constituted the inner circle of supporters of the local politician who had been elected to the local ward assembly for the first time only three years before. This "young" politician had successfully achieved his election without inheriting—or being actively supported by—the local political machine of a now-retired politician whose followers continued to dominate the institutional structure of Miyamoto-chō's chōkai: men in their sixties, seventies, and eighties who had led the neighborhood since the immediate postwar years.

The older leaders were generally "self-made men" who had founded their own businesses just before, during, or after World War II and who were now (at least by local standards) prosperous, successful elder statesmen. The younger leadership faction, conversely, was largely made up of second- or third-generation entrepreneurs whose inherited businesses were often larger and more prosperous than those owned by the elder group. Interestingly, the younger group included several *mukoyōshi* (adopted sons-in-law): outsiders whose entry to the neighborhood came when they married the daughters of established local entrepreneurial families.

The two factions of leaders were only slightly divided by political affiliations, in the broader sense of the term. Both the young politician and the older, now-retired one were members of the same conservative party, and therefore the young politician— by virtue of his office, once elected—was accepted by (and equally acceptable to) all factions of Miyamoto-chō's conservative leadership. The two factions of leaders were not separated by any significant differences in political philosophy, and they were equally committed, both pragmatically and in principle, to the neighborhood as the means and more significantly as the ends of political action.

But however much the two groups agreed in general political philosophy and on the importance of the neighborhood, they differed in their views on the exercise of political power within Miyamoto-chō, they differed in who their supporters were and how they mobilized them, and most consequentially they differed in how they felt the chōkai and other neighborhood institutions should revitalize themselves in the face of indifference on the part of many residents.

Not surprisingly, perhaps, the older generation of leaders tended toward a fairly authoritarian political style. No longer involved with electoral politics, they were not overly concerned with marshaling or mobilizing larger numbers of supporters. In any case, they subscribed to a view of leadership in which age, seniority, and the status conferred by offices previously held provided leaders their clout. Once decisions were made by the inner circle of upper leaders, orders were simply issued to those lower in standing. The consent of the governed was not at issue, and as far as considering changes in the chōkai's organization or activities to revitalize it, the older leaders generally argued that practical, pragmatic, unadorned services were what the residents wanted and were what the chōkai should strive harder to deliver. The younger leaders disagreed. Many of them themselves bridled at the older generation's authoritarianism and recognized that other residents, potentially interested in community activities, were alienated by this style. But the younger leaders also held a different view of politics, in so much as they were closely linked to the young politician's election campaigns. They were very much aware that residents did not automatically recognize the older leader's legitimacy and that to attract greater support for the chōkai, it had to exert some appeal that would catch residents' interest. The young leaders recognized the advantages of broadening the basis of chōkai support and participation, both for the chōkai itself and also for the goals of the young politician. A larger, more vibrant chōkai could be used both to recruit support for the young politician and to reward his backers by opening the organization up to them.

The young leadership faction had two constituencies particularly in mind. The first were younger men, in their thirties and early forties, who would infuse new blood into the chōkai and its activities, thus enabling the chōkai's work to be spread around and ensuring that there would be a future generation of committed leadership. The second group were the women of Miyamoto-chō. The support of women was not of critical importance to the young leaders in terms of revitalizing the chōkai (for they, no less than the older faction, saw men as indisputably natural leaders), but it was important for the faction's wider political goals.

The young politician had begun his career in neighborhood politics as the president first of the elementary school PTA and then of the local junior high school PTA, and so he was well known to and well liked by many of the women of the neighborhood. In his political activities, such as trips to hot springs organized for several busloads of local supporters, women outnumbered men, and he courted locally prominent women for their support. Teachers of arts and crafts such as tea ceremony, flower arrangement, and dance—with their coterie of devoted middle-aged female students—were especially favored by the young politician's attention.

In the view of the young leaders, new and different strategies to increase the visibility of the chōkai were necessary if new supporters were to be attracted. Its conventional activities—traffic safety campaigns, recycling, pesticide spraying, and the like—were too inconspicuous and already too much taken for granted by residents to be an effective rallying point, especially for the younger residents they hoped to attract. Instead, the young leaders seized on the festival as an eye-catching means to build support for the chōkai and for themselves.

In May 1982, the young leaders' faction formally launched a drive to raise funds for a new mikoshi. Since these "neotraditionalists" were opposed by the "pragmatists" of the older leadership who felt that reconstruction of the neighborhood hall was a higher priority,[8] the young leaders formed their own separate organization, which they called the Mikoshi Hōken Jikkō Iinkai (Action Committee for the Presentation of a Mikoshi). Within three months of the group's formal inauguration, the younger faction of leaders was able to raise more than ten million yen (approximately U.S.$50,000 at then-current exchange rates) in cash and in pledges from 408 local households. Table 1 provides a financial statement for the mikoshi campaign.

This in itself was a greater show of interest and participation in local life than the activities of the "regular" neighborhood association under the old leadership had ever been able to mobilize, and the new mikoshi organization gave recognition and leadership positions not only to the long-established "loyal opposition" but also to younger men who had previously disdained any participation in local institutions dominated by the old guard and to women whose enthusiastic support for the new venture was a key to its success.

By September 1982—in time for that year's festival—the newly created Mikoshi Action Committee had commissioned and taken delivery of the largest, most elaborate mikoshi in the area. Leaders of the fund-raising campaign argued that a major objective was to increase participation in the festival—and by extension in neighborhood affairs—by making the local festival more impressive and exciting. But they also pointed out with pride that Miyamoto-chō's new mikoshi was more impressive than the adjacent neighborhood's hand-built one. And they talked with unconcealed pleasure about the failure of another adjoining neighborhood to meet the challenge.

TABLE I   FINAL FINANCIAL STATEMENT OF THE *MIKOSHI HŌKEN*
           JIKKŌ IINKAI[a] (ACTION COMMITTEE FOR THE PRESENTA-
           TION OF A MIKOSHI) 1982–1984 (IN YEN)

	BUDGETED	ACTUAL
Donations[b]	8,000,000	10,622,500
Interest		26,317
Total Income	8,000,000	10,648,817
Mikoshi and paraphernalia[c]	5,200,000	5,552,300
Refurbishing *taiko* drums	1,000,000	350,550
Mikoshi maintenance[d]	1,000,000	153,526
Ceremonial expenses[e]		148,600
Fund-raising costs[f]	800,000	183,809
Honoraria *(sharei)* for mikoshi carpenters		128,000
Festival clothing *(hanten, tenugui)*		1,368,271
Transportation		33,373
Interest on loan		65,442
Total Expenditures		7,983,871
Balance on Deposit		2,664,946

NOTES:

[a] Financial statement prepared for the municipal authorities on August 28, 1984, at the formal dissolution of the committee.
[b] Donations collected from 408 households.
[c] Mikoshi paraphernalia includes stand for mikoshi, wooden collection box, and all metal fittings.
[d] Mikoshi maintenance includes renting hall for the mikoshi during the festival, cleaning, storage, and minor repairs.
[e] Ceremonial expenses include consecration of the new mikoshi at the shrine.
[f] Fund-raising expenses include printing, copying, postage, and other office expenses.

The new mikoshi indeed changed the character of the festival and the scale of neighborhood residents' participation in it. For the first time in many years, large numbers of teenagers and young men in their twenties avidly joined in the mikoshi processions; and in a sharp break with the neighborhood's past practices, women too were allowed to join in.[9] The festival became livelier, more boisterous, and continued on far later into the evenings than had been the case a few years earlier. One unanticipated consequence of the new mikoshi was that the young leaders who had

contrived to have it built found themselves no longer able to participate in carrying the mikoshi itself. The weight and size of the
new mikoshi and the energetic frenzy of the young men and
women carrying it simply were too taxing for middle-aged men:
they would plunge in for five or ten minutes at a time to take a
turn carrying the heavy beams supporting the mikoshi but
couldn't match the stamina of young men able to carry it for
hours, shouting until their voices were lost, bouncing the mikoshi
up and down until their shoulders and backs were black and blue.
The "young" leaders therefore increasingly were relegated to the
sidelines of the processions in supervisory roles. And so the two
leadership factions found themselves equally observers and managers of the festival, rather than its direct participants, united in
any uneasy alliance between the older leaders who actually ran the
festival organization and the young leaders who controlled the
mikoshi organization.

During the summer of 1984, two years after the Mikoshi
Action Committee had been formed and at the end of its legal
charter to solicit funds for philanthropic purposes,[10] there were
convoluted negotiations over the reconciliation of the two rival
organizations. With an unspent surplus of about two million yen
and the enthusiastic gratitude of many residents who thought the
new mikoshi and the excitement it generated were the best thing
to have happened in years, the young leaders were in a position to
set the terms for the reconsolidation of neighborhood institutions.

Despite the displeasure of the older leaders at the split,
but with a large bankroll and the support of a majority of local residents, the young mavericks rejoined the regular chōkai, reoccu
pied high positions of leadership, and set up the surplus two million yen from the mikoshi in a separate budget under their
control.[11]

The organizational rift was healed, and the generational
factions of leaders were reconciled. But the mikoshi campaign had
unleashed other forces and other interests as well. The festival that
year (1984) became the arena for other sets of conflicts, also
couched in terms of who could legitimately claim to represent and
participate in traditional communal life.

In their drive to build a new mikoshi the young leadership
faction had recruited the enthusiastic support of what one might
call the underclass of Miyamoto-chō—the day laborers and con-

struction foremen who have loose ties with the underworld and
who quite consciously view themselves as the true heirs to the
rough-and-tumble lifestyles of premodern shitamachi, where festivals of rough workmen were punctuated by drunkenness, brawl-
ing, and general licentiousness.

In Miyamoto-chō, the laborers and the labor bosses saw
the new mikoshi as a vehicle for asserting their role in community
life, which in their opinion had been in the hands of conservative,
"respectable," and wealthier merchants and manufacturers far
too long.

The construction workers saw the mikoshi as theirs and
by their participation sought to open the festival up—making it
much less controlled, much more frenzied and raucous, much
more drunken. To them the festival should no longer be simply a
neighborhood event, but an opportunity to invite in—and to
impress—their friends and associates from throughout Tokyo.

Thus, for the first time, in 1984 Miyamoto-chō's festival
was joined—or crashed—by large numbers of outsiders. To respectable residents, these outsiders were terribly *osoroshii* (scary):
men with deep knife scars on their faces; men whose backs were
elaborately tattooed; men who stripped down to loincloths to whirl
the mikoshi through the streets; worst of all, men who ignored the
orders and directions of constituted local authority.

Respectable members of the community stayed away, and
things came to a head on the second day of the festival during a
heavy rainstorm. Neighborhood leaders ordered that the mikoshi
be kept inside for fear the rain might damage the structure and its
decorations. The laborers protested and demanded the mikoshi be
brought out.

Suddenly, an argument broke out between a neighborhood leader, a merchant, and the local labor boss. Within seconds
the merchant was jumped by half a dozen laborers who stomped
him as he lay in the gutter, his festival garb covered with mud.
The fight lasted only a few seconds; but all around, parents pulled
their children home, and shutters noisily clattered down.

Eventually the rain broke, and the mikoshi made its
rounds. The workmen were allowed to carry it, but they were surrounded by the burliest men the respectable leadership could mus-
ter; and when the procession passed the shopfront of the festival
leader who had been beaten to the ground, a phalanx of "respect-

able" leaders formed a conspicuous but passive human shield in front of the shop's plate glass windows to guard against a sudden lurch of the heavy mikoshi.[12] The festival continued uneventfully but sullenly. And quickly, new regulations were drawn up to control the participation of outsiders and to keep the festival firmly under the control of the now reunited "respectable" leadership, both the young leaders who had built the new mikoshi and the old leaders who had initially opposed it.

Later that night, several of the young leaders gathered in a nearby bar to drink and discuss the festival. Inevitably their discussion centered on the brief outburst of violence and the angry mood that lingered afterward. One of the men, himself in the construction business, mused aloud to the group:

> It's all a matter of social status. Tanaka-san [the local labor boss] has been having a hard time lately because of the downturn in the construction industry, and he has trouble finding enough work to keep all his laborers busy. They've been getting restless. Tanaka needs to be able to show them he is still important and can still command respect. That's why he brought his guys to the festival today and that's why when he got into an argument with Uratsuji-san [the humiliated merchant] he couldn't back down. He has to show his guys that he is an important man in the community and can control the festival.

Although speaking for the benefit of the other leaders, not particularly for me, my informant had neatly summarized his analysis in terms to gladden an anthropologist. Of course, in this bull session, he was speaking only about the quest for status, leadership, and control on the part of the "marginal" underclass of local society. But I believe his point applies as well to the more general significance of traditional events in community life.

For the "respectable" old middle-class leadership of Miyamoto-chō is also a marginal group, at least in the eyes of new middle-class Japanese salarymen and bureaucrats. Thus for old middle-class merchants it is equally important to be able to demonstrate their own sense of status, leadership, and control. And the arena of community life provides them with the ideal forum in which to do so, just as emphasizing their grasp of tradition is the ideal tool.

Since community is acknowledged by everyone—insider

and outsider, resident and bureaucrat, merchant and white-collar worker alike—to be an integral part of the mercantile shitamachi tradition, to the extent that Miyamoto-chō's old middle-class can forge links—and here I use forge in several meanings—of continuity to the heritage of shitamachi, they are able to enhance their social standing by assuming culturally legitimate and unassailable roles.

In this manner they are able to create and control a social arena in which they call the shots and in which they can justify their exclusion of new middle-class residents on eminently legitimate grounds—their failure to honor traditional values of community participation.

Through events such as the festival, a line is clearly drawn between Miyamoto-chō and the wider society, symbolically setting the neighborhood apart.

And thus, the old middle-class argues that the systems of ranking that apply in the wider society are null and void within the neighborhood. As residents, the white-collar worker, the symphony musician, and the teacher count for no more and no less than the pharmacist, the baker, and the *tōfu* maker.

Whether outsiders or dissenting insiders like it or not, they are presented with a vision of community and a community social structure that is a fait accompli—a community structure that because of its resonance with tradition is unassailable. Residents and outsiders can choose not to participate, or they can mount a radical critique of Japanese tradition, as do Communists and members of some religious groups that oppose Shintō. But on its own terms the cultural legitimacy of the symbolism invoked in support of the neighborhood's status quo cannot be shaken.

Thus by accentuating the traditional—most dramatically but not exclusively through the festival—local events serve to imbue Miyamoto-chō and those vying for standing and control with the legitimacy that tradition so amply bestows.

Notes

During 1979–1981, my research in "Miyamoto-chō" was generously supported by the Japan Foundation; the National Science Foundation (grant number BNS 7910179); the National Institute of Mental Health (fellowship number MH 08059); and the American Council of

Learned Societies-Social Science Research Council Joint Committee on Japanese Studies. Additional research was conducted during three subsequent visits: in September 1983, with support from Sigma Xi; during the summer of 1984, made possible by the Japan Foundation and the Wenner-Gren Foundation for Anthropological Research; and, during the summer of 1986, with support from Columbia University and the Northeast Asia Council of the Association for Asian Studies. I also lived in Miyamoto-chō again from September 1988 to August 1989 while conducting research elsewhere in Tokyo.

Additional analyses of Miyamoto-chō's historical development and contemporary social life can be found in Bestor (1985, 1989, 1990a, 1990b).

I am grateful to Ardath W. Burks, Takie S. Lebra, Victoria Lyon-Bestor, Robert F. Murphy, Elliott P. Skinner, Robert J. Smith, and Michio Suenari for comments made on various versions of this essay. Portions of this chapter were previously published in an abridged Japanese-language version as: "Tōkyō no aru machi ni okeru kattō, dentō, seitōsei," in *Minzokugaku Kenkyū*, vol. 54, no. 3, 1989.

1. Miyamoto-chō is a pseudonym.

2. Throughout this essay I refer to the *ku* ("ward" or "borough") government as the municipal administration, in distinction to the prefectural government of *Tōkyō-to,* which only rarely is in direct contact with neighborhood-level institutions or issues. Present-day Tokyo is divided into twenty-three ku, each of which has a limited degree of political and administrative autonomy (see Steiner 1965 for a detailed discussion of Tokyo prefectural and municipal governance). While I use "ward" government and "municipal" government more or less interchangeably, I find it necessary to differentiate these terms because there are municipal functions that are not part of the ward government. Shinagawa ward, in which Miyamoto-chō is located, is of average size, with a population (in 1988) of 345,000 (Shinagawa-ku 1988).

3. In 1988, the ward as a whole contained approximately 160 distinct and recognized neighborhoods (as defined by the existence of chōkai) plus an additional 35 or so apartment complexes that have organized local residents groups, called *jichikai* (see Shinagawa-ku 1988, 240–245), but the ward assembly contains only 40 seats. Thus, neighborhoods able to elect a local candidate are regarded as having secured a highly advantageous resource.

4. The lyrics of the folk song appear in Bestor (1989, 301–302).

5. The following accounts of Miyamoto-cho's festival are based on my observations, interviews, and participation during the matsuri held in 1979, 1980, 1983, 1984, and 1988.

6. In Miyamoto-chō the only government involvement in the festival comes in the form of parade permits issued by the police depart-

ment to the festival organizers for the mikoshi processions. Generally, a couple of officers, and sometimes a woman traffic-control officer, are detailed to direct the flow of traffic through and around the processions.

7. In determining status positions within the hall, the "inner" wall, farthest from and facing the street, is more prestigious than the "outer" wall, closest to and facing away from the street. The "bottom" and "top" of the room are respectively closest to and farthest from the entryway.

8. This position, of course, was a reversal from the previous generation's struggles with the ward government, when the old neighborhood hall was seen as a central symbol of the community. By the late 1970s and early 1980s, however, most other neighborhoods in the area had built new halls, and Miyamoto-chō's older leaders had come to see their hall as impractical, obsolete, and embarrassingly shabby in contrast. They argued that a new hall was a practical necessity that would enable the chōkai to more efficiently serve the neighborhood's residents, while the partisans of the new mikoshi argued that it would attract more people to take an interest and participate in neighborhood affairs, to the ultimate benefit of the chōkai.

9. During the festival in 1980 the middle-aged members of the women's dance troupe were allowed—apparently for the first time—to carry the mikoshi for one short circuit up Miyamoto-chō's shopping street at the end of the regular festival. With the new mikoshi young women were actively recruited to join in the procession, and many of the older women of the neighborhood reacted with a sort of gleeful envy, telling me how glad they were that this had come about and how sorry they were that they were now too old to join in the fray.

10. To publicly solicit funds, the mikoshi committee had legally registered itself with the municipal authorities and had received authorization to conduct a two-year fund-raising campaign.

11. Although the budget initially was earmarked for maintaining the mikoshi and contributing to festival activities, ultimately much of it was spent to further the goals of the older leadership faction as well, including rebuilding the chōkai hall, which was done in 1986. The neighborhood's representative to the ward assembly, himself a central figure in the young leadership faction but on good terms as well with older leaders, arranged a grant to the chōkai from the ward government to build a new community hall (as part of the ward's machi-zukuri program). The required matching funds from the neighborhood were provided in part out of the mikoshi surplus.

12. I was among the men quickly drawn up to shield the windows, in tribute as much to my height and weight as to my close personal ties to the leaders of the young leadership faction.

References

Bestor, Theodore C. 1985. "Tradition and Japanese : tion: Institutional Development in a Tokyo . *Ethnology* 24 (2): 121–135.

———. 1989. *Neighborhood Tokyo*. Stanford, Calif.: Stanf Press.

———. 1990a. "Tokyo Mom-and-Pop." *The Wilson Quarte.* 33.

———. 1990b. "The *Shitamachi* Revival." *Transactions of the . of Japan* 5 (4): 71–86.

Cohn, Bernard. 1983. "Representing Authority in Victor. In *The Invention of Tradition*, edited by E. Hobsl T. Ranger. Cambridge: Cambridge University Press.

Nakamura, Hachirō. 1980. "The Concept of Community Tra in Japan." In *Asian Perspectives on Social Development*, S. Koyano, J. Watanuki, and H. Komai. Tokyo: Japa logical Society.

Shinagawa-ku. 1988. *Shinagawa-ku no tōkei* (Statistics of Shinagawa Tokyo: Shinagawa-ku.

Steiner, Kurt. 1965. *Local Government in Japan*. Stanford, Calif.: St. University Press.

CHAPTER 2

The Spatial Layout of Hierarchy: Residential Style of the Modern Japanese Nobility

Takie Sugiyama Lebra

Social relations are ordered in and across space as well as time. Put in Giddens' (1984) terms, "structuration" involves space-focused "regionalization," in conjunction with time-focused "routinization." The spatial representation of social hierarchy in particular, whether physical or symbolic, literal or metaphorical, is widely recognized and often taken for granted particularly in its vertical dimension, namely high and low, above and below, upstairs and downstairs, and so on. Barry Schwartz (1981) argues the universality of "vertical opposition" as conceptualized in line with structuralism (without, however, presuming it to be inherent in the structure of the mind). I extend Schwartz's vertical dimension to other dimensions to show how the actual operation of a hierarchy can deviate from the linear vertical model. Suggestive in this light is Feinberg's (1988) proposition of two contrastive models of spatial hierarchy, derived from two Polynesian outliers, Anuta and Nukumanu. One is "linear" and "unambiguous," while the other is "circular" and "relativistic" where high and low are reversible. This essay takes Schwartz and Feinberg as a point of departure to further elaborate the spatial design of status and hierarchy. In the concluding section, I suggest that the spatial analysis can generate a clue to what might be called "dyarchy," as it is applied to the hereditary elite of Japan including the emperorship.

The spatial focus makes much sense in dealing with the Japanese concepts of hierarchy since spatial references are a common alternative to personal names or pronouns for Japanese speakers in address as well as in reference. Avoiding direct use of a personal name, Japanese use spatial terminology to indicate respectful distance, and indeed, a spatial reference often amounts to an honorific. To mention a few out of countless examples of status-indicative spatial nomenclature: The literal equivalent for "Your (or his) Excellency" is "Lord Palace" (tonosama), the lordly status symbolized by the palace where the addressee resides as its master. A common term for identifying a royal prince or princess is miya[sama] (venerable house), miya also referring to a shrine for gods. The special honorific reserved exclusively for emperor and empress, the equivalent for His or Her Majesty, is heika, literally meaning "below the stair," an instance of reflexive twist in which the sacred personage is identified by the low position taken by an imaginary retainer speaking upward to the august one seated above the stair. The same reflexive logic holds for some other spatial terms like denka, kakka, and gozen, all meaning "your (or his) highness." Spatial terminology is not limited to "respectable" persons: an ordinary man may be referred to by his relative or acquaintance in terms of the city or district of his residence, as, for example, "Hiroshima is coming to stay with us." Even widely used terms for "you" and "I" literally mean spatial directions, for example, anata or sochira (over there) for "you" and kochira (over here) for "I." Such spatial nomenclature sounds natural to Japanese; most of their family names, after all, originated from the names of districts, locations, or landmarks.

Japan today is an egalitarian society as far as hereditary status is concerned, with no legally sanctioned ascribed elite except the imperial family. The following analysis will touch upon the imperial status, but most of the data come from a more anachronistic source, namely, the abolished nobility, whose life is only recalled and whose status is only ritually reenacted by those who have outlived their titles or by their descendants. The legally outmoded nobility, I claim nevertheless, is culturally contemporary (Lebra 1992), as much as the legally obsolescent ie (stem-family household) or the outcaste status is. For this reason, tense switch will become necessary from time to time. My analysis is centered on the "domestic" space as it interlocks with the "public" space.[1]

The Historical Background of the Nobility

By the nobility is meant the status group called kazoku, "the flowery lineage," the term applying at once to the group as a whole, each constituent family, and the head of the family to whom the title belonged, which definition allows the term to appear in singular or plural. As a legal entity the kazoku was formally established in 1884 and thrown out of existence in 1947 together with the royal lineage group, the kōzoku (except the emperor and his closest family), under the new constitution that replaced the 1889 Constitution of the Great Empire of Japan. The kazoku ranked immediately below the royal lineage group headed by the emperor and stood tall above the rest of the nation. The latter was further graded into gentry called shizoku (primarily of samurai-vassal origin) and commoners (heimin), and remnants of the outcaste variously renamed. For my present purpose, however, all three can be classified as nonelite or "commoners."

The kazoku was an institutional creation, felt necessary by leaders of Meiji Japan (1868–1912) after the old aristocracy was brought to an end through the Meiji Restoration. Originally and informally the kazoku consisted largely of two major categories of old aristocrats: (1) the former court nobles, generally known as kuge, who had attended the imperial court of the Kyoto Palace until the Restoration; (2) the former feudal domain lords, commonly called daimyō, who had centered at the Edo (Tokyo) Castle of the shogunal court and their respective provincial castles. Later, in 1884, when the kazoku was formally established, a new group of men joined the ranks, much to the dismay of the kuge and daimyō; the new group was elevated because of their recognized contributions and performances through and after the Meiji Restoration. These achievers came primarily from modest-ranking former samurai-vassals. Indicative of their respective origins, the three categories were named in popular vernacular as kuge-kazoku, daimyō-kazoku, and kunkō- or shin-kazoku (kunkō and shin mean "meritorious" and "new").

The above composition alone suggests two contrastive purposes involved in the creation of this modern aristocracy. On the one hand, the kazoku was to provide a symbolic continuity in hierarchy; it was thus meant to be conservative, propitiatory of the discontented old elite, particularly the daimyō, who had lost most of their former privileges, power, and wealth through the Meiji reform. On the other hand, this reorganization of aristocracy was to perform progressive functions as well. First, it allowed a continual assimilation of "new blood" with fresh energy into the "hereditary" elite to cope with the urgent tasks of modernizing the country. Second, the men of such diverse backgrounds were now integrated into a single "peerage," symbolic of a newly centralized national state under a single sovereign, the emperor. One of the kazoku privileges was that of membership—automatic or internally elected—in the House of Peers, one arm of the bicameral parliament established in 1889.

Kazoku were classified into five ranks, named after the five nobility ranks of ancient China but conceptually modeled on the European aristocracy. The five paralleled prince, marquis, count, viscount, and baron. These ranks were allocated, subject to promotion, according to pre-Restoration status, loyalist contributions to the cause of the Restoration, and subsequent performances in various fields of activities and professions. When the source of information is to be specified in the following account, the pre-Meiji status and nobility rank may be combined, such as "a son of daimyō-viscount."

The former kazoku continues to maintain its visible identity as a social club in the heart of Tokyo; from time to time it publishes records of itself as one of its major activities. The most comprehensive set of genealogies, published by the club (Kasumi-Kaikan 1982–1984), indicates there have been 1,011 kazoku families in total, including those that have become extinct or have lost kazoku titles for one reason or another since the inception of this institution. Initially about 500, the membership thus doubled, which means that the category of "new" kazoku, a small minority at the beginning, eventually came to outnumber the kuge- and daimyō-kazoku.

The kazoku privileges and duties both centered upon the emperor. They had special access to the imperial household such as social or ritual contact as host or guest, durable intimacy stemming from having been playmates and classmates with princes or princesses, opportunities (or obligations) of marriage with members of the royalty including the emperor, high-level employment in the court, and so on. Theoretically the nobility titles were awarded out of "the imperial benevolence," and they were transmitted to successors with the imperial sanctions. In return, the kazoku as a group was expected to dedicate itself as a human bulwark *(hanpei)* for the imperial house (Lebra 1992 for detail).

I have been in contact with surviving members and

descendants of the former kazoku intermittently since 1976. Uninterrupted fieldwork was conducted for five months in 1982, for ten months in 1984–1985, primarily in Tokyo, with occasional trips to other parts of Japan. Surviving members of kazoku, their descendants, and families were interviewed for their life histories. In addition to this retrospective, reconstructive set of information, direct observations were made of contemporary group activities and "events" involving former kazoku or their successors as central figures. Further, I was able to contact (not exactly "interview" in all cases) a limited number of royal princes and princesses. By the end of my last field trip (1989), I had met more than one hundred individuals. All my informants have outlived their own or their forebears' aristocratic titles, but modifiers like "former" will not always be given in the following account.

The Spatial Hierarchy of Residence

Kazoku households, even though they were a small group of "peers," were diverse, as is already clear from the above three-fold categorization of kazoku composition. They varied in genealogical depth—from a kuge whose "first" ancestor appears as a god in the Kojiki, the mytho-historical chronicle compiled in the early eighth century, down to an upstart of "obscure" or "lowly" origin. A more conspicuous variation existed in wealth; here the category ranged from a rich daimyō-kazoku[2] commanding hundreds of acres of real estate—enormous by the Japanese, if not by the European or American, standard—and several dozens of servants, down to a pauperized kuge who refrained from social activities because he/she could not afford proper accoutrements, whether attires, vehicles, or a quality retinue. Financial giants, who too were eventually ennobled, stood in contrast to modest salaried men. Further, the lifestyle differed extensively along the continuum from extreme Westernization ("We had our shoes on indoors") to adherence to "the age-old Japanese style of life," as represented by the residential architecture. In addition to intra-group variation, one must consider a tremendous change that took place within the sixty-three-year span of kazoku existence: "My mother was still wearing *ohikizuri* [outer garment of kimono with train]," said an informant, "like many other women. But such was stopped overnight by the Russo-Japanese War [1904–1905]."

Besides that war, my informants identify two more major turning points: the great earthquake of the Kanto region (1923) and World War II.

All these variations and changes defy a generalization about spatial design. Nevertheless some patterns, admittedly always to be qualified by exceptions, do emerge, probably thanks to two factors: first, some more or less standardized culture of the elite was developed and learned at Gakushuin, a special school system catering to royal and kazoku children and other selected upper-class children; second, a high frequency of intermarriage and interadoption (Lebra 1989) within this status group contributed to a sense of shared kinship and cultural homogenization. Given the above diversity in life conditions, such standardization reflected shared mental constructs rather than uniformity of physical layout. The same vocabulary was uttered by informants with various backgrounds in reconstructing their residential architecture.

Residential Locations

First, I locate the kazoku residential space in a larger map. The Restoration government maneuvered the old aristocracy to settle permanently in Tokyo. Further, for any ambitious men who were later to rise to nobility ranks through merit, the new capital seemed the only place to provide opportunities. In other words, there were good reasons for the kazoku population to concentrate in Tokyo (although a few among the kuge stayed on in Kyoto).

Since this initial resettlement, there have been many residential relocations, as told by my informants, either by choice or by necessity. And the war, Tokyo air raids, evacuation, and postwar radical taxation upon properties ruined their residential grandeur, forcing most of them to forgo their estates considerably or entirely and to live in cramped sections of their former servants' quarters or to disperse into rural areas.

Today, one might think that there would be no geographical pattern of residence that distinguishes the former kazoku. It was found out, however, that former kazoku still concentrate disproportionately in Tokyo. Of all the households whose addresses are known (N = 916 according to Kasumi-Kaikan 1982–1984), as many as 57 percent reside in prefectural Tokyo, whereas the percentage for the whole nation is only 11.9 percent (Jichishō Gyōsei-kyoku 1984). The second most settled prefecture is Kanagawa, adjacent to Tokyo, where many kazoku used to own resort villas along the coast of Sagami Bay; these became their permanent homes when their main estates in Tokyo were lost. Here, the percentage for the kazoku is 16.7 percent, compared with 6.5 percent for the nation. In sum, 73.7 percent of kazoku live in these two prefectures while the national representation is only 18.4 percent.

Prefectural Tokyo divides into the urban center situated in the eastern portion facing Tokyo Bay, and the vaster rural area stretching westward. Taking all the prefectural households as 100, we find 86 percent of kazoku households reside within the urban limits, while only 74 percent of the general population do so. More telling is the pattern of concentration within urban Tokyo, which breaks down into twenty-three wards *(ku)*. We find 66.6 percent of the kazoku households residing in the twenty-three wards concentrated in five wards (Minato, Shibuya, Setagaya, Meguro, and Shinjuku) whereas only 24.3 percent of the general residents live in the same wards. Conversely, eight other wards (Katsushika, Sumida, Arakawa, Adachi, Kita, Kōtō, Edogawa, and Itabashi), have 2.6 percent of kazoku, 35.2 percent of the general residents. These figures confirm our impressions that there is a class cleavage in residential geography within the city limits between what are vaguely and misleadingly designated *yamanote* (hillside) and *shitamachi* (downtown).

The yamanote-shitamachi dichotomy is far from clear or consistent, partly because the boundary and internal division of urban Tokyo has changed extensively since the initial installation of the 15-ku system in 1878. Twenty more ku were added in 1932, and this total of 35 ku was reorganized into the present 23-ku system in 1947. (It should be noted that these changes were occasioned by the two events of Tokyo devastation: the 1923 earthquake and the 1945 air raids). The result is that there are many areas that cannot be characterized as either yamanote or shitamachi. Nevertheless, Japanese adhere to this dichotomy because these designations are strongly symbolic of class divisions more than denotative of geography. Seidensticker (1983), while limiting his analysis to the old 15 wards, calls the two regions "high city" and "low city," combining physical altitude and social class. He takes us back to the historical origin of this division:

When in the 17th century the Tokugawa regime set about building a seat for itself, it granted most of the solid hilly regions to
the military aristocracy, and filled in the marshy mouths of the
Sumida and Tone rivers, to the east of the castle. The flatlands
that resulted became the abode of the merchants and craftsmen
who purveyed to the voracious aristocracy and provided its
labor. (1983, 8)

So there is a reason why the yamanote region is associated
with the *buke yashiki* or *daimyō yashiki,* "mansions of the ruling
class." The former kazoku, despite many relocations, continue,
albeit in less density, to cluster in the choice areas of the "high
city." That such geographical condensation must have been much
more pronounced in prewar times can be inferred from the previous residences revealed in interviews. Most frequently mentioned were the two wards of the old city: Azabu and Akasaka,
both presently part of Minato ward. These comprised the heart of
old yamanote. *The Tale of Akasaka,* a popular essay by Kōbata
(1984), for example, is primarily about the former elite.

Confinement

The above-sketched residential geography is the first sign
of the spatial confinement in which the kazoku life was led. Confinement meant one's relative seclusion from the outside world,
remaining in the "high city," in one's status group, in one's household. A daughter of a daimyō-marquis recalled that, while her
"unusually liberal parents" allowed her as a child to visit areas
like Asakusa (a popular entertainment district of shitamachi, not
to be confused with Akasaka) on occasions like local festivals if
escorted by "several maids," they themselves would step into such
a place "under absolutely no circumstances." To this day, some
upper-class yamanote residents are strangers to the heart of shitamachi even though they are familiar with major American and
European cities. So an author who only recently discovered the
wonder of shitamachi confesses, "Yes, Asakusa was more remote
than New York" (Inukai 1989, 37).

In this seclusion the sexes were not equally confined; girls
and women were more strictly bound by this rule of spatial confinement than boys and men; the boys in fact were allowed and
sometimes encouraged to enter the social wilderness of the outside

world. Older women informants particularly recalled their girl-hood as secluded within the enclosure of the estate. Some were frustrated, but most accepted the seclusion as "natural"; thcy did not become awakened to the "freedom of mobility" until after their marriage to possibly "liberal" husbands or after the war. The old ohikizuri garment epitomizes the woman's indoor life and immobility.

What stands out in kazoku life histories in sharp contrast to those of average Japanese is the insignificance or total absence of neighbors. This is pointed out as a characteristic of the yamanote lifestyle in general and was more pronounced among the upper class. There was almost no contact with neighbors beyond perfunctory greetings in accidental encounters in the residential vicinity until wartime, when everyone was forced into a neighborhood association and had to line up for rationed foods. Even children did not find their playmates among neighbor children. A fifty-five-year-old woman, daughter of a count, recalled that when she was a young girl she lived temporarily in an area where she heard the sound of neighbors for the first time in her life. Neighbor children came to invite her to join them in play, but she did not know how to respond. She was curious about them and enjoyed watching them, but she had no wish to participate in their play. That the lack of neighborly contact may have had something to do with the Gakushuin subculture was suggested by a daughter of a baron: she somehow lost the freedom of playing with neighbor children when she began to attend Gakushuin.

The only neighbors whose names and homes my inform-ants remembered were fellow kazoku, Gakushuin classmates, high government officials, financial giants, and the like. All this is consistent with the previously stated geographical clustering of kazoku residences in selective areas. Whcn there was contact with neighbors, the usual characteristics of neighborliness—such as mutual and easy visibility, unannounced visits, mutual help in emergencies and so on—were missing. "There was no easy way of having *tsukiai* (interaction) with your neighbors. You couldn't just drop in, saying 'Hi, here I am!' " Even between classmates it was impossible, I was told, to visit one another at home on the spur of the moment: parents on both sides had to be informed first, and then visiting was scheduled. An adult visitor was bound, not only by such an appointment rule, but by the dress code and gift-giving obligation. All this class-bound tsukiai was devoid of the "natural," informal, spontaneous sociability typical of shitamachi or rural neighborhoods. One of the old institutions essential to shitamachi neighborliness is the public bathhouse, where bathers enjoy "naked" tsukiai. Yamanote also has public bathhouses, and many club houses built by ward governments for the elderly have bathing facilities in them. A ninety-one-year-old woman of kuge origin, married to a wealthy commoner, would shudder, said her daughter-in-law in response to my suggestion, at the idea of bathing together with neighbors.

No household being self-sufficient, seclusion was far from complete, and in fact there were constant interchanges between inside and outside the house but only in a way minimizing the free exposure of the family to the outer world. Routine domestic labor was supplied internally by a pool of servants, and specialized services such as hairdressing were provided by regularly hired professionals. Necessary goods like food and clothing were delivered by house-calling salesclerks (goyōkiki) of certain stores. Not a few informants recalled their curiosity about such salesmen, hairdressers, or gardeners as the only "windows" to the outside.

Even when members of the kazoku family had to go out, exposure to the outside world was curtailed, first, by means of transportation. To commute to school, go shopping, or visit any other place, many of my informants walked, if the distance was short enough, or took public transportation, "like everyone else." If the train was divided by grades, they were likely to take a higher-class car. High-ranking and wealthy families used private transportation. Historically, the vehicles changed from early Meiji on (see Seidensticker 1983), and my informants talked about their family-owned vehicles shifting from horse carriages to jinrikisha (rickshaw) to automobiles. Today, car ownership is no longer a status symbol, but in prewar Japan it was a special luxury.

It may sound strange, but private transportation was another factor inhibiting access to the outside world. The vehicles were driven by a privately employed driver who usually lived within or near the family compound and who thus served as a guard as well as a driver. The most adventurous mischief a girl could perpetrate was to steal a moment to get away from the watchful eyes of a servant driver. Under these conditions, it was difficult to meet people outside, even one's own kin. The wife of a count, seventy-six years old, recalled that, after marriage, she was not free to visit her mother, ironically because she had to be chauffeured around wherever she went. Apparently, she was bound by the idea that married women belonged exclusively to their husbands and in-laws and therefore could see their natal kin only surreptitiously. It was not until World War II, when she lost this private convenience and had to use trains, that she acquired freedom of mobility and contact.

Whether one walked or took private or public transportation, the most commonly practiced pattern was chaperonage. Servants escorted the children from home to school and back home, at least up to about the third grade but in some cases throughout high school, much to the embarrassment of their charges. In the case of a female servant, she waited sewing in an escorts' room *(tomo-machi beya)* of the school until the end of the school day. Daughters were not the only ones chaperoned; some families assigned male escorts to their young sons. Adults, too, were shepherded by servants. In shopping, it was the accompanying servant who discharged all the actual transactions with store clerks, leaving the master or mistress aloof from or ignorant about money. Even the newlywed couple was escorted by an entourage on their honeymoon, said some of my older informants chuckling. After the last escort servant was lost, "I still kept forgetting to carry a wallet."

Kazoku women, and to a lesser extent, men, too, even when they stepped out of the house, were thus insulated from the outside world, precisely because the private transportation and chaperonage kept them from being left alone. Insulation and the lack of privacy were two sides of the same coin. Only through the war and postwar collapse of the old hierarchy did they gain unrestrained freedom for external self-exposure and privacy. It might be noted that insulation, while a constraint, was also a protection. The protective function was sometimes fulfilled to conceal "embarrassments." One of my informants had a mentally retarded brother who was protected from public exposure by being educated and cared for at a school built privately by the family.

The selectivity of destinations for commuting or traveling further inhibited exposure. A large majority of the children attended Gakushuin. Some parents chose other schools, but these were similarly exclusive, catering to the upper or upper-middle class, and therefore they also narrowly circumscribed classmate contact.

Traveling away from Tokyo meant staying at private resort villas or prominent hotels that accepted regular patrons only. Kazoku shopped at particular stores where the head managers would meet and attend the elite shoppers; occasional eating out meant going to special restaurants or hotels; and reputable theaters provided entertainment. Most often mentioned were the Mitsukoshi department store at Nihonbashi, the Imperial Hotel, Tokyo Clubhouse, Imperial Theater, Seiyōken (the first Western hotel, built in 1867 in Tsukiji—the initial district for settlement by foreigners[3]—which later opened a Western restaurant in Ueno)— places that are no longer elitist but used to appeal to the yamanote taste. The Peers' Clubhouse (Kazoku Kaikan) was another center of recreation of kazoku families. For hospitalization, St. Luke's (in Tsukiji) and imperially sponsored Red Cross hospitals were mentioned most.

The Domestic Space

The foregoing discussion on seclusion was concerned with boundaries between a kazoku person and the external world, external in a double sense to his/her household and to his/her status. Attention is now called inward to spatial boundaries within the residential premises. It will be shown that the above seclusion from the external sphere was reproduced within the domestic sphere.

One can imagine the magnitude of the previous estates of the kazoku from what have replaced them: school campuses, parks, golf courses, government buildings, foreign embassies, rental office buildings, hospitals, hotels, art galleries, sports arenas, wedding halls, new billionnaires' dwellings, condominia, and so on. The group of "Prince Hotels," owned by a parvenu family, the Tsutsumi, is indeed, in part, a replacement of estates of the imperial house, royal princes, and kazoku. According to one prince, his family had a lot of 30,000-*tsubo,* which roughly corresponds to 1 million square feet (1 tsubo equals 35.5 square feet). The prewar main premises of my kazoku informants ranged widely from one extreme of 100,000 tsubo to the other of less than 100 tsubo, but most stood between some thousands to several hundreds of tsubo. One of the largest main estates (commanding 38,000 tsubo) employed twenty-two gardeners. In addition, many of them had resort villas on the Shōnan seashores (e.g., Hayama, Zushi, Kamakura, Oiso) or highlands (Karuizawa, Nasu, etc.) as well as other real estate. The Maeda, the richest of all kazoku, owned, in addition to a 50,000-tsubo main residential estate (a large part of which comprises the present Komaba Park of Meguro ward), secondary estates *(bettei)* in Kamakura, Karuizawa, and Kanazawa (the castle town of its former province), ranches and forests in Hokkaido, and more lands in Kyoto and Korea (Sakai 1982, 120). Some of the new kazoku did very well, too, taking over old daimyō estates. Haru Reischauer (1986) writes that Matsukata Masayoshi, her grandfather, who rose from a modest samurai to count and eventually to prince, owned, in addition to the residential house in Shiba ward, which had formerly belonged to Matsudaira Sadanobu, a famous daimyō, a twenty-two-acre lot (called Matsukata Hill) in Azabu ward (1986, 104–105), summer homes in Kamakura, and 4,000 acres of wasteland in Nasuno, which was developed into farms, pastures, forests, and the like (117–118).

In a questionnaire, I asked about prewar and present landownership. Several respondents did not know the prewar ownership, and more respondents, now living in condominia or rental housing, wrote "none" for present ownership. For a comparison, only those responses that indicated some forms of private landownership are tabulated. Table 1 compares the total areas of

TABLE I   LAND AREAS IN PREWAR AND PRESENT OWNERSHIP

TOTAL AREA *(TSUBO)*	PREWAR OWNERS (N)	PRESENT OWNERS (N)
100 or fewer	7	35
500 or fewer	16	32
1,000 or fewer	13	5
5,000 or fewer	21	6
10,000 or fewer	6	1
50,000 or fewer	7	1
100,000 or fewer	1	0
200,000 or fewer	1	0
600,000 or fewer	1	0
N. Total respondents	73	80

NOTE: 1 acre = 1,224 *tsubo;* 10,000 *tsubo* = 8.16 acres.

land owned, including nonresidential lands, during the two periods.

The seventy-three prewar owners held on average approximately 16,700 tsubo each. Some had very extensive holdings, including several estates and/or forests combined. The postwar reduction is phenomenal, the average of the present eighty owners being roughly seven hundred tsubo, 4.2 percent of the prewar figure. Since the sample excludes apartment or rental dwellers, the actual percentage is even lower.[4]

The imperial house surpassed all in the possession of estates. As of 1937, it controlled roughly 627 million tsubo (over one-half million acres), including the central Tokyo palace (637,170 tsubo = 520.5 acres), eleven secondary or detached palaces, and many forests, which were a main source of its "private" revenue (Kodama 1978, 314–315).

The kazoku main dwelling in Tokyo consisted typically of two architecturally distinct parts—Japanese- and Western-styled —either as two separate houses *(nihonkan* and *yōkan)* or as two sections of a single house. While there were purely Japanese houses, some kazoku, including the Maeda, had an entirely Western house. This is one of the visible indications of how yamanote residents, upper class in particular, in contrast to the conservative, poorer shitamachi people, were influenced by the Meiji slogan of "Civilization and Enlightenment" and lured into the Western way of life, which in turn sharpened their status distinction. And this is why many kazoku houses, after the war, were commandeered to serve as lodgings for high officers of the Occupation forces. It might be noted in this conjunction that the heart of "high city" where kazoku residences congregated has been densely populated by foreign nationals and embassies.

The Three-Dimensional Boundaries

The spatial demarcation of residence was multidimensional, geographically, and symbolically marked. The boundaries were associated with the ranks, functions, or sex of the occupants. I detect three partially overlapping dimensions even though these do not completely match the mental map held by my informants. The first was the universally recognizable "vertical opposition." Some areas of the premises were conceptualized as low and marked off from high areas. The personnel of the premodern imperial court, for example, used to be dichotomized between *den-jōbito* (literally, "people up on the palace floor," namely, nobles who were allowed into the emperor's living quarters) and *jige* ("down on the ground," i.e., nonnoble retainers).

The kazoku family occupied the upper domain *(kami)*, the servants the lower domain *(shimo)*. These vertical terms referred both to the areas and their respective occupants—master family and servants. Within the family, the uppermost area was quarters for the head of the household (and his wife); it was some distance from the nursery, which was at the lower end of the upper domain; in some households the head of the household or the family as a whole was designated *o-kami* from the humble standpoint of a servant (shimo).[5] Servants, maid-servants in particular, who as a whole constituted the shimo domain, were further broken down into kami and shimo: upper maids *(kami-jochū)* attended the master family; lower maids had little contact with the master family; they *(shimo-jochū)* worked around the kitchen and/or waited upon the upper maids. The living room and bedrooms of the head and his wife thus constituted the uppermost area, the kitchen area the lowermost. Occupancy varied with time: involving shifts and bedtime. Kami-jochū, for example, belonged to two levels: while attending the master family they waited for calls in a room close to the uppermost quarters, and therefore they were designated *otsugi* (the adjacent room);[6] at bedtime, they would withdraw, except one on duty in some cases, into the maids' living quarters, which was another lower point of the domestic space.

The vertical opposition, universally recognizable, sounds simple, but it remains largely metaphorical. What is more important and what complicates the spatial analysis is the lateral opposition of *omote* and *oku,* which was interlocked with the vertical opposition of kami and shimo in an intricate fashion. Vertical metaphor in fact translated into the literally physical space spreading laterally. The boundary between omote and oku to which every informant drew attention in describing his/her residence turned out not to be so sharp and self-evident as it appeared in the informant's mental map. In the intricacy of this boundary lies, I argue, a clue to the Japanese conception of ascribed hierarchy.

Omote and oku may be translated as "front" and "interior" respectively. The front versus interior opposition appeared as a logical dichotomy to my informants for good reasons. First, the two sections were architecturally separated, situated either in two distinct parts of a single house, removed from each other and connected by a long hallway, or in two separate buildings. Further, the dichotomy between omote and oku was strongly associated with the sex of occupants of the respective spaces: the omote refers not only to the frontal space but also to male servants, and the oku to female servants of the interior. The omote versus oku opposition further corresponded to that of the "public" versus the "private" sector of the house. The omote staff managed the house in relation to the outside world, and thus the space was also called "office"; the oku staff was in charge of the private life of the kazoku family.

The question is where the master family belonged in this lateral dimension, or how the vertical dimension of kami/shimo was related to the omote/oku dimension. It would make no sense to say that kami is to shimo what omote is to oku because the kami person, the lord of the house in particular, belonged to both oku and omote. Conversely, some of the lowest personnel seem to have belonged neither to omote nor to oku. The confusion is untangled when the omote/oku opposition is further broken down into two subdimensions. The opposite of the front is not the interior but the rear, and the opposite of the interior is the exterior, not the front. The two dimensions are thus restated as front/rear *(omote/ura)* and interior/exterior *(uchi/soto)*. These two can then be neatly paralleled with the above/below *(kami/shimo)* dimension: there were rough alignments between above, front, and interior on the one hand, and below, rear, and exterior on the other.

Figure 1 implies that the uppermost person (the head of the house) belonged to the innermost and frontmost domains whereas the lowest person (janitor or kitchen maid) occupied the outermost or the rearmost areas.[7] Other residents intermediary in status, whether family or servants, would find themselves somewhere in between in variable permutations of the three dimensions. While assigned to one domain for usual occupancy, there were varying degrees of freedom or obligation to cross the boundary. An upper maid was in the interior, as mentioned above, in attendance to the master and family; hence she was called *oku-jochū*[8] (interior maids) or otsugi as well as kami-jochū; but she would retire at night to her living quarters closer to the exterior or rear, unless she slept by a child in her charge (Lebra 1990). An upper managerial male servant, usually occupying the exterior,

FIGURE I   THE TRI-DIMENSIONAL HIERARCHY OF SPACE

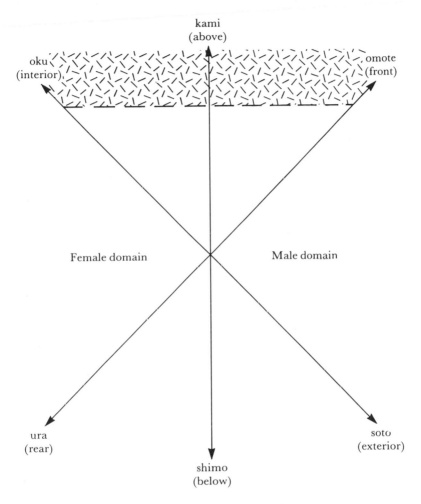

The shaded area is occupied by the head of household.

would be privileged to enter the interior to discuss "public" affairs with the master. Among the "exterior" personnel, some were higher, closer to the front, with greater access to the interior, than others, like rickshaw pullers, who were closer to the rear pole.

While some personnel were free on occasion to cross the

boundaries, rules of segregation were otherwise adhered to. Between the interior and exterior there were various degrees of sex segregation, more strict among high-ranking or traditional kazoku. During the night in particular, sex segregation was stringently enforced, as symbolized in some households by a special door, opening from one to the other region, which was locked at night from the interior side.

All boundaries for segregation give rise to marginals or anomalies. The interior versus exterior sex segregation produced an anomalous situation for male members of the family occupying the female domain, the interior. The head of the household, the foremost example of such anomaly, was exempted from the segregation code (indeed he was *the* innermost person) for a reason to be stated below, but sons were not. In some households, especially shogunal and high-ranking daimyō houses, sons at age seven (the supposedly marginal stage when a child was still totally dependent upon his parents and interior maids and yet began to assume sexual identity) were, according to the Confucian decree *(Danjo nanasai ni shite seki o onajū sezu)*, removed from the interior to the exterior to be waited upon by young male attendants called *shosei* (student-servant) or removed to all-male dorms away from home (Lebra 1990). Complete removal of a son from the interior was rarely practiced, however. A son's marginality was well exemplified by a royal informant whose ordinary day was marked by crossing the boundary inward and outward: in the morning, the prince would wake up in his exterior bedroom, enter the interior to have breakfast with his family, go to Gakushuin, come home after school, study and play in the exterior, go back to the interior for dinner and stay there until bedtime, and sleep in the exterior.

Sex segregation was related to the difference in marital status between male and female servants. The male staff, except the shosei, were married and commuted to the office from their private residences ("tenements") provided by the master and situated on the periphery or in the vicinity of the premises. The female servants, unmarried, lived and slept within the interior to be available for calls around the clock.[9]

In conjunction with the interior-exterior sex segregation, there was a rule of vertical segregation within the interior. Lower areas, closer to the rear, were tabooed to higher persons (as higher, front areas were tabooed to lower). Women informants in particular recalled rooms they would not go near. Servants' quarters were avoided by the master family, especially the head and his wife. The wife, coming from another family, thus often knew nothing about the rooms and hallways reserved for the maids whereas the children, who were more free to move about, were more informed about the house design. This kind of spatial taboo was more rigid for the lowest section of the house, centered on the kitchen. A daughter of a wealthy baron recalled having been told not to walk by the kitchen. When she had to, she ran fast. There was no exchange of words between the lady of the house and lower servants. A daughter of a kuge-prince, married to a royal prince, did not know where the kitchen was and never talked with either the kitchen maids or the janitors. One day, she accidentally caught sight of a kitchen maid, who, too frightened either to bow or to run away, froze with her face turned away. No wonder that many informants could not give the exact number of house servants, "because I don't know how many lower maids we had."

The spatial taboo was reciprocated by the servants. They stayed away from the rooms occupied by the master except when they were in attendance. The head of the house seated in the uppermost/innermost room was spoken to by a servant kneeling outside the room behind the door.

Here, too, we come across anomalies such as old-time concubines, known as *oharasan* (uterine ladies) or, again in a spatial metaphor, as *sokushitsu* or *owaki* ("side room" ladies). When a concubine mothered the heir, her status was raised from that of an attendant, but not all the way up to the kami. She was residing elsewhere, but when she visited her "master's" house, she had no room to occupy, "neither in the otsugi nor okami section" and so was found "standing around the hallway." Her spatial marginality was sometimes translated into a seated position and posture, as recalled by a woman whose father-in-law, the head of a collateral royal house, was mothered by a uterine lady: "Every one of us was seated in a chair, but this woman [when she visited us] alone sat on the floor and knelt, thanking. Members of the family all referred to her by her maiden name without *san.*" The uterine lady occupied the same space as the master family, but at the same time her body, posture, and speech were telling that she did not belong "upstairs."

Kitchen maids personified the lowest end in the vertical

opposition, as well as the rearmost position in the front-rear opposition. At the same time, they were marginal to the interior-exterior boundary, and thus spatially uncertain. According to a shogunal descendant, they were "loitering around the kitchen area as if there was no fixed place to belong to."

The outdoor area of the premises was also subject to the segregation code. Some daughters were not even allowed to step out into the garden unless escorted by servants; playing within the grounds, most sons and daughters found playmates among the children of the exterior staff, but some of them were forbidden to have such contact. There were boundaries in the premises inside which kazoku children were confined, the area of the servants' tenements being especially tabooed (which taboo only tempted some daring children to break it).

The Front-Interior Double Occupancy

Thus far no question has been raised about the seemingly contradictory nature of the master's double occupancy of the frontmost and innermost regions. Hosting distinguished guests or being invited as one of such guests was among the most regular activities of the head of a kazoku house. Banquets and entertainments were held in the frontmost section of the house, namely, the reception hall built away from the interior, as well as in the landscaped garden (for a "garden party"). In consideration of foreign dignitaries or the Westernized royals and peers to be invited, some households would use the Western-style section or house primarily for such receptions. Accompanied by his wife, the master was most conspicuously present in the frontal section when hosting an entertainment or ceremony. The personnel in both the exterior and interior were mobilized to prepare the master (and lady) to present himself in the front.

Symbolic of the front-rear hierarchy was the rank order of entrance gates and doors. The front gate, leading to the main entrance door, was reserved for the household head and his prominent guests; the lowest rear gate, which was behind the kitchen door, was for the lowest-ranking servants or outsiders like fish or produce venders. Others—such as lesser members of the family, lesser guests, sellers of more "clean" goods such as candy and clothing—used one of the side or "inner" gates, which ranked somewhere between these two extremes. The importance of the gate hierarchy to the sense of order can be inferred from the complaint of a woman quoted by her niece: "It used to be that only my father-in-law and husband walked through the Grand Gate. But now everything is mixed up and confused."[10]

The lateral hierarchy of front versus rear thus correlates with the vertical hierarchy of above versus below. The structure of "above : below : : front : rear" is also found in the models presented by Schwartz (1981) and Feinberg (1988) respectively. What does look problematical in the Japanese case is the addition of another lateral hierarchy: interior versus exterior. The lord of the house, while seated in the front and thus on display face-to-face with distinguished outsiders, was also the resident of the innermost region of his household, hidden from outside. Even within a front-staged reception room, the highest person was seated at the innermost center. In this connection one might recall that in a samurai movie the hierarchy is best dramatized by an extremely elongated hall where rows of vassals seated according to ranks prostrate themselves toward the lord, who is hardly visible, sitting at the farthest inner end.

For the hereditary elite, royal and noble alike, the double occupancy of the ceremonial front and the hidden interior was inevitable. First of all, the status of the hereditary elite was both public and private—public because of their symbolic eminence in the national hierarchy, private because their status was deeply rooted in the family, kinship, ancestry, "blood." In other words, the public status presented in the front domain was inseparable from the family life led in the innermost domain protected from the public view. In this connection, it is significant that guests were categorized differently, according to a daimyō-viscount, on the basis of the above duality of hereditary status: public guests—high officials, kazoku peers, royals, foreign ambassadors and ministers, and so on—were invited into the formal reception hall (front); private guests—kin of the master family—were privileged into the parlor of the interior for intimate contact. Visitors lower on both scales (public status and kinship proximity), those who were neither public enough nor private enough—such as low-ranking former vassals or tradesmen—were met and dealt with in the lower guest rooms attached to the exterior and hosted by the house staff, not the head of the household.

The front-interior separation is unavoidable or even necessary also as a matter of presentational strategy familiar to us through Goffman's writing in dramaturgical sociology. To play a ceremonial role on the front stage effectively requires the concealment from the audience of what goes on behind the stage. Writing about the British royalty, Hayden (1987) discusses the monarch's "two bodies"—"body natural" and "body politic"—which should be kept apart. "The Queen's body politic is relentlessly on display" while "Her body natural is assiduously hidden by 'the impenetrable secrecy' of the Palace" (1987, 11). The natural body is manifested, to put it in Douglas' down-to-earth terms, by "organic eruption" such as excretion, vomiting, spitting. The "purity rule" is to keep nature from culture, organic from social (Douglas 1975, 213). One might add "erotic eruption," which could require multiple bedchambers within the interior, as in the case of polygyny[11] practiced by my informants' forebears. For Elias (1978), concealment of the natural body and its functions from the public self amounted to the "civilizing process" marking modern European history.

The front-interior separation was all the more necessary for the eminently public elite, who played a central role on the front stage and therefore needed extra relaxation offstage. The natural body had to be protected as much as the public body, through the separation of the two bodies.

Dyarchy

What does all this add up to in terms of the overall hierarchy? Because of the omote-oku double occupancy, royalty or aristocrats necessarily depended upon the retinue to mediate between spheres. As a front-stage, ceremonial actor, the master had to be propped up and guided by the stage producers. As an occupant of the interior, he depended upon exterior personnel and outside counselors to manage his external affairs and relations. Furthermore, his positional interiority often even kept him from playing a front role, and this spatial dilemma stemming from double occupancy was resolved by the institutionalized surrogacy by kin or head servants. The "surrogate worship" *(godaihai)* at the ancestor shrines or temples was a major responsibility of the head maid in high-ranking kazoku households. In the imperial household, a chamberlain on duty does the same at the palace shrine every morning as the surrogate for the emperor, and imperial messengers *(chokushi)* are sent out from time to time in the same capacity of imperial surrogacy to the Ise shrine and other imperially sponsored shrines *(chokusaisha)* and temples away from the capital.

The lord master was thus more or less kept out of touch from or control of the "real" space which lay "down below," "outside," or "behind." This was all the more true, the higher the position and therefore the more interiorized its holder was. It followed, then, that the "authority" of the master—unless he was an unusually strong character determined to make decisions and exercise authority by himself, to be autonomous, and thus to deviate from the conventional norm of the ascribed elite—was destined to become ritualistic, symbolic, or empty. Actual decisions tended to be made, power to be exercised, budgets to be allocated, the stage to be "produced," by the high-ranking subordinates who were free to move between exterior and interior, front and rear, up and down. A typical lord would leave everything to his subordinates, telling them, as the cliche goes, "Do it as you think best" *(yoki ni hakarae)*. It was this situation that gave rise to a dyarchy with duocephaly—a symbolic head and a managerial or operational head.

Against the backdrop of dyarchy, it is understandable that informants held ambivalent feelings toward their former servants. On the one hand, the latter were recalled with warmth as having been helpful, caring, loyal, dependable, indispensable, more intimate than one's family, and so on. The prosperity of the house was generously credited to the loyalty and managerial acumen of the staff. The master-servant bond is still surviving, in some cases, into the descendant generations, even though their contemporary socioeconomic statuses may well have been reversed.

On the other hand, negative remarks were heard as frequently. The head maid was recalled as domineering, more oppressive to a bride than the worst example of mother-in-law, and the top manager was resented as laying an iron hand over budgetary matters, overruling the master's request. "In those days, the lord could say nothing to his employee-subordinates," said a daimyō-countess regarding her father-in-law. What went on backstage or outside the premises was kept secret until a household crisis erupted. Postwar bankruptcy was attributed, in addition to the extraordinary property taxes and the loss of status privileges, to the managerial servants who took advantage of the master's financial naïveté, and "cheated" and "robbed" him. These contrasting views of the former subordinates reflect two different roles played by one party of the dyarchy in relation to the other: supportive and complementary on the one hand, expropriative and usurpatory on the other.[12]

The dyarchy took a dramatic form with the imperial institution because the emperor represented the unparalleled charisma of the hereditary status. While required to be spatially split, the body is nevertheless "indivisible" (Giddens 1984), needless to say, and it was in the indivisible body that the hereditary charisma resided. The general tendency would then be to isolate the charismatic body by pushing it further inward. In other words, interiority tended to encompass the other dimensions.[13]

Generally, then, the responsibilities involving decisions and executions that were vested in the status holder would have to be left to his subordinate surrogate. Spatially, if one was confined in the interior and front, the other dominated the exterior, rear, and, above all, intermediary areas. One embodied the status, the other implemented it; one authenticated the decision made and executed by the other. Historical examples of dyarchy are legion and at many levels, notably the emperor and his regent, a shogun and his regent, the imperial court and shogunal government, a *shoen* proprietor and local manager, a daimyō and his chief vassal, the emperor and *genrō*. One represented symbolic/cultural hegemony, the other politico-economic domination. We can extend this type of dyarchy to the aristocratically affiliated *iemoto,* schools of art. An iemoto was (and still is in some cases) topped by a court noble who does not practice the art as authenticator of professional licenses; classes are actually taught and led by the practicing iemoto master of the art (Lebra 1991).

The two parties were interdependent, complementary, or instrumental to one another, but the duplex arrangement also opened the way to a reversal of the hierarchical order to the point of virtual subversion or usurpation. Nevertheless, the formal structure of dyarchy was not destroyed, neither party supplanted the other to claim a *mono-archy*—a true monarchy. Again the imperial institution provides the best illustration. The imperial authority was expropriated, but not annihilated. The Tokugawa ruler could and did demonstrate the shogunal hegemony over the imperial court, and yet even at the peak of its power, he needed *shōgun senge,* the imperial authorization for shogunal investiture. The murder of an emperor did not mean that the murderer wanted to put an end to the "sun dynasty" but to replace the victim by another member of the same family. Emperor Hirohito, supposedly targeted by ultramilitarists, would have been replaced by Prince Chichibu, his brother. The dyarchy contributed to the preservation of the "symbolic capital" (Bourdieu 1977) carried by the imperial dynasty. The Japanese monarchy thus may be said to owe its place as the world's longest-lived dynasty to the *dy*archy itself, whereas a true *mon*archy would have been short-lived.

It was the purpose of this essay to throw light upon this historical legacy of dyarchy from the standpoint of the spatial demarcation of hereditary hierarchy. The hereditary elite was characterized as an embodiment of the "public" eminence on the one hand and of the private identity embedded in kinship and ancestry on the other. This duality was represented by the spatial oppositions of residence such as interior-exterior and front-rear. The head of the house as the hereditary-status holder was to divide his indivisible body between the front-public and interior-private space, with a strain toward interiorization. It was concluded that the spatially constrained charisma of hereditary status contributed to the production and reproduction of the dyarchy. It might be speculated that the dyarchical legacy explains the cultural survival (or revival) of the hereditary status of the nobility and royalty, a status that is legally, politically, and economically empty.

Notes

The long-term research that underlies this essay has been supported at various stages by the Joint Committee on Japanese Studies of the American Council of Learned Societies and the Social Science Research Council, the Japan Foundation, the University of Hawaii Japan Studies Endowment, the University of Hawaii Fujio Matsuda Scholar award, and the Wenner-Gren Foundation. I wish to take this opportunity to express my heavy sense of indebtedness.

1. Robben (1989) analyzes the domestic space in a Brazilian fishing community. Employing Bourdieu's "practice" theory, the author connects the domestic architecture with "sea" and "street," the private

with the public space. I find it a good demonstration of the productivity of domestic-space analysis.

2. Through the Restoration, the daimyō lost most but not all of their domainal wealth in terms of rice revenue. The retention of even a fraction showed the significance of the pre-Restoration estate, so that a bigger daimyō house was that much wealthier than a smaller one after the Restoration. Further, with the fraction that was later commuted into bonds and cash, some daimyō houses reemerged with enormous wealth through well-advised investment and financial management (mismanagement threw some others into bankruptcy). No longer a domainal lord, the former daimyō possessed such wealth as his "private" property.

3. This is a good example of the discrepancy between the status-symbolic meaning and the physical location of the yamanote-shitamachi division. Tsukiji is a definitely shitamachi district, but in early Meiji it emerged as a geographical forerunner of "Civilization and Enlightenment" because it was selected for foreign settlement, to cater to the westernized yamanote taste.

4. Even the prewar figures show how little land the Japanese aristocracy commanded, compared, for example, with their British counterpart who own(ed) tens of thousands of acres. One thousand acres (more than 1 million tsubo) would be "not much" for a British baron (Perrott 1968, 34) but would be beyond a dream for most Japanese princes.

5. The term *okami* was used for the late Shōwa emperor privately by his entourage as well as by the empress. The same term was used for kazoku household heads according to several informants. (Likewise, *ue-sama* was also used for a top person like the shōgun, *ue* being identical to kami as *shita* to shimo). Kami also means gods. Resemblance between a god and a high-status personage can be also shown in the usage of *miya*, which means both a shrine and royal person. Such resemblance stems from spatial symbolism.

6. This is one meaning of otsugi given by several informants; another was suggested in vertical terms as "second to or lower than the head maid."

7. While a janitor's low position is understandable in view of the location of refuse collection at the rear end, outdoors, of the premises, why a kitchen maid was so low may not be as obvious. The kitchen was subdivided between the section, often with a lowered floor, closest to the rear door, where rice was cooked, and the more frontal section with an elevated floor, which was occupied by the male chef in command of assistant cooks engaging in "professional" cooking. The kitchen maid(s) specialized in rice cooking and thus was called *meshitaki* (rice cooker); she may have also cleaned bathrooms. It is interesting that the upper-class

households considered rice cooking unskilled, peripheral to the whole repertoire of culinary art, and thus to be relegated to the *hashitame,* lowly maids. Some aristocratic daughters were tutored in fanciful French or Chinese cookery, but they had no idea how to cook rice. For middle-to-lower-class women, rice cooking was a skilled job to be mastered as a required curriculum for bridal training. This class difference may reflect the differential weight of rice itself as a staple.

8. In a household where the hierarchy of maids was more elaborated, the term *oku-jochū* was reserved for the head maid, also known as *jijo-gashira* or *rōjo,* who supervised the whole female retinue and/or carried an exclusive right to wait upon the head of the house.

9. From this circumstance one can surmise the vulnerability of a maid to sexual "harassment" by a male member of the family unless the segregation rule was imposed. The rule was less stringent among court nobles *(kuge)* than warriors *(buke).* A son of a prominent kuge kazoku, viewing the family history with a scholarly detachment, discussed how his ancestors typically had experienced sex in their adolescence with live-in maids-in-attendance, called *ie nyōbō,* long before their formal marriage with noblewomen. Pregnancy led to the discharge of the "hand-laid" maid, and the child thus born out of wedlock was, according to this informant, dumped into certain Buddhist temples as a priest or nun. The informant thus disclosed the mundane side of prestigious royal or noble temples, commonly called *monzeki.*

10. The symbolic significance of entrances and doors was noted by a student of Victorian England's aristocracy as well. "All business and trade inquiries went to the back door. The front door was opened by a servant correctly mannered and dressed to suit the status of the family. . . . In larger houses, the Servants Hall was sometimes used to hold special categories who were halfway between back and front door status, e.g., the doctor, schoolmaster, important tradesmen or unimportant kin" (Davidoff 1973, 87).

11. "Polygyny" is not quite an accurate term since there was clear status inequality between the principal wife and secondary consorts.

12. This argument has some implications for male-female relations. The imperial and aristocratic world was definitely male-centered, and yet women played important roles, as shown in this essay, for good reasons. We have seen how the master was placed in the innermost section of the residence, which was also a predominantly female domain. The male master depended upon female servants to take care of his corporeal needs. Some male servants, too, helped the master in similar capacities, but it was taken for granted that women were better equipped for domestic caretaking chores. (It might be further footnoted here that female service seems indispensable for gods' well-being also. Closest to

the Amaterasu of the palace shrine, it turns out, are female ritualists, called *naishōten*, who, according to an informant, "as caretakers" could enter the *nainaijin*, the holiest and innermost chamber, which was off limits even to the emperor.) The kazoku recollections suggest that the master's overall dependency made some higher-ranking maids, head maids in particular, quite powerful and domineering. Can we speculate, then, that all-around servility, as embodied by a female servant, or even a housewife in the commoner class, may lead to a reversal of hierarchy, in this limited sense, between male master and female servant or between husband and wife?

13. An analogy may be drawn from a Shintō god in that the interiorized, hidden emperor was like a god whose presence, forever invisible, is symbolized by a shrine. Even when the god is brought out to make a tour around the community under his jurisdiction in an annual festival, he is transferred by a mystic rite from his residential shrine into a temporary portable shrine *(mikoshi)* with no moment of exposure. This kind of spatial confinement of a god is likely to have magical implications because invisibility is a genesis of supernatural potency, as argued by Luhrmann (1989). As if to ensure invisibility and thereby maximize magical efficacy, mystic Shintō rites are conducted in the dark, during the night or before dawn. Like a god confined in the hidden interior of a shrine, the emperor was in no position to use his potency, instead only to have it available to a magician who was outside the shrine, or, in a Japanese metaphor, by "the carrier of the mikoshi," who invoked to his advantage the name of the august one inside and invisible.

Not that emperors were voiceless like gods. The Shōwa emperor expressed his opinions for or against what went on outside the palace, oftentimes in his name, by means of *gokamon* (imperial questioning) (Titus 1974). He did so, however, only through his closest entourage *(sokkin)* like the lord keeper of the seal, genrō, and grand chamberlain. The sokkin not only represented the emperor but influenced his will and coached his conduct—and for this reason were targeted for assassination as *kunsoku no kan* (evil men of the imperial entourage) by the radical right wing of military officers, culminating in the February 26, 1936, coup. Even at the *gozen kaigi* (the nonconstitutional conferences, in the emperor's presence, of topmost state leaders to make important decisions to determine the state's destiny), the emperor was there to listen, not to speak, or only to authenticate, not to make, decisions by his presence. Frustrated, the Shōwa emperor attempted to speak up but was politely discouraged by the sokkin, or if he did speak against the sokkin's advice, he was gently overruled by the conferees.

As has been well documented (Kido 1966, 1223–1224; The

Pacific War Research Society 1968, 34–35), the Shōwa emperor broke the tacit rule of silence to have his voice heard and heeded on August 10, 1945, at the gozen kaigi to decide whether Japan should accept or reject the Potsdam Proclamation. He could do so because Prime Minister Suzuki solicited His Majesty's opinion to break the tie in the vote.

References

Bourdieu, Pierre. 1977. *Outline of a Theory of Practice*. Cambridge: Cambridge University Press.

Davidoff, Leonore. 1973. *The Best Circles: Women and Society in Victorian England*. Totowa, N.J.: Rowman and Littlefield.

Douglas, Mary. 1975. *Implicit Meanings: Essays in Anthropology*. London: Routledge & Kegan Paul.

Elias, Norbert. 1978. *The History of Manners*. Vol. 1: *The Civilizing Process*, translated by E. Jephcott. New York: Pantheon Books.

Feinberg, Richard. 1988. "Socio-Spatial Symbolism and the Logic of Rank on Two Polynesian Outliers." *Ethnology* 27:291–310.

Giddens, Anthony. 1984. *The Constitution of Society: Outline of the Theory of Structuration*. Cambridge: Polity Press.

Hayden, Ilse. 1987. *Symbol and Privilege: The Ritual Context of British Royalty*. Tucson: University of Arizona Press.

Inukai Tomoko. 1989. *Tomoko no nihon suteki sengen* (Tomoko's discovery of Japan's wonders). Tokyo: Jōhō Sentā Shuppankyoku.

Jichishō Gyōseikyoku (Administrative Bureau, Home Ministry), ed. 1984. *Zenkoku jinkō: setaisū-hyō, jinkō dōtai-hyō*. (The national population: tables of households and demographic trends). Tokyo: Kokudo Chiri Kyōkai.

Kasumi-Kaikan, ed. 1982–1984. *Kazoku kakei taisei* (The complete compilation of kazoku genealogies). 2 vols. Tokyo: Yoshikawa Kōbunkan.

Kido Kōichi. 1966. *Kido Kōichi nikki* (The diary of Kido Kōichi). 2 vols. Tokyo: Tokyo Daigaku Shuppankai.

Kōbata Yoshiko. 1984. *Akasaka monogatari* (The tale of Akasaka). Tokyo: Aki Shobō.

Kodama, Kōta. 1978. *Tennō: Nihonshi shōhyakka 8* (The emperor: a short encyclopedia of Japanese history, no. 8). Tokyo: Kondō Shuppansha.

Lebra, Takie Sugiyama. 1989. "Adoption among the Hereditary Elite of Japan: Status Preservation through Mobility." *Ethnology* 28: 185–218.

————. 1990. "The Socialization of Aristocratic Children by Commoners: Recalled Experiences of the Hereditary Elite in Modern
Japan." *Cultural Anthropology* 5:78–100.
————. 1991. "Resurrecting Ancestral Charisma: Aristocratic Descen-
dants in Contemporary Japan." *Journal of Japanese Studies* 17:59–
78.
————. 1992. *Above the Clouds: Status Culture of the Modern Japanese Nobility.*
Berkeley and Los Angeles: University of California Press.
Luhrmann, T. M. 1989. "The Magic of Secrecy" (1986 Stirling Award
Essay). *Ethos* 17:131–165.
The Pacific War Research Society. Compiled 1968. *Japan's Longest Day.*
Tokyo: Kodansha International.
Perrott, Roy. 1968. *The Aristocrats: A Portrait of Britain's Nobility and Their
Way of Life Today.* London: Weidenfeld and Nicolson.
Reischauer, Haru Matsukata. 1986. *Samurai and Silk: A Japanese and Amer-
ican Heritage.* Cambridge: Harvard University Press.
Robben, Antonius C. G. M. 1989. "Habits of the Home: Spatial Hege-
mony and the Structuration of House and Society in Brazil."
American Anthropologist 91:570–588.
Sakai Miiko. 1982. *Aru kazoku no showa-shi* (The Shōwa history of a
kazoku). Tokyo: Shufu to Seikatsu Sha.
Schwartz, Barry. 1981. *Vertical Classification: A Study in Structuralism and the
Sociology of Knowledge.* Chicago: University of Chicago Press.
Seidensticker, Edward. 1983. *Low City, High City: Tokyo from Edo to the
Earthquake.* New York: Alfred A. Knopf.
Titus, David A. 1974. *Palace and Politics in Prewar Japan.* New York:
Columbia University Press. Translated into Japanese by Otani
Kenshiro as *Nippon no tennō seiji* (Tokyo: The Simul Press, 1979).

CHAPTER 3

Christmas Cakes and Wedding Cakes: The Social Organization of Japanese Women's Life Course

Mary C. Brinton

To the social scientist's eye, the apparent orderliness of the life course is one of the most striking features of contemporary Japanese society. How does one become aware of this orderliness? In my case, it happened neither through delving into statistical sources nor constructing deductive hypotheses, but rather from picking up clues and impressions from daily interaction. Three examples come to mind.

At a social gathering of university-educated Japanese women in 1984, I found myself engaged in a discussion of cultural differences in marriage and childbearing with one of the women present. In the middle of the conversation, she offered her own frank and spontaneous summary of Japanese life cycle stages: "It is like a life plan that we [Japanese] have" (Brinton 1988). The normative significance of this statement impressed me. What American would offer such a succinct statement on the "life plan" of Americans?

A second example of attention to life cycle orderliness was demonstrated in a Japanese newspaper ad for a bank. The headline ran, "Where are you in life right now?" Underneath were drawn five succeeding swirls, each encircling in sequence, one by one, the following: "*kekkon* (marriage), *shussan* (birth), *jūtaku* (owning a house), *kyōiku* (education), and *rōgo* (old age)."

The third example is more specific in its reference to the appropriate timing of a specific life event, marriage. In a lecture in Tokyo in 1985 I demonstrated with comparative data for the United States and Japan a social fact of which I had become increasingly aware through living in Japan: Japanese women marry "on schedule" to an extent unimaginable to American women. After I proudly displayed my data, one member of the audience excitedly piped up: "What you are saying is expressed by a Japanese riddle: Why are women like Christmas cakes?" My blank expression led him to continue, as other members of the audience laughed in anticipation: "Because they are popular and sell like hot cakes up until twenty-five and after that you have a lot of trouble getting rid of them" (Brinton 1992).[1]

The first story suggests a strong awareness that to be Japanese implies following a life event schedule, the second story indicates the natural ordering of life events, and the third humorously suggests the consequences should a woman choose not to begin a particular life stage (marriage) on time. Together, these stories suggest a strongly sanctioned regularity to the life course. What does this regularity tell us about social organization in Japan? How is structure imparted to the life course by the key social institutions through which the individual passes in his or her life? What features of the Japanese life course differ from American life course(s)?

The goal of this essay is to answer these questions and to reach toward a theoretical goal as well. I argue that contrasts between the structure of the life course in Japan and the United States reflect differences in the structure of basic social institutions in the two cultural settings. Analyzing the life cycle and making the link upward from individual behaviors to the level of social organization facilitates theorizing about how future changes in Japanese social institutions will reverberate back down to individual lives.

The essay focuses on women's life course transitions among educational institutions, the family, and work organizations in Japan and the United States. The metaphor of a "stakeholder" is relevant. I use the term to refer to an individual who has a stake in exercising some control over the life course transitions of another person.[2] More so than for American women, the lives of Japanese women are influenced heavily by stakeholders. Key individuals such as parents and employers play an active role in shaping crucial life course transitions. The socially embedded lives of Japanese women and the more self-directed lives of American women are important not so much because of what they reveal about cultural differences in individualism and internalized norms but because of what they reveal about the social organization of American and Japanese societies. In short, the lives of both groups of women reflect underlying social structure.

The first part of the essay discusses the American bias in life course research and how this bias hinders cross-cultural comparisons. Three features of life course transitions (variance, reversibility, and age-congruity) are identified as useful for cross-cultural comparison. These features summarize key differences between Japanese and American women's life courses. In the second section of the essay I explore how women's life cycle patterns reflect the structure of central social institutions in Japan and the United States—the educational system, the links between the educational system and the labor market, and the relation between the family and the labor market. The third section concludes with thoughts on how future changes in Japanese social institutions may affect women's lives.

The Embeddedness of the Life Course in Social Organization

A number of studies have examined how the life course is organized differently in industrial societies (see for instance, Featherman and Sorensen 1983; Hogan and Mochizuki 1985; Morgan, Rindfuss, and Parnell 1984). Hogan and Mochizuki considered whether industrialization and modernization have had similar consequences for the life course of men in Japan and the United States. They found little evidence of similar life course changes in the two societies and concluded that cultural differences exist in the response to modernization. For instance, age at marriage declined between the two cohorts of American men born in 1908–1912 and 1923–1927 (corresponding to men marrying during the Great Depression and men marrying during the baby boom) but remained invariant for Japanese men. The sequencing of the life course shows almost no variability for Japanese men: more than 90 percent of men complete school, begin working almost immediately, and marry after they are established in their careers. While this pattern was followed by about three-quarters of American men born in the early twentieth century, it was followed by only about 60 percent of those born in 1933–1942 (Hogan and Mochizuki 1985).

Likewise, Morgan, Rindfuss, and Parnell (1984) find less variability in Japan than in the United States in women's age at initiation of childbearing, the duration between marriage and first birth, and the incidence of childlessness. They conclude that "Japan has been successful at adapting industrialization to fit its existing social institutions" (1984, 27) and argue that it would be erroneous to conclude that modernization gives rise to the same marriage and fertility patterns in all cultures.

These descriptive studies demonstrate that the timing and sequencing of events is more predictable for the Japanese than the American life course. They suggest the necessity for a theoretical perspective that delineates how culture, apart from the general processes of industrialization, affects the life course. But they stop short of posing an explanation for the observed differences in life course patterns. An important objective of life course research should be to explain the social-structural sources of differences in life course behavior or to link what Plath has called "structural time" and "lifecourse time" (1983, 4). What differences in the relationships among social institutions in Japan versus the United States result in life course differences? Who are the symbolic stakeholders in individuals' decisions? How does the role of stakeholders differ across societies?

This series of questions reorients the life course perspective from an individualistic approach to a more social-institutional one. American researchers of the life course have usually treated the individual as a fairly independent decision maker responding to a set of choices regarding significant role transitions according to a normatively defined "life script." The transition to adulthood, for example, has typically been conceptualized in terms of exit from school, exit from the parental household, entry into marriage, entry into the labor force, and entry into parenthood. The exercise of control over entry and exit into each stage has been assumed to be an individual matter, subject to the goals and intentions (even if suggested by societal or subcultural norms) of an autonomous social actor.

A perspective that analyzes Japan or other cultures with the American assumption of individual actors who are relatively unconstrained by the motivations of others risks failing analytically. The social organization of Japanese society compared to American society provides more stakeholders in individuals' life course transitions into and out of social institutions. The life course and the rules that govern it in a given society are closely related to these stakeholder relationships among people and to the relationships among social institutions as well (Meyer 1986a, b).

Features of Life Course Transitions

Three dimensions of the life course specified by Modell, Furstenberg, and Herschberg (1976) are particularly useful in cross-cultural comparisons. These are the dimensions of *spread* or *variance, reversibility* of entrance and exit from specific institutions (e.g., marriage or the labor force), and *age-congruity.* *Spread* refers to the amount of time it takes for a given proportion of the population to make a particular transition. For instance, one could calculate the length of time it takes the middle 50 percent of the population to marry. A short spread indicates greater conformity in behavior among individuals than a long spread. *Reversibility* signifies whether entrance into a role or state tends to be reversed (by exit) at a later date. For instance, men generally exhibit irreversibility in their labor force status—once they begin their work lives, they remain in the work force until retirement. Women's work pattern in many societies exhibits reversibility, involving multiple entrances and exits from the work force. Finally, *age-congruity* refers to the degree of overlap between statuses. Greater age-congruity means that the individual simultaneously occupies several statuses at the same age, for example, he or she marries before leaving school rather than waiting until school completion to marry. Conversely, age-incongruity of certain statuses implies that individuals in a population do not simultaneously occupy those statuses. Instead, they exit one stage or state before entering another.

How do these concepts apply to the Japan–United States comparison? My argument in capsule form is that the timing of life course transitions in Japan is more *irreversible* than temporary, exhibits little *variance* or *spread* across individuals, and is *age-incongruous* (exhibiting very little overlap between the spreads of two or more transitions). The postadolescent period and adulthood are clearly demarcated by discrete, nonoverlapping transitions. Irreversibility, low variance, and age-incongruity symbolize the control exercised by stakeholders in the Japanese family (e.g., parents, spouses) and in other institutions such as the work organization (e.g., employers).

In contrast, the life course transitions of American women tend to be *reversible* rather than permanent, to exhibit a fair amount of *variance* or *spread* across individuals, and to be *age-congru-ous* (exhibiting overlap between the spreads of two or more transitions). Reversibility, variance, and age-congruity symbolize the relative openness and fluidity of positions in social institutions and the relative absence of stakeholders in the life course beyond the individual and the state.[3]

The Changing Life Course of American and Japanese Women

In a survey of historical changes in the life course of American women, McLaughlin et al. (1988) identified a decline in control over the life course by both the family of origin (for the transition to adulthood) and the family of procreation (for transitions within adulthood). This characterization was supported by a number of observations:

1. American women are spending a smaller proportion of their lives in family households. A large part of this decline is attributable to sharp increases in the proportion of women living alone among both younger (age 18–34) and older (age 65 and over) women.

2. American women are spending a smaller proportion of their lives married.

3. The control of the family over the regulation of sexual behavior has declined. This is illustrated by increases in premarital sexual behavior and in rates of cohabitation.

4. The family's role as a regulator of the *timing* of labor force participation has declined. The previous pattern where women's labor force participation was restricted to the periods prior to marriage and after the last child left home was replaced first by a continuation of employment after marriage and then with continuous participation after the birth of the first child. In short, family events that only thirty years earlier marked periods of eligibility and ineligibility for the labor force have become less and less significant.

These and other changes in the life course of American women represent a decline in the control of the family over many of the most significant aspects of the life course. Marriage and the family now compete with other institutions in the provision of social and economic rewards to women. Along with this, the family loses some of its ability to control the behavior of its members: parents and husbands become less important as stakeholders. This gradual loss of control is mirrored by the increasing involvement of the state in the control over the life course, not through direct legalistic means such as regulation of age at marriage, but rather through the assumption of more and more of the caretaker functions formerly assumed by the family. Unemployment insurance, social security, and other benefits that accrue to the individual at critical life transitions make it less economically imperative that individuals live their entire lives within families that, in effect, sponsor or guarantee the individual's decisions regarding marriage, education, and employment. The appearance of greater individual control over life course decisions is thus highly related to the increased role of the state as a guarantor. Control previously shared by the individual and primary institutions such as the family has not shifted wholly into individual hands. It has come to be shared by the individual and a more removed institutional actor in the form of the state.

Japan represents a contrast to this. The family of origin continues to play a central role both as a supplier of individuals to the "marriage market" and as a supplier of individual labor to economic organizations. The family plays a greater mediating role between the individual woman and formal institutions in Japan. Japanese parents in particular are greater stakeholders in life course decisions than American parents. In part this greater parental participation is due to the highly competitive, age-graded nature of the Japanese educational system. Successful competition in the series of contests at different junctures in the educational ladder and in the contest at the point of initial entry into the labor market is critical for individual economic and status rewards. Educational failures cannot be retraced and made up at later ages. Parents therefore feel pressure to help their children succeed. Furthermore, the preferred mode of labor market organization in the postwar period has been the internal labor market in which employers make investments in workers' human capital through on-the-job training (Koike 1983; Shimada 1981). In short, individual decision making in Japan is highly influenced by stakeholders such as parents and employers.

The social relations between Japanese women and the stakeholders in their fate are closer than in the United States.[4] The stakeholders might be thought of not as puppeteers holding the strings to individual action but rather as directors working from various parts of the stage. In the United States, these directors have instead become members of the audience.

Education, Labor Market, and Family

Education

The purpose of women's education in Japan's rapid industrialization phase, which began in the Meiji period (1868–1912), was to produce "good wives, wise mothers." At the same time that female education developed along the formula of preparing women for entry into a good marriage, male education developed along the formula of preparing men for placement in a work organization where more specialized training would occur. Post–World War II reforms consolidated men's and women's tracks together through the high school level. Beyond high school, sex segregation was reasserted within the very structure of the contemporary educational system: junior colleges came to function mainly as marriage preparation schools (for women), vocational schools were oriented toward technical training (principally for men), and universities were attended more heavily by men than women and supplied white-collar labor to large firms and to the government (Fujimura-Fanselow 1985; Nakata and Mosk 1987).

The Japanese educational system offers general educational preparation and certification to enter a subsequent organizational context. For men, this is the work organization; for women, it is marriage. As stakeholders or directors, Japanese parents hope for different levels of educational attainment for sons and daughters. They also view the purpose of education as different, depending on the sex of the child. Among parents who want to send a son to university, 41 percent see the primary goal as general education; the corresponding proportion for parents who want to send a daughter to university is 62 percent (Japan, Office of the Prime Minister 1982b). Conversely, 27 percent of parents want their son to get a university education for the purpose of obtaining job qualifications, and only 16 percent of parents who feel university is important for a daughter cite this as the primary reason.

That university education does not solely constitute job

preparation for women is underscored by figures for the proportion of Japanese women who enter the labor force upon school graduation: in 1987, this figure was 71 percent for junior high school graduates, 86 percent for high school graduates, 84 percent for junior college graduates, and 77 percent for university graduates. University-educated women were thus the second *least* likely to become employed upon graduation (Japan, Ministry of Labor 1988). In their discussion of women's life course, Hogan and Mochizuki conclude that "one of the most outstanding features of Japanese women compared to women in other developed countries has been that increased education is not uniformly associated with a stronger career orientation" (1985, 16). This point is underscored by Tanaka's finding of little change in the employment behavior of successive cohorts of highly educated Japanese women (1987).

In contrast, the primary reason stated for enrollment in higher education among American women in 1980 was job preparation (McLaughlin et al. 1988). In response to the increased demand among older American women for career-oriented higher education and the desire to combine education with family commitments, educational institutions have initiated more part-time student programs (primarily in female-dominated program areas).

In summary, a central purpose of women's education in contemporary Japan is preparation for family roles. As such, we would expect educational enrollment to occur almost exclusively before marriage, and the pattern of returning to school after marriage should be extremely rare. In the United States higher education for women has become more and more directed toward preparation for entry into the labor force. The timing of American women's education may exhibit more overlap with other roles such as wife and mother.

Figure 1 shows school enrollment figures for Japan and the United States in 1980. The left graph illustrates the relationship between age and enrollment; the right graph presents data on the marital status of enrolled women in each country. Enrollment declines rapidly with age in both countries, but the decline is much more rapid in Japan than in the United States. By age 25–29, only 1 percent of Japanese women are enrolled in school. In the United States, 14 percent of women 25–29 are enrolled in

Enrollment Status by Age
Japan and the United States (1980)

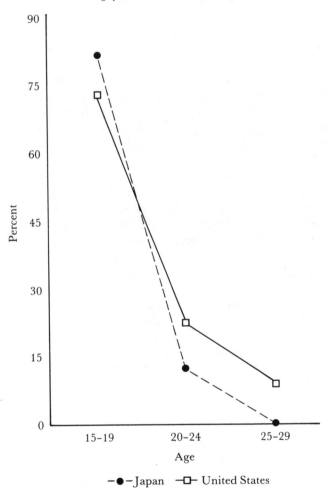

−●−Japan   −□− United States

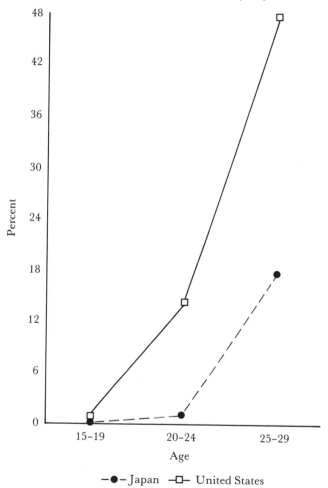

Percent Married among Students
Japan and the United States (1980)

Sources: U.S., Bureau of the Census, 1982; Japan, Office of
the Prime Minister, 1980a.

school either full- or part-time. Enrollment is clearly more age-graded in Japan than in the United States. Japanese educational enrollment by age demonstrates the *irreversibility* of school-leaving. Enrollment stretches over a greater number of years in the United States than in Japan, reflecting both increases in the number of years devoted to education and an increasing tendency for individual women to *return* to school after having once left it. These two phenomena are not separable by looking only at enrollment rates by age. But women aged 25 and above currently constitute more than 40 percent of female college students in the United States (McLaughlin et al. 1988). So figures on enrollment at older ages for large numbers of American women show both the return to school for some women and the continuation in postgraduate education for others.

Coupled with a lack of reversibility of the school-leaving decision in Japan is strong *age-congruity* between school enrollment and marriage. The right-hand graph of Figure 1 shows the percent of Japanese and American female students who are married. Not only do American women spread school enrollment over a longer time, but they are more likely to be married at the same time. Almost half of all American women aged 25–29 who are in school are married. In Japan, enrollment after age 25 is rare to begin with, and even rarer for married women. Enrollment in postsecondary education and concurrent marital responsibilities are largely incompatible in the Japanese context.

Relation between the Educational System and the Labor Market

To better understand the different roles the educational system plays for women in the two countries, it is necessary to consider differences in the labor market. Some American workplaces have career ladders with positions based on recruitment from inside the organization; others are constituted by positions into which individuals of different ages are recruited from other organizations or from school. The American educational system in recent years has demonstrated increasing flexibility in terms of being a resource to which individuals turn at different points in their lives for additional training and certification, and then reenter the labor force (Evans 1986).

The Japanese educational system, by contrast, essentially sponsors individuals directly into positions in work organizations

(Japan Institute of Labor 1990; Rohlen 1974). The ideal career consists of upward mobility through the hierarchically arranged positions in an organization. Despite recent broadening of the external labor market as a result of economic downturns and structural changes in the Japanese economy, enterprise-based internal labor markets remain a central model of economic organization in Japan. Comparative studies continue to document lower rates of job changing in Japan than in the United States (Hashimoto and Raisian 1985). Large private firms with internal career ladders have been popular choices for male graduates from Japan's top universities (Ushiogi 1986). A 1983 survey reported that 62 percent of male university seniors aspired to employment in a large firm, up 11 percent from 1975 (Nihon Recruit Center 1983).

In Japan, the importance of placement for men in a good work environment upon school graduation is shown by patterns of institutional sponsorship whereby schools maintain close ties with businesses in the community (Azumi 1969; Rosenbaum and Kariya 1989). The close relation between schools and individual firms in Japan occurs across secondary and tertiary levels, not just in selected universities and professional schools as in the United States. Employers have a strong interest in recruiting from top schools at each level because students have already been sorted via the school entrance exams from high school onward. Acceptance to a good school is a prerequisite for entering a good firm, and the content of schooling is regarded as quite incidental to future work. Securing a commitment from a good employer is equivalent to future job training and career sponsorship by that employer (Miyahara 1988).

The tight connection between the educational system and the labor market is not ideally suited to the dual demands of work and family. In fact, the careful channeling of male students into an organizational setting where they will receive employer sponsorship via on-the-job training is mirrored by the channeling of women into marriage or into temporary jobs that will give them a sense of the outside world and at the same time fill a company's needs for low-cost clerical labor (Brinton 1989; Clark 1979; Upham 1987). Japanese employers have argued that statistical discrimination (Arrow 1973) against women is rational because investment in on-the-job training for men will pay off (especially in the context of men's low interfirm mobility rates), whereas investments in women will be wasted when they marry or give birth and quit the labor force (Upham 1987). Enterprise-based internal labor markets act in combination with strong age-at-marriage norms to render it "rational" for women to exit from the labor market after a few years of work experience. As McLendon notes, "When a young woman gets a job she is encouraged to think of the workplace not as the first stage of a working career but rather as a way station on the route to marriage" (1983, 156). Employers are stakeholders in men's career mobility in the firm, and stakeholders in women's mobility into marriage and out of the firm. The employer is in effect hiring or directing women into marriage. A manager in a major electronics company expressed the symbolic passing of the stakeholder role from parents to employer: "Parents give us their daughters to take care of for a period before marriage, and we are responsible for them" (Brinton 1992). Some employers assume the role of hiring as clerical workers attractive young women to become possible future brides for their promising young male employees. It has not been uncommon for prestigious firms in Tokyo to make a consistent practice of never hiring women who lived alone during college, for fear that such women have sullied reputations and would make poor mates for their male employees.

The age patterns of female labor force participation reflect Japanese and American differences in the ways that women coordinate the demands of marriage and work. Figure 2 shows patterns for three different time periods. The Japanese data indicate little change in the overall level of participation over the 1960–1984 period and in the extent to which labor force participation is responsive to the assumption of the roles of wife and mother. The American data for the years 1960 and 1970 were similar to the Japanese data. Labor force participation increased until age 20–24 and then declined by age 25–29. The sharpness of this decline was not as great as in Japan, but the general sensitivity of women's labor force participation to family events is clear. Employment before marriage was followed by exit from the labor force after marriage. Reentry to the labor force occurred after the last child left home. In other words, labor force participation was a reversible decision.

The 1984 American data, however, are quite different. By

that point the female pattern of labor force participation by age had become similar to the male pattern, with little evidence of a decline in labor force participation in response to marriage or the birth of the first child. Labor force participation for many women in the United States is now an irreversible, lifetime decision.

The absolute levels of labor force participation in Japan and the United States are not directly comparable because in Japan the labor force includes a larger number of married women working as unpaid members of family businesses. The inclusion of unpaid family workers in the Japanese data actually attenuates what would otherwise be an even *steeper* decline in participation rates during the ages 25–34 when marriage and the first birth are most likely to occur. The second age peak of labor force participation for Japanese women (age 40–44) is largely representative of female part-time workers and/or workers with short-term employment contracts.[5]. It is not indicative of either the resumption or commencement of a career, but represents instead the supplemental character of work to a woman's primary set of obligations: her family.

Relation between the Family and the Labor Market

Initial entrance into the labor force is not synonymous with entrance into a career for most Japanese women (Brinton 1988; Lebra 1984; McLendon 1983). I have already noted the age-incongruity (incompatibility) between education and marriage as life stages in Japan and the irreversibility of the school-leaving decision. The pattern of age-incongruity between marriage and employment is also stronger in Japan than in the United States, reflecting the fact that entry into marriage constitutes a Japanese woman's primary commitment, expressed euphemistically in Japanese as her "lifetime employment" *(shūshin koyō)*. If a woman reaches the age of twenty-five without marrying, stakeholders such as parents, former teachers, employers, and friends typically assume the responsibility of introducing her to suitable partners (Lebra 1984). Hence the origin of the Japanese Christmas-cake riddle.

Greater stakeholding on the part of Japanese than American parents should be evidenced in a longer period of single daughters' cohabitation with parents and a lower propensity to live alone. Figure 3 shows the proportion of single women 25–34

FIGURE 2 LABOR FORCE PARTICIPATION BY AGE IN JAPAN AND THE
UNITED STATES (1960–1984)

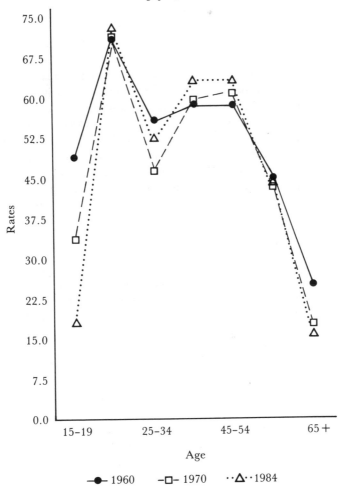

Labor Force Participation Rates by Age
Japan, 1960–1984

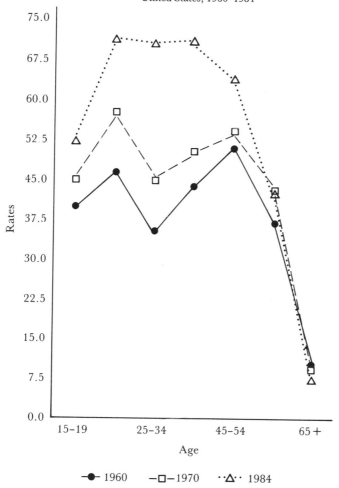

Labor Force Participation Rates by Age
United States, 1960–1984

Age

●— 1960   —□—1970   ··△·· 1984

Sources: U.S., Department of Labor, Bureau of Labor Statistics, 1985; U.S., Bureau of the Census, 1986; Japan, Ministry of Labor, Women's Bureau, 1985.

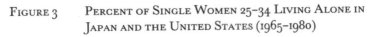

FIGURE 3   PERCENT OF SINGLE WOMEN 25–34 LIVING ALONE IN
            JAPAN AND THE UNITED STATES (1965–1980)

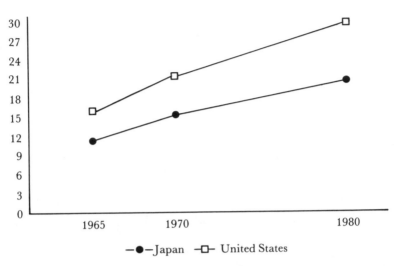

—●—Japan   —□— United States

Sources: U.S., Bureau of the Census, 1965; idem, 1971; idem, 1981;
Japan, Office of the Prime Minister, 1965; idem, 1970a.

living alone in the United States and Japan. The proportion is
increasing in both countries, but it remains substantially higher in
the United States. Rates of cohabitation (with an unmarried partner of the opposite sex) have also increased dramatically in the
United States (McLaughlin et al. 1988), but this trend is scarcely
visible in Japan. The living arrangements of single American
women in their twenties and thirties are largely distributed
between the two statuses of living alone and living in a cohabitation relationship. Japanese women's patterns consist of living
alone or residing with parents. These data suggest less family control over single women in the United States than in Japan.

    If the individual rather than the family is the stakeholder
in the United States, we would also expect marriage to be a more
reversible state and expect marriage timing to exhibit more variance across individuals. The divorce rate, since it measures the
prevalence of exits from marriage, is an appropriate indicator of
reversibility. So, as a second indicator of individual rather than

familial exercise of control over marriage, we can compare the divorce rate in the two countries. Figure 4 shows the comparison since 1940. The divorce rate in the United States began a steep increase in the mid-1960s. It is now roughly four times as high as the Japanese divorce rate, which also began to increase in the mid-1960s but at a much slower pace. Marriage is a more reversible decision in the United States than in Japan.

Finally, Figure 5 indicates a sharp disjuncture in the amount of variance or spread in age at marriage in the two countries. The number of years required for the middle 50 percent of a cohort to marry has remained around four in Japan over the past thirty years. The year 1950 is used as the starting point to show how slight the change in Japan has been over a substantial period of time. Though the variance in age at marriage has always been somewhat higher in the United States, it has shown a particularly sharp increase since 1970. These data offer additional evidence for the view that entry into marriage is more tightly controlled in

FIGURE 4   DIVORCES PER THOUSAND PERSONS IN JAPAN AND THE UNITED STATES (1940–1984)

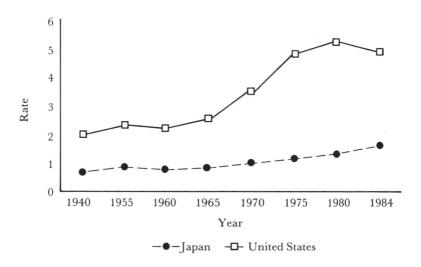

Sources: U.S., Bureau of the Census, 1975; idem, 1986; Japan, Ministry of Labor, Women's Bureau, 1985.

FIGURE 5   NUMBER OF YEARS REQUIRED FOR MIDDLE FIFTY
PERCENT TO MARRY IN JAPAN AND THE UNITED STATES
(1950–1980)

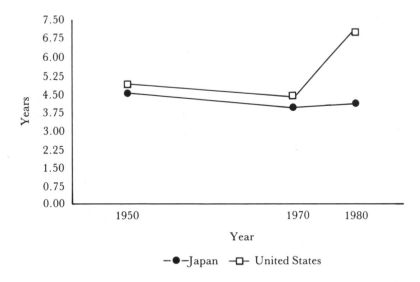

Sources: U.S., Bureau of the Census, 1983; Japan, Office of the Prime
Minister, 1950; idem, 1970b; idem, 1980b.

Japan and that there is an overriding set of rules to which individual women and their families conform.

The irreversibility and invariance of the marriage decision in Japan is coupled with age-incongruity or nonoverlap between educational enrollment and marriage, as we have shown. This nonoverlap has persisted despite rapid social change. Figure 6 shows changes in the percent of women never married at age 20–24 in the United States and Japan. (*Never married* refers to women who are single, not *unmarried* as a result of divorce or widowhood.) With the exception of the immediate post–World War II period, the proportion never married in this age group has climbed in Japan (and mean age at marriage has increased). The proportion never married in this age group in the United States remained stable or declined through 1960, then began to increase. At all time points, mean age at marriage has been higher in Japan than in the United States. Thus as women's education increased in Japan,

FIGURE 6   PERCENT NEVER MARRIED AT AGE 20–24 IN JAPAN AND
THE UNITED STATES (1890–1980)

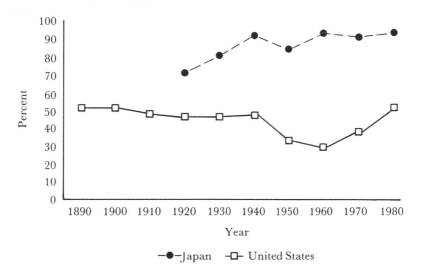

Year

—●—Japan   —□— United States

Sources: U.S., Bureau of the Census, 1983; Japan, Office of the Prime Minister, *Kokusei chōsa* (Population census), various years (Tokyo: Statistics Bureau).

age at marriage also climbed (Kumagai 1984). Education and marriage have remained separate and sequential statuses to a much greater extent than in the United States.

The permanence of the marital relationship and the relative invariance across individual women in the timing of marriage mark it as the key institution that Japanese women enter in their transition to adulthood. In addition, childbirth is a much more inevitable consequence of marriage and a more integral aspect of adulthood for Japanese women than for American women (Coleman 1983; Lebra 1984; Morgan, Rindfuss, and Parnell 1984). The proportion of all American women reaching age fifty without experiencing motherhood varied across the 1890 to 1930 birth cohorts from a high of 22.5 percent to a low of 5.5 percent (Uhlenberg 1974). This proportion varied almost imperceptibly in Japan, from 6.8 percent to 5.6 percent (Watanabe 1986).

In contrast to the irreversibility of marriage, the decision

to participate in the labor force represents one of the few reversible decisions in Japanese women's life course. Comparative attitudinal data illustrate the difference between American and Japanese women's views on the most desirable combination of work and marriage (Japan, Office of the Prime Minister 1982a). Forty-two percent of American women cite continuous labor force participation as ideal, whereas this pattern is cited as ideal by only 18 percent of Japanese women. In contrast, the preferred pattern stated by Japanese women (44 percent) is to work until childbirth, then leave the workforce and return when children are older. This pattern is preferred by 39 percent of American women. Very low proportions of women in either country think it is best for women not to work at all (1 percent of American women and 7 percent of Japanese women), but a much larger proportion of Japanese than American women feel that women should quit at either marriage or childbirth (26 percent of Japanese women and 10 percent of American women).

Conclusion

Japanese women's life course transitions are characterized by irreversibility, age-incongruity, and low variance in timing across individuals. These characteristics reflect the structure of the educational system, work organizations, and marriage as well as the strong influence of stakeholders. Entry into positions in both the Japanese educational system and marriage is carefully timed and typically occurs only once in a lifetime. On the one hand, parents and other stakeholders play a hand in an individual woman's success in the marriage market. On the other hand, educators are important stakeholders in seeing that graduates are properly placed into an employment relationship. The work organization considered ideal by the majority of people has been an internal labor market consisting of positions that are filled from within the organization. These positions are almost entirely restricted to men because they involve employers' investments in employee training and an expectation of service to the firm uninterrupted by the demands of marriage and childrearing. Employers are important stakeholders in filling these internal labor market slots. The labor market structure therefore nearly precludes continuous participation by Japanese women in the paid labor force. Women exhibit a pattern of dropping out and reentering a secondary labor market of part-time and temporary positions at a later age.

In contrast to the strict sequencing of life course transitions in Japan, Modell, Furstenberg, and Herschberg (1976) and others have argued that American youth are faced with a variety of complex coordination decisions in a briefer period of time than has been true historically: it is now possible to hold several statuses simultaneously. American women's life course decisions have become less directed by the family or other primary institutions. Age barriers to reentry to educational institutions or to work organizations are minimal, and the recognition of individual variation in the timing of life course transitions is built into social institutions (the educational system, work organizations, and the institution of marriage) in the form of greater openness in the positions within these institutions. The economic success or prestige of an organization in the United States is not necessarily harmed by the circulation of new entrants into positions in the organization.

The relative flexibility of the American social-institutional setting is connected with life course patterns that show women alternating their energies among education, family, and labor force activities across the life cycle and frequently overlapping these activities rather than being involved exclusively in only one at a time. The transition into and out of the roles of spouse and student are increasingly reversible, occurring more than once in life. The timing of these transitions also varies considerably across individual women, who have become the principal stakeholders or directors in their own life course decisions.

It is important to recognize that the cluster of phenomena discussed for Japan is not repetitious of an earlier point in American history. The life course is affected by the historical development of social institutions within specific cultural settings. Whereas age at marriage has risen across the twentieth century in Japan, it has dropped in the United States (Cherlin 1981; Kumagai 1984). The same holds true for age at first birth. Educational attainment has risen in both countries. But Japanese women complete their education "on schedule," whereas an increasing number of American women return for additional schooling after marrying, divorcing, or entering the labor force. In short, recent historical changes in Japanese patterns of timing in life course transitions have largely acted to *maintain* discrete life stages in the individual woman's life. Changes in American timing have combined to form complex overlaps in life stages.

All of this does not mean that Japanese women's life course is static and unchanging. Changes in the family, the educational system, and the labor market will most certainly be reflected in the structure of women's life course. For instance, the Equal Employment Opportunity Law passed in 1985 has resulted in the creation of multiple tracks for young women in some large companies rather than the sole traditional noncareer track (Nishiyama 1988). If career opportunities in large firms and in multinational companies open up for Japanese women, greater age-congruity may emerge between marriage and employment for Japanese women. Although this situation has already occurred for a small group of women, it is unlikely to become widespread without concomitant changes in the nature of the family and in husbands' expectations that wives bear almost full responsibility for housework and childcare. Unless these expectations change, women may simply marry later and leave the workplace at that point rather than struggling to adopt an age-congruous pattern between employment and the early stages of marriage.[6]

A second example of a recent institutional change in Japan that could produce changes in women's life course is the proliferation of adult education opportunities geared toward married women in their thirties and forties. As long as these educational activities remain relatively valueless in the labor market, their primary function will be self-improvement and diversion for women whose children have already entered school. But as service industries expand and create a greater demand for information- and computer-related skills that can be taught through educational courses rather than on-the-job training, educational institutions will try to attract more mid-career women (and men) for training.[7] These are but a few of the reasons why Japanese women's life course transitions may show greater age-congruity in the future. We will need to pay close attention to changes in Japanese social institutions and the role of stakeholders in order to make such predictions.

Notes

An earlier version of this essay with more American material was presented with Steven D. McLaughlin at the annual meeting of the American Sociological Association, Chicago, August 1987.

1. There is also the metaphor of a "discount sale" for women who have passed the marriageable age. The Christmas-cake riddle is becoming obsolete as age at marriage rises in Japan. But it is too early to tell whether the strong norm about marrying "on time" is significantly altering or not, even though the meaning of "on time" may be changing.

2. The concept of the stakeholder in relation to life course decisions is closely related to Sorensen's (1986) description of "closed" positions in a social system. As described by Sorensen, open positions are those for which access is open to all individuals meeting the requirements for entry. Access to these positions is therefore determined by the characteristics of the individual. Closed positions are those with limited access to individuals meeting certain organizational membership requirements. They are often sponsored positions, hence, the tie to the notion of a stakeholder with an interest in smoothing the transition of an individual into the position.

3. In this essay I draw from a variety of published data sources, but microlevel data on cohorts will be essential in future work. Comparison of subgroups within the American population is also an important further direction. In the cross-national comparison made here, I preserve the cultural and ethnic heterogeneity of the United States because it is one of the distinctive characteristics of the country.

4. This statement applies to men as well.

5. Part-time work is an ambiguous concept in Japanese, with many supposedly part-time employees working more than forty hours a week. But I use the term here to refer to work that is truly part-time.

6. A less likely scenario is that more women will choose to remain single—a different strategy that also results (by default) in a lack of age-congruity between employment and marriage. The proportion of women stating that lifelong "singlehood" would be acceptable has risen dramatically in recent years (Tsuya 1988). But it is unclear yet whether such attitudes will translate into greater numbers of women actually remaining single across their lifetimes.

7. The University of the Air (Hōsō Daigaku) in Chiba prefecture is an example of a government-sponsored educational institution that attracts older men and women.

References

Arrow, Kenneth. 1973. "The Theory of Discrimination." In *Discrimination in Labor Markets,* edited by Orley Ashenfelter and Albert Rees. Pp. 3–33. Princeton, N.J.: Princeton University Press.

Azumi, Koya. 1969. *Higher Education and Business Recruitment in Japan.* New York: Teacher's College Press.

Brinton, Mary C. 1988. "The Social-Institutional Bases of Gender Stratification: Japan as an Illustrative Case." *American Journal of Sociology* 94:300–334.

———. 1989. "Gender Stratification in Contemporary Urban Japan." *American Sociological Review* 54:549–564.

———. 1992. *Women and the Economic Miracle: Gender and Work in Postwar Japan.* Berkeley: University of California Press.

Cherlin, Andrew. 1981. *Marriage, Divorce, Remarriage.* Cambridge: Cambridge University Press.

Clark, Rodney C. 1979. *The Japanese Company.* New Haven, Connecticut: Yale University Press.

Coleman, Samuel. 1983. "The Tempo of Family Formation." In *Work and Lifecourse in Japan,* edited by David W. Plath. Pp. 183–214. Albany: State University of New York.

Evans, Robert, Jr. 1986. "The Transition from School to Work in the United States." In *Educational Policies in Crisis: Japanese and American Perspectives,* edited by William K. Cummings. Pp. 210–239. New York: Praeger.

Featherman, David L., and Aage B. Sorensen, 1983. "Societal Transformation in Norway and Change in the Life Course Transition into Adulthood." *Acta Sociologica* 26:105–126.

Fujimura-Fanselow, Kumiko. 1985. "Women's Participation in Higher Education in Japan." *Comparative Education Review* 29:471–489.

Hashimoto, Masanori, and John Raisian. 1985. "Employment Tenure and Earnings Profiles in Japan and the United States." *American Economic Review* 75:721–735.

Hogan, Dennis P., and T. Mochizuki, 1985. "Demographic Transitions and the Life Course: Lessons from Japanese and American Comparisons." Paper presented at the annual meeting of the American Sociological Association, Washington, D.C.

Japan. Ministry of Labor, Women's Bureau. 1985. *Fujin rōdō no jitsujō* (Status of women workers). Tokyo: Government Printing Office.

———. 1986. *Fujin rōdō no jitsujō* (Status of women workers). Tokyo: Government Printing Office.

———. 1988. *Fujin rōdō no jitsujō* (Status of women workers). Tokyo: Government Printing Office.

Japan. Office of the Prime Minister. 1950. *Kokusei chōsa* (Population census), vol. 4. Tokyo: Statistics Bureau.

———. 1965. *Kokusei chōsa* (Population census), vol. 2, part 4. Tokyo: Statistics Bureau.

———. 1970a. *Kokusei chōsa* (Population census), vol. 8, part 1. Tokyo: Statistics Bureau.

———. 1970b. *Kokusei chōsa* (Population census), vol. 4. Tokyo: Statistics Bureau.

———. 1980a. *Kokusei chōsa* (Population census), vol. 4, part 1, div. 3. Tokyo: Statistics Bureau.

———. 1980b. *Kokusei chōsa* (Population census), vol. 2, part 1. Tokyo: Statistics Bureau.

———. 1982a. *Fujin mondai ni kansuru yoron chōsa* (Opinion survey on women's problems). Tokyo: Office of the Prime Minister.

———. 1982b. *Kyōiku ni kansuru yoron chōsa* (Opinion survey regarding education). Tokyo: Office of the Prime Minister.

Japan Institute of Labor. 1990. *Japan Labor Bulletin* 29:5–8.

Koike, Kazuo. 1983. "Workers in Small Firms and Women in Industry." In *Contemporary Industrial Relations in Japan,* edited by Taishiro Shirai. Pp. 89–115. Madison: University of Wisconsin Press.

Kumagai, Fumie. 1984. "The Life Cycle of the Japanese Family." *Journal of Marriage and the Family* 46:191–204.

Lebra, Takie Sugiyama. 1984. *Japanese Women: Constraint and Fulfillment.* Honolulu: University of Hawaii Press.

McLaughlin, Steven D.; Barbara D. Melber; John O. G. Billy; Denise M. Zimmerle; Linda D. Winges; and Terry R. Johnson. 1988. *The Changing Lives of American Women.* Chapel Hill: University of North Carolina Press.

McLendon, James. 1983. "The Office: Way Station or Blind Alley?" In *Work and Lifecourse in Japan,* edited by David W. Plath. Pp. 156–182. Albany: State University of New York Press.

Meyer, John W. 1986a. "The Self and the Life Course: Institutionalization and Its Effects." In *Human Development and the Life Course: Multidisciplinary Perspectives,* edited by A. B. Sorensen, F. Weinert, and L. Sherrod. Pp. 199–216. Hillsdale, N.J.: L. Erlbaum.

———. 1986b. "Levels of Analysis: The Life Course as an Institutional Construction." Paper presented at the annual meeting of the American Sociological Association, New York, N.Y.

Miyahara, Kojiro. 1988. "Inter-College Stratification: The Case of Male College Graduates in Japan." *Sociological Forum* 3:25–43.

Modell, John, Frank F. Furstenberg, and Theodore Herschberg. 1976. "Social Change and Transitions to Adulthood in Comparative Perspective." *Journal of Family History* 1:7–32.

Morgan, S. Philip, Ronald R. Rindfuss, and Allan Parnell. 1984. "Modern Fertility Patterns: Contrasts between the United States and Japan." *Population and Development Review* 10:19-40.

Nakata, Yoshifumi, and Carl Mosk. 1987. "The Demand for College Education in Postwar Japan." *Journal of Human Resources* 22: 377-404.

Nihon Recruit Center. 1983. *Daigakusei (danshi, joshi) no shūshoku dōki chōsa* (Job-seeking behavior of male and female university graduates). Tokyo: Nihon Recruit Center.

Nishiyama Misako. 1988. "Josei rōdōsha to fukusenkei jinji—jūnan na rōdō shōgai ni tsuite" (Women workers, multilinear personnel management, and flexible work life). *Shakaigaku Hyōron* (Japanese sociological review) 39:22-37.

Plath, David W. 1983. "Life Is Just a Job Resume?" In *Work and Life-course in Japan,* edited by David W. Plath. Pp. 1-13. Albany: State University of New York Press.

Rohlen, Thomas. 1974. *For Harmony and Strength.* Berkeley: University of California Press.

————. 1983. *Japan's High Schools.* Berkeley: University of California Press.

Rosenbaum, James, and Takehiko Kariya. 1989. "Market and Institutional Mechanisms for the High School to Work Transition in the U.S. and Japan." *American Journal of Sociology* 94:1334-1365.

Shimada, Haruo. 1981. *Earnings Structure and Human Investment: A Comparison between the United States and Japan.* Tokyo: Kogadusha Limited.

Sorensen, Aage B. 1986. "Social Structure and Mechanisms of Life-Course Processes." In *Human Development and the Life Course: Multidisciplinary Perspectives,* edited by A. B. Sorensen, F. Weinert, and L. Sherrod. Pp. 179-197. Hillsdale, N.J.: L. Erlbaum.

Tanaka, Kazuko. 1987. "Women, Work, and Family in Japan: A Life Cycle Perspective." Ph.D. dissertation, University of Iowa.

Tsuya, Noriko. 1988. "Changes in Marriage and Family Formation among Contemporary Japanese Women." In *Summary of the National Opinion Survey of the Family in Japan.* Pp. 65-77. Tokyo: Nihon University Research Center.

Uhlenberg, Peter. 1974. "Cohort Variations in Family Life Cycle Experiences of U.S. Females." *Journal of Marriage and the Family* 36:284-292.

Upham, Frank K. 1987. *Law and Social Change in Postwar Japan.* Cambridge: Harvard University Press.

U.S. Bureau of the Census. 1965. Marital Status and Family Status:

March 1965. *Current Population Reports,* series P-20, no. 144. Washington, D.C.: U.S. Government Printing Office.

———. 1971. Marital Status and Family Status: March 1970. *Current Population Reports,* series P-20, no. 212. Washington, D.C.: U.S. Government Printing Office.

———. 1975. *Statistical Abstract of the United States: 1975.* Washington, D.C.: U.S. Government Printing Office.

———. 1981. Marital Status and Living Arrangements: March 1980. *Current Population Reports,* series P-20, no. 365. Washington, D.C.: U.S. Government Printing Office.

———. 1982. School Enrollment—Social and Economic Characteristics of Students: October 1981 and 1980. *Current Population Reports,* series P-20, no. 400. Washington, D.C.: U.S. Government Printing Office.

———. 1983. Marital Status and Living Arrangements: March 1983. *Current Population Reports,* series P-20, no. 389. Washington, D.C.: U.S. Government Printing Office.

———. 1986. *Statistical Abstract of the United States: 1987.* Washington, D.C.: U.S. Government Printing Office.

U.S. Department of Labor. Bureau of Labor Statistics. 1985. *Employment and Earnings,* vol. 32, no. 1. Washington, D.C.: U.S. Government Printing Office.

Ushiogi, Morikazu, 1986. "Transition from School to Work: The Japanese Case." In *Educational Policies in Crisis: Japanese and American Perspectives,* edited by William K. Cummings. Pp. 197–209. New York: Praeger.

Watanabe, Y. 1986. "The Life and Death of Mothers and Children: A Life Course Analysis." Tokyo: Institute of Population Problems, Ministry of Health and Welfare.

CHAPTER 4

Life on Obasuteyama, or, Inside a Japanese Institution for the Elderly

Diana Lynn Bethel

Japanese elderly stand at the edge of a great divide in the course of twentieth-century Japanese history. They have contributed to the evolution of Japanese society from a premodern agricultural economy to the postmodern present. They have witnessed the reigns of four emperors and two world wars, as well as the transformation of rickshaw to bullet train; of the traditional rice diet to pizza, spaghetti, and Big Macs; and of the prewar authoritarian family to the "my-home-ism" of the nuclear family. They are repositories and survivors of a Japanese past rendered obsolete by postwar denunciation of the family system, guarantee of equality between the sexes, and a new ideology of individualism, which asserts the right for young (as well as old) to pursue their lives free from intergenerational interference.

Institutionalization of the elderly highlights the disjuncture between the cultural norm of filial piety (and its expression in the ideal of coresidence) and a changing social reality. Though the fact of institutionalization is traumatic at any age or in any culture, cultural context shapes the experience of institutionalization and the design of the institutional environment. This essay examines the experience of institutionalization and construction of home society and culture by residents and staff in one Japanese old age home. It depicts the character of an emerging social institution in Japanese society patterned on familiar cultural models, new norms tailored for an older population, and conflicting agendas of staff versus residents in a contest of power and self-determination.

Background

In the 1980s public awareness suddenly focused on the "old people problem" (*rōjin mondai*). Demographers predicted rapid population aging up through the first decades of the twenty-first century and warned of the social and economic impact on Japanese society. Social policies were revised as the government sought to ease the economic pressures stemming from overextended pension programs, free medical care for the elderly, and expenditures for institutional care (Campbell 1979). The popularity of books and movies on aging and care of the aged reflected public concern (Ariyoshi 1972; Fukazawa 1964; Imamura 1983; Inoue 1982; Niwa 1962).

Coresidence is the Japanese ideal for life in old age. In traditional perceptions of the Japanese life course, old age is a time when the eldest son assumes responsibility for his parents in their later years. It bestows increasing freedom from family and work responsibilities (Benedict 1946) as well as the leisure to develop the inner self in the later years (Rohlen 1978). During these postretirement years, one would be able to reap the returns from many years of hard work and sacrifice invested in one's children. The Confucian ethic of filial piety and the virtue of repaying one's obligations *(on),* ingrained by the prewar educational curriculum (Lanham 1979), sanction this idyllic image of Japanese aging.

Institutionalization violates the traditional ideal of coresidence. Although the majority of Japanese sixty-five years of age and over (approximately sixty percent) live with their children, coresidence has gradually declined since the 1960s (Kōseishō 1990; Ōkurashō 1991). Socioeconomic, demographic, and cultural forces such as (1) rural to urban migration in the industrialization process, (2) increasing longevity of older Japanese, (3) postwar decline in fertility resulting in fewer children to look after aging parents, (4) the increase of women (the traditional caretakers of the elderly) in the workforce, as well as (5) changing cultural attitudes (Kumagai 1984; Maeda 1983) have made the ideal increasingly difficult to achieve. These trends have led to an increase in the number of institutions for older people, from 690 in 1963 to 2,814 in 1984 (Kōseishō 1990). This population of institutionalized older people most acutely faces the discontinuity between cultural ideal and social reality—between the ideal of cor-esidence versus institutionalization.

Four types of homes for the elderly exist in Japan: (1) the nursing home (*tokubetsu yōgo rōjin hōmu*—for the bedridden and mildly mentally impaired) (Campbell 1984); (2) the "protective care" home (*yōgo rōjin hōmu*—for low-income elderly); (3) the "low-cost old age home" (*keihi rōjin hōmu*—for those with modest but sufficient means); and (4) the "full-cost" retirement home (*yūryō rōjin hōmu*—for those with substantial financial resources). The first three types are public institutions funded by a combina-tion of national, prefectural, and local government sources, in addition to a sliding scale of individual resources usually deter-mined by ability to pay. Institutions of the fourth category are pri-vate and can be extremely costly.

The home chosen for this study is a protective care facility (yōgo rōjin hōmu). As a social welfare institution of the second type, it requires that residents be of low economic status. It is situ-ated in a declining coal mining area in the mountains of Hokkaido. The Aotani Institution for the Elderly (Aotani Rōjin Hōmu) in which this study was conducted has a maximum capac-ity of one hundred residents. The number of residents fluctuates between seventy-five and eighty people, approximately half wom-en and half men. The residents range in age from fifty-seven to ninety-one, with an average age of seventy-seven. Residents are assigned three or four to a room; couples have their own smaller, two-person room. Three male administrators from the city office oversee the official and clerical responsibilities while ten female staff are in closest contact with the residents and take care of the daily operations of the home.

Research on the Aotani Institution for the Elderly was conducted over a period of fifteen months, from July 1985 to October 1986, as well as during two brief visits in the summer of 1988. Of the fifteen months spent living in the small community in which the institution is located, I lived for eight months in the institution as a resident. I am extremely grateful to the city Social Welfare Department for providing me this rare opportunity and to the staff of the institution who reluctantly admitted me on the con-dition that I abide by all the rules governing residents and receive no special privileges. Residents were aware that I was a student researching the lives of Japanese institutionalized older people.

They befriended me as a surrogate granddaughter as well as a fellow resident submitting to staff authority and pursuing meaning and fulfillment in a confined situation.

Most residents were happy to tell me about their lives, but only a few permitted me to tape our conversations. Accordingly, most of the interview data were collected during informal visiting over tea and refreshments. The staff were also cooperative in discussing the institution, the residents, and their philosophies of care for the elderly. The name of the institution as well as personal names appearing in this paper are all fictitious.

Psychological adjustment to life in Aotani is hindered by popular images of institutions for the elderly. Early twentieth-century poor houses and post–World War II social welfare institutions for the poverty-stricken remain in recent living memory. Residents must reconcile their belief in the traditional Confucian value of filial piety and the cultural ideal of coresidence with their own deviance from the norm.

The Confucian tale of Obasuteyama reflects an age-old ambivalence toward responsibility for aging parents (Plath 1972). Legend tells that, long ago in some areas of Japan, eldest sons were forced to cast out elderly family members who no longer contributed to the family economy. An aging parent was taken to a deserted mountain called Obasuteyama and left there to perish from starvation and exposure. In contemporary Japan, the mention of institutions for older people conjures up these images of desolation and abandonment.

For residents of the institution, the story of Obasuteyama ·is a symbolic metaphor (Lakoff and Johnson 1980) representing the pathos and unfulfilled expectations of their later years. It serves as an explanation for their own institutionalization, a harsh reality encapsulated and objectified by its transformation into a symbol of suffering and sacrifice.

Residents may be admitted to Aotani because of advancing age, economic hardship, family conflict, refusal to migrate with younger family members in search of employment, or even a desire for more freedom to live their own lives separately from their children. Whatever the reason, residents are sensitive to the social stigma associated with institutionalization. As a reaction to this stigma, residents respond defensively, vigorously affirming the advantages and benefits of the institutional home life. Willing or not, they have been thrown together in an unfamiliar social universe to either adapt or wither as social beings. Those who realize this begin socially and emotionally to immerse themselves in the dynamic and intricate society of institutional life.

Cultural Constructs of Aotani Society

The conceptual world of Aotani is structured by the need to transform the impersonal facility into a hospitable environment that recognizes and nurtures individual worth and social intimacy. A discourse of family creates an aura of intimacy and helps mask the austere and unpleasant aspects of institutional life. Concepts of community, including the cultural understandings involved in the use of fictive kinship and recognition of age and seniority hierarchies, shape the social world of the institution. The ethic of mutual aid, as well as the tendency to defy authority, also contribute to the construction of the Aotani social environment.

The familial image is a tool used both consciously and unconsciously by Aotani staff as well as residents. The staff use it to cultivate a sense of intimacy in staff-resident relations. New residents are routinely assigned to a staff woman. When Mrs. Minamisawa (age seventy-eight) entered the facility, Mr. Kitami, the assistant director, told her, "Think of your care giver as your daughter-in-law. If you need to have something done, ask her to help. If you have a problem, confide in her. She will take care of you, probably better than your own daughter-in-law."

Care givers also employ family-related concepts in their interactions with residents. Mrs. Katō, a care giver, thinks of Aotani as a family *(kazoku)* and the staff women as mother figures. "Members of a family must try to understand each other's feelings. That's why care givers have to take on the mother role *(haha no yakume)* and cultivate 'a mother's heart' *(haha no kokoro)*." They must develop a maternal sensitivity to older people and be able to discern when residents are troubled by reading the expressions on their faces and sensing their moods. For Mrs. Katō, this "mother role," altruistically compassionate and intuitively sensitive, is the saving grace that transforms the impersonal institution into some semblance of a home and family.

Residents create a sense of solidarity and belonging through references to family and householdlike qualities of the institution. They use terms such as "We all eat from the same ricepot" and "We all use the same entrance *(genkan)* and live under the same roof."

Fictive kin terms also enhance feelings of belonging. Befu and Norbeck (1958) observed that kin terms of address are used only for senior relatives. Similarly, in their use of kin terms, care givers often refer to the elderly in their charge as "grandmother of my 'house' " *(uchi no bāchan),* that is, a resident of a room for which they are responsible. Several care givers even refer to their charges as mother *(okāchan)* or father *(otōchan)* as further expressions of familiarity and affection. These usages are based on an addressor-centered perspective of the age and social status differences between addressor and addressee.

A teknonymic usage in which the addressor takes the child's point of view has been identified by Lebra (1976) as "vicarious kin" terminology. This is illustrated by some of the older men who call the younger ones "older brother" *(onīchan),* in the same way a father would when referring to his oldest son. Several of the older men also call some of the care givers "mother." Sometimes residents refer to each other respectfully as grandmother *(obaba)* or grandfather *(ojiji).* On other occasions the same terms are transformed into insults by tone of voice and omission of the honorific "o." By taking a child's point of view, residents place themselves lower in the age hierarchy. This self-effacing function eliminates barriers of formality and social distance to allow expression of social intimacy.

The difference in chronological age, or in vicarious age, between addressor and addressee approximates age distances in a typical family, making the superimposition of kin terms in a group of unrelated elderly people and their care givers a natural extension of family and community interaction.

By beginning the relationship with an informal address pattern, care givers intend to bypass the stiff and formal social rituals between strangers. As an informal relationship develops, the care givers become closer to and more in touch with the older people's problems.

A resident's use of kin terms reveals the nature of friendship circles and relationships with acquaintances. Kin terms are multifunctional in their clear delineation of the age hierarchy, as well as in the way they help create a familial atmosphere. The creation of a hierarchy (implying social distance) seemingly contradicts the funtion of expressing social intimacy. The two functions are resolved by the complementary nature of hierarchy and social intimacy in which age awareness conveniently structures the expression of respect, familiarity, or intimacy within one's social circle.

Mrs. Otake, a staff woman, uses kin terms for their humor value. She calls some of the residents by their first names, adding the suffix *"chan."* A kind of infantilization, the "chan" suffix is normally reserved for children and indicates a social intimacy reserved for family relationships and for relationships among those who have grown up together. Sometimes Mrs. Otake uses this form of address to point out a nonconforming resident for public ridicule, for example, during mealtime, when all the residents are assembled in the dining room. Mrs. Otake is somewhat of a clown and makes the most of this comic incongruence of feigned intimacy between adult strangers *(tanin)*. By using the address style normally reserved for young children, she adds another dimension to the repertoire of age-related address terms used in the home. Her endearing antics earn her also the fond name of "Otake-chan."

Community Model

As an institution, Aotani is an impersonal entity that operates by schedules, rules, and regulations. Within this formal structure residents create their own informal structure to help them adapt and survive in a difficult setting.

Historically, in traditional rural communities in Japan, age grades were a distinctive part of community social organization (Norbeck 1953). Each age grade had its own function in community life. Remnants of this social structure still persist in many contemporary rural communities. Keith (1981) describes age as an often overlooked principle of social organization. In Japanese social groups, however, age concepts have long been recognized as central features of social interaction (Norbeck 1953; Rohlen 1974; Lebra 1976). The Aotani home community, in which individuals are distributed along an age continuum spanning thirty years or more, illustrates both the subtle distinctions that place residents in a hierarchy of age and seniority and the horizontal solidarities of age identification.

In Aotani, as in other types of organizations (Rohlen 1974; Tobin 1989), people who enter around the same time form a stratum identified by time period and feel a sense of camaraderie based on their common experience as newcomers. As junior members (based on date of admission to Aotani) of a seniority system in which authority and prestige accompany length of residence, they face the double ordeal of adapting themselves to the rigors and regimentation of the institution as well as integrating themselves into its social fabric.

Residents also use chronological age and age grade identification to establish ties to the Aotani social environment. An automatic bond is created among people of the same age. By identifying shared characteristics such as age they begin to construct their social support network of peers. Residents keep track of the ages of friends in their social networks. With each passing year they count their losses and celebrate the longevity of survivors. Those whose birthdays fall in the same month also develop a sense of camaraderie. At the monthly birthday party, they are treated as special guests. As is the custom, one month's birthday group summoned Mr. Sakata, who owns an automatic camera (bakachon), to record the occasion on film. The little group, each one dressed in her best kimono or his best suit, gazes solemnly from the resulting photograph. Added to personal albums containing other such memorabilia of home events and social relationships, pictures affirm their lives and ease feelings of being abandoned and forgotten. They also serve as gifts to send to one's children and/or relatives to assuage concerns (or maintain the fiction) that grandma or grandpa is well and enjoying life at Aotani.

At each month's special birthday dinner the celebrated birthday residents are hosted at the head table in the dining hall. Friends pour their drinks (juice or the alcohol of their choice) and offer congratulations and best wishes for a long and healthy life. The care giver serving as master of ceremonies selects residents to sing congratulatory provincial folksongs (minyō) or popular ballads (enka) for dinner entertainment. Any given month's birthday people develop a group identity (e.g., as "January people") and a sense of common experience over the years as their minisocial convoy (Plath 1980) makes its way through life spent in the institution. The little group journeying together through time is a metaphor for the institution itself, a band of people insulated in a communal environment in which they create a rich and diverse social life. When asked what were the most interesting aspects of life at Aotani, most residents expressed their eager anticipation of the monthly birthday parties and other special celebrations. Special food is served, and residents who display their singing talents bask for a brief moment in the applause of their peers' approval. Birthday parties and other group celebrations affirm a communal identity and add a touch of festivity to the humdrum of daily routine.

Public and Private Domains

Personal privacy in the home exists only within the mind. Staff enter rooms without knocking, and residents' only personal space consists of a small area in front of their own clothes closets. Despite the public nature of this group living facility, degrees of public and private space are clearly delineated. The outside world is separated from the interior as shoes are taken off at the entrance to the building and kept in a large shoe cabinet *(geta bako),* just as in a private residence. This custom highlights the private residential nature of the Aotani community in contrast to the outside world. Once inside the facility, the use of slippers demarcates public and private spheres within the home geography. Slippers are worn in the public areas—which include the dining hall, hallways, infirmary, and the like—but are shed at the door to the private space of residents' rooms.

Each floor, including its hallways, is also a social unit. Residents are divided into two strata, "first-floor persons" and "second-floor persons," based largely on their physical health status. Those on the second floor must be able to negotiate the stairs. In the second floor lounge men play checkers and Chinese chess, and old books, magazines, and newspapers line the wall. This area is inaccessible to those who cannot climb up and down the stairs. Second-floor residents, then, tend to be younger and/or stronger; the weaker and more frail residents reside on the first floor. The first floor has no lounge per se, so residents gather on the benches lining the main hallway or in front of the two television sets in the large dining hall.

On each floor, two hallways extend in opposite directions from the center of the building. A sense of identification and relatedness among residents of a hallway unite them in a network of cooperation and communication. As a result, each hallway maintains its own geographical integrity. It is a mini-neighborhood in which residents interact more extensively with their neighbors than with people residing elsewhere. The territorial boundaries of each area are respected: residents refrain from going into other "neighborhoods" unless they have specific business with someone who lives there.

Sex-segregated restrooms and a common washroom are shared by residents whose rooms line each hallway. Each personal room is akin to a household in this hallway neighborhood. As the day begins, residents greet their neighbors on the way to and from the restroom. Plans for the day, invitations to tea, and neighborly conversation are exchanged as residents wash their faces, rinse small laundry items, or wash tea cups for morning tea.

Home residents adhere to the common-sense principle for community living, *"Mukō sangen, ryō donari."* This homily admonishes them to cultivate neighborly relations with the three households across the way and the two on either side. Home residents take care to maintain friendly relations with their close neighbors. These relationships impart peace of mind, because in emergencies, they constitute networks of mutual aid. They also are the foundation for friendship networks.

Each room is separated from the hallway by a sliding door. During the day, a doorway curtain establishes a symbolic barrier shielding the inhabitants from the eyes of passersby. The entry to the room is a zone separating the "inside" (i.e., the room) from the "outside" (ie., the public hallway). To one side, a small geta bako cabinet stores residents' shoes and extra slippers. From the entryway off the hall, one steps up onto the slightly raised floor of the room, as into a house or apartment.

Within the room, a low folding table set up during the day is the focal point of social interaction. It plays a pivotal role in defining the temporal structure of public and private space in the room. When it is folded up and set aside, residents are usually engaged in solitary activities such as reading, taking a nap, or caring for their belongings. In most rooms, the table is set up only at certain "social" times of the day, usually before meals, when roommates and friends gather to snack and wait for the signal to converge on the dining hall for mealtime.

Age, Seniority, and Family in the Room Context

The room is the basic social unit of the Aotani society. Relationships between roommates are characterized by a householdlike hierarchical structure, including a system for division of labor and a sense of mutual responsibility for each other.

The age and seniority system orders social relationships. When this cultural format is followed, interactions are harmonious. Irresolvable differences arise when residents do not take their "proper" place in the social hierarchy based on age, sex, and seniority. The system functions most effectively when the older person knows how to use authority and fulfill the role in a magnanimous and paternalistic manner and the younger person observes the proper deference.

In Mrs. Kajima's room, for example, the age hierarchy follows the norm: the eldest has the highest status, the youngest, the lowest status. By following the traditional pattern, conflict is avoided, and a smoothly functioning system results. Eighty-five-year-old Mrs. Kajima is the eldest and most senior of the roommates. Mrs. Miyashiro is the next oldest (age seventy-nine); Mrs. Moriya (age seventy-three) is the youngest. Mrs. Kajima's dignified and amiable personality win her the esteem and deference of her roommates. She wields the power of her status benignly.

Mrs. Moriya chuckles, "Since I'm the youngest I get asked to do all the errands. The other day Mrs. Kajima said, 'Get the chopsticks for the *takuan* (pickled radish). They're in the cabinet.' So I went to the cabinet, but before I got there Mrs. Miyashiro said, 'No, they're in the drawer,' so I turned around and headed to the dresser. Mrs. Kajima insisted, 'No, I'm sure they're in the cabinet,' so I turned around again. They had me going in circles until I was dizzy and out of breath! I told them, 'I wish you two would make up your minds. I may be the youngest, but I'm not exactly a spring chicken!' We all burst out laughing. It was so funny because we're all old ladies."

All three ladies get along well, and their room radiates an inviting atmosphere. Kin terms reflect their friendship. Mrs. Moriya explained, "When no one else is around and just the three of us are together, I call Mrs. Kajima *'kāchan'* (mother) and Mrs. Miyashiro *'nēchan'* (older sister). They're older than me and are like my older sisters. It makes me feel like we are family."

Sometimes on women's bathing days (scheduled three times a week), Mrs. Miyashiro scrubs Mrs. Kajima's back and washes her hair. Other roommates and friends do the same for each other, just as they have for family members and friends in neighborhood public baths throughout their lives. The bathing period gives the women a chance to relax with each other while soaking in the large communal tub, and is thus a familiar family and community experience. It provides a context for expressing closeness. One typical day Mrs. Katō, the care giver on bath duty for the day, came into the bathing room with pant legs rolled up, taking requests for assistance. She joked and teased, simultaneously entertaining the older ladies as she scrubbed their backs.

Not all roommates are so congenial. In Mrs. Okayama's room, the air is strained: her roommates resent her heavy-handed manner. Mrs. Okayama is one of the oldest residents of the home. At age eighty-nine, she is legally blind, but she still shuffles up and down the hallway every day for exercise. As the longest residing woman in her room as well as the oldest, Mrs. Okayama directs the way things are done in the room. Her roommates chafe at her bossiness. To make matters worse, she berates Mrs. Yokoyama (age seventy-six) constantly for her forgetfulness. Mrs. Honma, her other roommate, expresses her discontent in hushed tones. "When you first come into the home and are placed in a room, you have to figure out how to fit in and follow the customs *(shikitari)* of that room. The roommates who have been there longest will tell the newcomers what to do and how to do it. Some people will teach you kindly, but others are bullies. Aotani is a very lonely place if your roommates are mean."

Age-dominance is vehemently resisted in Mr. Hirano's room. Mr. Hirano, a retired railway man, is more than twenty years older than his two roommates. Mr. Ishikawa (age fifty-eight), the youngest, is proud of his youth. Previously a lumberjack and construction worker who blazed trails and dug tunnels through the Hokkaido wilderness, he still maintains his former drinking habits. Mr. Ishikawa loses patience with Mr. Hirano, claiming that the older man is *katai* (stubborn and demanding). Their arguments escalate into yelling matches, especially when Mr. Ishikawa has been drinking. Normally, however, the two men avoid each other as much as possible.

Contributing to the Common Good:
Self-affirmation and Social Integration

Shared family and community images enacted in the subspheres of the institution such as the room, hallway neighborhood, and work groups facilitate the social integration of newcomers. Initially, newcomers resist joining a community of "old people," but soon the desire for social recognition and approval takes priority. Resourceful residents create their own social niche of distinction. Mr. Akatsuka learned to paint during his last stay in the hospital. The nurses had encouraged him and even requested watercolors of the flowers by his bed or the mountain view from his window. At Aotani, residents come to him with requests for pictures to give as gifts to their grandchildren and friends. Mr. Akatsuka also paints pictures for people he thinks need cheering up. He says he wants to comfort Mrs. Shibutani, whose mental faculties seem to be deteriorating rapidly. When she receives a picture from him she lights up, and that, he says, is his greatest reward.

Mr. Sakata possesses one of the few snapshot cameras in the home. His picture-taking services are greatly appreciated. The first set of pictures of an event is displayed in the main hallway so residents can order reprints for their albums. Occasionally, residents ask Mr. Sakata to take pictures of them with visiting relatives. At tea, roommates and friends bring out albums and reminisce about significant social events such as the annual Aotani talent show. In this way, Mr. Sakata's photography records Aotani's history and enhances residents' sense of identification with each other and the institution.

Recognition and social approval also come from adhering to commonly esteemed values, such as demonstrating one's commitment and dedication to the common good. The local municipal code specifies that Aotani's residents are required to work four hours of "light labor" per day. Accordingly, all able residents receive work assignments. Tasks range in degree of rigor from dusting the Buddhist altar to vacuuming the hallways and cleaning the restrooms and are assigned according to each resident's physical capability. Most residents conscientiously apply themselves to their tasks with a sense of mission. Social reputations are

built as residents display their seriousness of intent and willingness
to contribute to the common good through their work responsibilities. When a resident is hard at work, passersby in the hallway
recognize their efforts with the standard greeting, *"Gokurōsan!"*

Mr. Kitsutani takes great pride in his work. He claims
that the first floor men's restrooms are spic and span after he
finishes cleaning ("much cleaner than when anyone else does this
job"). He beams whenever passersby commend him on his
efforts. Mrs. Onishi, assigned to washroom duty, complained
about how tired she was after cleaning the washroom. During her
assigned week, she had to rest all afternoon after only a few hours
of work each morning. She explained to her friends that the doctor
told her she could relinquish her cleaning responsibilities whenever she wanted. When she finally gave up her task at age eighty-
eight, everyone knew she had continued it for as long as she possibly could. Now she makes a point to praise other residents as they
work at their various jobs, thanking them for their efforts since she
is no longer able to help out.

Aotani residents represent a wide range of age and physical capacity. Cooperation and mutual assistance are offered to
people who are less physically mobile or strong. Mr. Nakagawa,
in his late fifties, is four feet tall, walks with a limp, and is border-
line mentally retarded. Residents are amused that he wears a
watch but can't tell time. He had trouble maintaining an independent lifestyle, so a social worker encouraged him to enter the institution. He makes himself useful by helping others. Filling this
niche helps him feel needed and responsible. For example, he
comes to Mr. and Mrs. Sakamoto's room every morning to pick
up their hot water jug and fetch water for morning tea. Mr. Sakamoto is partially paralyzed from a stroke and Mrs. Sakamoto has
her hands full just taking care of him. They are very grateful to
Mr. Nakagawa, who is always cheerful and usually stays to chat a
while.

Compassion and service to those weaker than oneself is an
ethic nurtured in the institution. Mr. Nakagawa's service helps
integrate him into a community of older people of which he is only
peripherally a part. The older people praise and reward him with
fruit and other treats as appreciation for his assistance. Women
explain that they try to help their older and weaker roommates as

much as possible, because they hope that when they get older, younger residents will do the same for them.

Power and Resistance

Residents are able to construct their social environment from familiar cultural concepts and thereby create a more hospitable environment. Yet, in the final analysis, this environment is a cultural construct imposed upon strangers. The adjustment to group living *(shūdan seikatsu)* is difficult—both because residents must learn to live with strangers at very close quarters and because their lives are tightly regulated for ease of supervision. Mrs. Kajima advises, "If you just follow the rules, this is a nice place." But Mr. Iwakura confides darkly, "The only way to survive in this place is to have forbearance *(gaman)*. No matter what you have to endure, be silent and bear it." Newcomers can no longer set their own schedules or decide their own diet. The staff claims there are no rules, that residents need only be aware of others and avoid causing them problems *(meiwaku)*. Even so, a person who refuses to conform may be asked to leave.

The daily schedule structures daytime hours, and except for those who are convalescing in the infirmary, adherence is strictly enforced. According to the schedule, residents must rise at 6:00 A.M., when the morning wakeup music is broadcast over the public address system. They complete their daily tasks before breakfast is served. At exactly 8:00 A.M., residents file into the dining hall. They begin eating when the head staff woman gives the signal and must finish their meal within fifteen minutes. After that, they are given permission to leave the table. This same pattern is followed for lunch (served at 12:00 noon) and dinner (served at 5:00 P.M.). Residents are not allowed to go outdoors after dinner without special permission. Everyone must be in bed by exactly 9:00 P.M. Sometimes when the men are watching an exciting baseball game, they are made to leave before the game is over, amid much grumbling and complaining.

Many residents have difficulty adapting to their new lives in Aotani. They realize their powerlessness to make many of their own decisions regarding how to spend their time, what and when to eat, and other details of daily life. They know they must submit to the authority of the staff or forfeit their right to stay in the institution. In many cases, they have no place else to go, so they have no alternative but to adapt. Evading the rules and wishes of the staff is a major preoccupation for some residents. The younger men especially chafe under the authoritarian rules and regulations. In their refusal to be controlled, they devise ingenious strategies to maintain a modicum of freedom despite their decreased autonomy.

As one survival strategy, residents become astute observers of the staff, that is, of those who hold power over them. The older women anticipate needing staff support when they become frail and try to stay on good terms with them. Residents know which staff members are sticklers when it comes to enforcing the rules and who will let them get away with minor infractions. When Staff Woman A is on night duty, for instance, the men know they can finish watching the ball game before going to bed, but when it is Staff Woman B's turn, they do not even bother to ask. Mr. Komura knows that when it is Staff Woman C's shift, he can go out to the town and come back late without getting into trouble. The more lenient staff women are regarded as being on the residents' side. The rule sticklers are dealt with cautiously and discussed pejoratively in hushed tones.

A camaraderie of the oppressed thus unites residents in a common pursuit of freedom from restrictions and staff authority in their daily lives. Networks of resistance and mutual aid are created to facilitate rule violations. For example, alcohol consumption is prohibited except during supervised periods. For many of the younger men (in their late fifties and early sixties), drinking is an integral part of their social patterns. They furtively enjoy drinking together on forays into town, and within the facility they drink illegally in the privacy of their rooms. Networks of resistance aid residents in bringing liquor into the home without being detected by the sharp and watchful eye of the staff women and administrators.

Mr. Takahata had an especially active social life. When not imbibing at a local bar, he was at his woman friend's house in town. He did not appreciate the institution's 9:00 P.M. curfew and the restriction against leaving the facility after dinner without permission. He devised a scheme that would allow him to stay at his woman friend's house until the wee hours of the morning, then sneak back into the home to be present and accounted for at breakfast. He enlisted the aid of his friend Mr. Nozawa, who would unlock the side door for him so he could slip inside without being noticed. One day this plan backfired when the security guard discovered the unlocked door and locked it. Since Mr. Takahata could not get back into the building, he was exposed by his absence the next morning, and the whole story came out. For this transgression, Mr. Takahata was "grounded" for several weeks. But despite the occasional slip-up, most of the time residents successfully assist and cover for each other to achieve maximum autonomy within their restrictive environment.

Residents adhere to an ethic of resistance, an affirmation of their effectiveness as human beings and their will to remain in control of their lives. Through violating the rigid rules, men express their refusal to be dominated, especially by the care givers, who are younger than themselves. Networks of resistance form an integral part of the informal social structure of home life. They provide mutual aid to assist in covert activities and encourage the drive for self-determination. In their own networks, the ones who successfully evade the rules become heroes and popular figures. Perhaps this explains why Mr. Takahata was overwhelmingly elected president of the Residents' Association.

New Norms

When Mrs. Takashima and Mr. Koyama "got married" they had their picture in the local newspaper. Mr. Koyama is proud that Mr. Sakata's photograph captures their nuptial kiss. In the insular context of an institution, new values evolve unimpeded by societal pressures and inhibitions. More than 85 percent of the residents are single; not surprisingly, new norms regarding male-female relationships have developed. Although some staff frown on it, men and women who share a mutual attraction spend time with each other, and if the romance progresses they may even move in together in a common-law marriage arrangement.

In Japan, marriages among the elderly have been extremely rare. Norms are changing as members of senior centers and clubs break with convention and boldly live less restricted lives. In these contexts, less inhibited social relations among men and women are possible. Similarly, in the more insulated context of an institution, away from the social sanctions imposed by children and relatives, residents create social lives based on values and attitudes relevant to their own social and emotional inclinations.

Remarriage between older people is problematic. Children object to older parents' contemplating a legal union because such a union threatens their inheritance. Couples who wish to "marry," that is, enter into a common-law marriage, must first obtain the permission of their children. Aotani's director calls a meeting in which the residents and their children discuss the matter. Mrs. Takashima's and Mr. Koyama's families, for example, were brought together at the same meeting. Mrs. Takashima says, "We did everything properly. We asked the director to be our go-between and he talked to our children's families. Our children were opposed to our marriage at the start; but when they saw we were going to go ahead with it anyway, they decided it was no use opposing us and gave their consent."

As is customary for marriages in the society at large, the marriage-partners-to-be chose a respected person in the community—in this case, the director of the home—to give their union legitimation. They anticipated that his blessing would enhance their new status in the eyes of other residents and improve the chances that the "marriage" would be accepted. Their "wedding" was held at the monthly birthday dinner, and the newlyweds were officially introduced to the assembled residents as husband and wife.

New norms also evolve from the older people's perceptions of health, based on their experience of biological aging. Loss of physical strength and mental clarity diminish a resident's ability to contribute socially and physically to the daily life of the institution. Because the degree of involvement and contribution determines one's reputation and standing in the community, health status modifies the potency of the seniority principle in this social hierarchy. Despite the loss of standing that can result from loss of health, individuals are buffered from the criticism and insensitivity of the young by the understanding and sympathy of their peers. Residents tend to regard the aging process anxiously, but also with the assurance of acceptance by their peers.

Even though some younger men ridicule the more senile residents with rather nervous laughter, progressive forgetfulness is joked about and accepted as an inevitable process, even by the persons affected. Even as mental capacity declines, individuals maintain themselves as distinct social entities, whose personality and social skills are maintained. Mrs. Hata, for example, is friendly and talkative. She confides that her memory of recent events is fuzzy, but she enjoys relating snatches of her younger years as an immigrant to Sakhalin where the *Rosuke* (Russians) were neighborly and the sea was bountiful. Mrs. Makino bows and greets people politely, even though she is less sure of herself than she used to be and seems anxious about her memory loss. Even so, every day she sits on the benches lining the hallway and chats with acquaintances, still a part of the social setting.

Despite physical and sensory decline, residents who maintain a sense of dignity, composure, and responsibility for self-maintenance in the face of advancing disabilities are respected. Mrs. Sasaki, for example, is regarded as a model of internal strength. She is described as *shikkari shiteiru,* one who stands firm and perseveres against adversity with silent strength and courage. She endures her disabilities without complaining, in spite of advancing deafness and diminishing eyesight. Mrs. Ōya, in contrast, is described as *darashi ga nai* (the phrase implies a slovenly and self-indulgent attitude). The staff claims that she endangers her health by overeating, whines constantly, and has a defeatist attitude. Because of the way she manages herself, she fails to receive the respect from staff and peers that Mrs. Sasaki does.

Trajectories: The "Last Stop" and Beyond

Health status is the major criterion for maintaining residency in the home. Residents tend to think of the home as their "last stop on the train ride of life *(Jinsei no shūchaku eki).*" For most residents, however, it is merely a way station. Health status determines a resident's trajectory through the home. Over time, as residents' physical strength declines, second-floor residents are transferred to accommodations on the first floor. From these rooms, they can get back and forth to the dining hall more easily.

The infirmary is a membrane through which residents pass in and out of Aotani, some never to return. It serves as a holding station for those of marginal health unable to function at the level required. For those who become ill, depending on the severity of the illness, the infirmary is their last chance to hold on to their lives in the institution. If they recuperate successfully, they are allowed to return to their rooms; if not, they must leave for the hospital, because the staff cannot care for residents who require a lot of assistance in their daily lives. When there is hope of recovery, they may be readmitted to Aotani after discharge from the hospital. The infirmary then becomes a free zone in which they are temporarily freed from observing Aotani's strict schedule.

Residents hold to the belief that this is their last stop in life. Not wishing to be aging nomads, they believe they have finally found a place to die in peace. This belief is shaken when older residents around them traverse a trajectory through the institution and exit to the hospital, a nursing home, or the family, before going to their graves.

A death at Aotani brings a sobering reminder of the transience of life. Mr. Itami had been a coal miner in his younger days and had contracted black lung disease. After his wife died he had become intensely lonely and had developed a severe drinking problem. He was admitted to Aotani because he was incapable of maintaining a household and caring for himself. He had been drinking heavily the evening before he died. The next day, his thin, frail body was carried to the infirmary, where the staff women prepared it for mourning. One staff woman slowly beat the Buddhist bowl gong. The head staff woman gently bathed and clothed Mr. Itami in a pure white kimono, all the while whispering softly to reassure him not to be afraid on his journey to the other world.

After the preparations were completed, an announcement was made over the loudspeaker system, and residents began to line up to pay their last respects to his departing spirit. Waiting in a line extending from the infirmary the length of the main hallway, each resident in turn paused briefly to offer incense in front of the tiny altar placed at the head of Mr. Itami's bed. After the long line of residents had filed past the altar, a somber mood prevailed in the hallway where residents stopped to chat. Mrs. Ohara said, "He's lucky, he went so quickly. That's how I want to go." Her listeners all nodded solemnly in agreement.

The family came to take the corpse that morning. By bidding farewell to the deceased earlier in the morning, residents had marked a closure in their relationship with him. Mrs. Kawata remembered another occasion years before, when Mrs. Kamatani died during the night and first thing the next morning the family came to take the body. She and others were upset that they were unable to give their friend a proper send-off not only from the home, but from this life. They had not been allowed to perform the therapeutic farewell rituals that not only console the living, but make peace with the deceased and liberate their spirits to pass on to the next dimension.

At Mr. Itami's funeral, the institution was represented by an administrator, a care giver, and an individual selected from among the residents who was a close friend of the deceased. The customary funerary donation *(kōden),* a small sum of money, was offered to the family of the deceased on behalf of the institution.

The known universe for most residents consists of this world *(kono yo)* and the next *(ano yo).* Contact is maintained between the two realms vis-à-vis the Buddhist altar, a window allowing communication with the world beyond. The most important beings occupying the "next world" are deceased spouses, immediate family, and nameless ancestors extending back for generations. They exist in a paternalistic relationship to their descendants, offering protection to their loved ones who diligently revere their memory at the Buddhist altar.

Mrs. Saito says half in jest, "I wish my husband would hurry and come get me." Other residents also say they are waiting for either parents or a deceased spouse to deliver them to the next world.

Situated in a prominent position at the far end of the dining room, the Buddhist altar and a small Shintō god shelf represent the spiritual essence of the Japanese family and by extension, the Aotani family. Women are considered the caretakers of deceased family members and are responsible for observing the Buddhist rituals that give comfort to those in the next world. Every morning, small groups of women of the same sect gather to chant sūtra passages before the Buddhist altar. In contrast, a mere handful of men pause briefly before the altar.

The ashes of deceased residents whose relatives' whereabouts are unknown are interred in the Aotani grave. Their memorial tablets *(ihai)* are kept in the home Buddhist altar together with those brought by residents when they came to Aotani. In some cases, the tablets belong to residents who are the

only surviving member of their family. In other cases, they are
kept because the resident was the only one willing to care for the
spirits of deceased family members. On the first of each month
and on all major Buddhist holidays, a Buddhist priest comes to
chant sūtras and conduct the proper religious services. This practice ensures that the "Aotani ancestors" as well as residents'
deceased family members are honored with the proper rituals.

The Buddhist altar thus unifies the residents with their
predecessors in the institution as well as with deceased family
members. As a symbol of generational continuity, those who have
been denied their rightful place in their families in this world
anticipate that justice will prevail in the next. Through death, they
believe they will come to reside once again in the family circle,
albeit in the form of a memorial tablet in the family Buddhist
altar.

These Japanese elderly maintain their expectations for
family care, hence much bitterness arises from their feelings of
abandonment by their children. Reunification in the afterlife is a
comforting consolation. In contrast, future generations may hold
fewer expectations for family care. As Buddhist altars and religious observances become less central in household social rituals,
the nature of religious salvation in the afterlife may also be redefined. Family ties in the afterworld may be less related to the continuity of the family as older people become more emotionally
independent from their families in this life.

Conclusion

As nonfamily care becomes more likely for present and
future generations of Japanese elderly, models are needed that
illustrate a successful negotiation of the problems of aging, especially social and economic support and self-maintenance. Institutions for the elderly are alternatives to the supports of the biological family, and their residents are pioneers in exploring ways to
humanize institutional settings.

Life in a social welfare institution for the elderly is far
removed from the cultural ideal of growing old within the security
and warmth of the family circle. Institutions by nature tend to be
impersonal and efficiency-oriented; thus residents must live with
the regimentation necessary to ensure the smooth operation and

maintenance of the facility. From a broader perspective, every institution structures and limits the freedom of those who live within it, yet it is this same structure that makes possible the development of community. Without a social structure in which to develop, intimate social ties would not have a context in which to be formed.

Despite the sense of social stigma and preconceptions about institutions for the elderly that Aotani residents may have held, or more likely, because of this cultural baggage, their relief is all the greater at discovering a thriving community of peers with whom they can identify. The fear and shame of institutionalization is forged into a defiance of popular misconceptions of residents and institutions for the elderly and a resolute determination to affirm their new identities as Aotani residents. No longer isolated and alone with shrinking social support, nor ignored or feeling like a burden in their children's homes, newcomers begin to participate in the diverse and multilayered interactions of Aotani social life. Roles relinquished as part of the aging process in the mainstream age-integrated society are replaced with new roles and sources of self-affirmation.

The social patterns resulting from this interaction of roles and statuses illustrate the power of cultural symbols and concepts to provide models and a foundation on which to construct a new social universe, a new kind of social institution in Japanese experience. The haunting legend of Obasuteyama, which highlights feelings of abandonment and separation from family, intensifies the desire to embrace a new pattern of social relationships as an alternative to family ties. A discourse of family, which represents the intimacy, nurturance, and order in family relationships, is used as an ideal after which to pattern social relationships in the institution. Spatial concepts structure a sense of public and private space of an entire community within the geography of one building as well as condemn the institution to the periphery of social acceptability. In the struggle to define the boundaries of authority and submission, patterns of conflict and defiance also evolve as integral elements of the structural form of Aotani social life. New values cultivated in the insular institutional environment supplement familiar ones to answer the special needs and desires of people in their later years.

The institution and residents can be viewed within the

historical time frame of their long lives, bringing to the construction of their new social world the traditions and experiences of their families and communities. The concept of age hierarchy further articulates this time orientation, applied even within an age group labeled "old," as it structures social relationships based on age and its refracted expression in the seniority system.

Through intentional as well as unconscious design, the institutional environment is thus humanized, in the Japanese sense. The same basic design can be seen in other Japanese social structures. Historically, age grades have been an integral part of social relations in traditional communities in some parts of Japan (Norbeck 1953). The traditional *ie* (household) embodied the hierarchy of age and sex statuses as well as solidarity and primary in-group mentality. Rohlen's (1974) Japanese company, a contemporary mainstream social structure, also illustrates age grades in the form of incoming and advancing ranks of employees. A discourse of family solidarity and loyalty, aided by spatial concepts of in-group and out-group social boundaries, is the social glue in Japanese companies as well as in many other Japanese social groups.

Institutions for the elderly have existed for nearly a hundred years in Japan, but only in the past twenty or thirty years have they become overtly problematic in a changing Japanese society. Just as other social arrangements have evolved to meet new social needs, so the Japanese institution for the elderly has emerged as a social phenomenon in the wake of changing demography. It tweaks the Japanese conscience by virtue of its violation of traditional norms, which hold family care as the ideal for life in old age. Yet, looking past the stereotype of a gloomy custodial facility, we discover a bustling society of resourceful survivors who demonstrate perseverance, creativity, and dignity in embuing their existence in the institution with life-sustaining meaning.

Note

Research for the dissertation on which this chapter is based was supported by grants from the Institute of Culture and Communication of the East-West Center (Honolulu, Hawaii) and the University of Hawaii Japan Studies Endowment (funded by a grant from the Japanese government).

References

Ariyoshi Sawako. 1972. *Kōkotsu no hito* (A man of the trance). Tokyo: Shinchōsha.

Befu, Harumi, and Edward Norbeck. 1958. "Japanese Usages of Terms of Relationship." *Southwestern Journal of Anthropology* 14:66–88.

Benedict, Ruth. 1946. *The Crysanthemum and the Sword.* Boston: Houghton Mifflin.

Campbell, John Creighton. 1979. "The Old People Boom and Japanese Policy Making." *Journal of Japanese Studies* 5 (2): 321–357.

Campbell, Ruth. 1984. "Nursing Homes and Long-term Care in Japan." *Pacific Affairs* 57 (1): 78–89.

Fukazawa Shichirō. 1964. *Narayamabushikō* (Ballad of Narayama) (in Japanese). Tokyo: Shinchosa.

Imamura Shōhei. 1983. *Narayamabushikō* (Ballad of Narayama). Tokyo: Tōhei Films.

Inoue, Yasushi. 1982. *Chronicle of My Mother.* Tokyo: Kodansha.

Keith, Jennie. 1981. "Old Age and Age Differentiation: Anthropological Speculations on Age as a Social Border." In *Aging: Social Change,* edited by Sara Kiesler, James N. Morgan, and Valerie Kincade Oppenheimer. Pp. 453–488. New York: Academic Press.

Kōseishō (Ministry of Welfare). 1990. *Rōjin fukushi no tebiki* (Handbook on welfare for the aged). Tokyo: Rōjin Hoken Fukushibu (Department of Health and Welfare for the Aged, Ministry of Welfare).

Kumagai, Fumie. 1984. "The Life Cycle of the Japanese Family." *Journal of Marriage and the Family* 46 (1): 191–204.

Lakoff, George, and Mark Johnson. 1980. *Metaphors We Live By.* Chicago: University of Chicago Press.

Lanham, Betty. 1979. "Ethics and Moral Precepts Taught in Schools of Japan and the United States." *Ethos* 7 (1): 1–18.

Lebra, Takie Sugiyama. 1976. *Japanese Patterns of Behavior.* Honolulu: University of Hawaii Press.

Maeda, Daisaku. 1983. "Family Care in Japan." *Gerontologist* 23 (6): 579–583.

Martin, Linda, and Suzanne Culter. 1983. "Mortality Decline and Japanese Family Structure." *Population and Development Review* 9 (4): 633–649.

Niwa, Fumio. 1962. "The Hateful Age." In *Modern Japanese Stories,* edited by Ivan Morris. Rutland, Vt.: Charles E. Tuttle.

Norbeck, Edward. 1953. "Age-grading in Japan." *American Anthropologist* 55:373–383.

Ōkurashō (Ministry of Finance). 1991. *Chōju shakai taisaku no dōkō to tenbō*

(Policy trends and perspectives for a longevity-oriented society). Tokyo: Ministry of Finance, General Affairs Agency, Director General's Secretariat, Department for Policy for the Elderly.

Plath, David W. 1972. "Japan: The After Years." In *Aging and Modernization,* edited by Donald O. Cowgill and Lowell D. Holmes. Pp. 133–150. New York: Appleton-Century-Crofts.

——. 1980. *Long Engagements: Maturity in Modern Japan.* Stanford, Calif.: Stanford University Press.

Rohlen, Thomas P. 1974. *For Harmony and Strength: Japanese White-Collar Organization in Anthropological Perspective.* Berkeley: University of California Press.

——. 1978. "The Promise of Japanese Spiritualism." In *Adulthood,* edited by Erik H. Erikson. Pp. 129–147. New York: W. W. Norton.

Tobin, Joseph Jay, David Y. H. Wu, and Dana Davidson. 1989. *Preschool in Three Cultures: Japan, China, and the United States.* New Haven, Conn.: Yale University Press.

CHAPTER 5
Under the Silk Banner: The Japanese Company and Its Overseas Managers
Tomoko Hamada

This essay will illustrate the social relationship between Japanese managers at *honsha* (the Japanese corporate headquarters) in Tokyo and *kaigai-kogaisha* (a wholly owned Japanese overseas subsidiary) in the United States. It focuses upon the practice of *kaigai-shukkō* (temporary overseas assignment), using the case of Taihō Kaisha (Technology) (pseudonym), a company belonging to a very powerful industrial group *(keiretsu)* called the Heisei Group (pseudonym). The analysis of the mechanism of Japanese intercorporate alliances from the human resources angle will show how individuals within the system construct, change, distort, deny, and/or manipulate their perceived reality of corporate and intercorporate hierarchies.

First, at the structural level of social dynamics, I will analyze major aspects of the human resource management of the Japanese firm in terms of two personnel transfer systems called *shukkō* and *tenzoku*. Second, ethnographic data will reveal the subjective and multiple meanings of the overseas assignment and will illuminate the career development of Japanese managers overseas. Finally, I will discuss forces for organizational cohesion and human dynamics between the core (the parent firm) and the periphery (the child firm). Because human life is as complex inside an organization as outside, the organization must be analyzed from symbol-producing, comparative, and often competitive angles. Organizational reality as perceived and expressed by its members projects and is projected upon the political economy of the firm, where rivaling forces attempt to expand their relative power bases vis-à-vis the power center and other units.

While Japanese manufacturers are "internationalizing"

at a tremendous pace, each dominant corporate subculture (in this case, that of top management) attempts to achieve its goal through a unique set of cultural "equipment" for organizational integration. Some cultural patterns of domestic Japanese business that facilitate internationalization will remain as part of this equipment, while others will be changed, modified, or abandoned through new cultural learning. The patterns of the parent company–child company dynamics discussed here imply such possibilities.

Historical Background:
Japanese Overseas Direct Investment

Every year an increasing number of Japanese businessmen and their families leave Japan for overseas assignments. In the year 1986 alone, 58,951 Japanese left the country as *kaigai-shukkō-sha* (corporate transferees to overseas assignments). Already about two million Japanese businessmen and their families have been transplanted into foreign countries by Japanese companies. About a quarter million come to the United States.

Kaigai-shukkō has one literal meaning, but what it "means" for one person's career can be dramatically different from what it means for another's. For some it is a new opportunity for career advancement. Or it can be a training ground for future internationalists. But for others it is a temporary sidetracking of their long-term career marathon in a Japanese corporation. At its worst, it is a dead-end job.

Some Japanese businessmen leave their families behind when they are given such assignments without being notified in advance. They are called *tanshin-funin* (single-person assignment away from home). These extended assignments away from home, the bane of the contemporary working man, arouse particularly strong feelings. In 1986 a total of 175,000 businessmen were working away from home and their families on extended business assignments (both domestic and foreign). On an average, 217 employees out of every company employing 5,000 or more were on tanshin-funin that year. In an interview survey of 5,000 adult men and women by the Office of the Prime Minister concerning the tanshin-funin, 48.6 percent of Japanese male respondents replied that extended assignments away from home are unavoidable or "cannot be helped" *(shikataga-nai)* if there is a "compelling reason" *(yamu o enai riyū)*, while 44.0 percent thought tanshin-funin should not be made.[1] Because of their strong concern for their children's education, some businessmen leave their children behind so they do not become *kaigai-kikoku-shijo* (returnee children from overseas).[2]

The history of Japanese overseas direct investment is rather short, of about twenty to twenty-five years at a maximum. When Japanese firms started overseas investment in the late 1960s, a majority were to establish final assembly plants in developing countries, and/or to establish sales offices in developed countries. They established so-called "knock-down plants" or final assembly plants in Korea, Singapore, Malaysia, Taiwan, and other developing countries, using designs, machinery, and parts imported from Japan. Average investment during this period was small, about one million dollars. In the mid to late 1970s, when labor and energy costs surged in Japan, some Japanese firms started to move manufacturing bases and build complete manufacturing facilities in Asian and Latin American developing countries. In the 1990s, the mission of these Japanese businessmen often is to set up a new kaigai-kogaisha (overseas child company) in the United States or a European country and to engage in local manufacturing of products that were previously exported from Japan.

Partly because of local government restrictions on foreign direct investment, many Japanese overseas manufacturers at that earlier time were joint ventures with local concerns, in which the Japanese were minority owners. Those which entered Asian newly industrialized countries (NICs) and developing countries during this period aimed at expanding business in the global market and at exporting products back to the Japanese market.

In contrast, Japanese investment in industrially developed countries during the 1970s often meant the opening of wholly owned Japanese sales offices. These sales offices helped increase exports from Japan and their subsidiaries in developing countries to markets in the United States and Europe. Manufacturers of electrical appliances, semiconductors, bearings, industrial machinery, office equipment, watches, and foods were major movers during this period. Japanese direct investment flows throughout the 1970s remained around two to four billion dollars a year. This style of multinationalization—a search for cheaper labor, raw materials, and energy sources; a preference for joint ventures; a strong export orientation and multilateral trade aiming at Western markets—has been discussed as a manifestation of "Japanese" strategies in contrast to the earlier models of Western firms' multinationalization.[3]

In the 1980s a dramatic shift occurred in Japanese direct investment partly because of the strong yen, whose value more than doubled vis-à-vis the dollar, and partly because of the increasing trade surplus and mounting trade friction between Japan and Western countries. In 1981 Japanese investment abroad hit a record $8.9 billion, a 90.3 percent increase over the previous year. The torrent of capital flows from Japan followed year after year in the 1980s until the recession of 1991 temporarily stopped it. Japanese invested $7.7 billion overseas in 1982, $8.1 billion in 1983, $10.1 billion in 1984, and $12.2 billion in 1985. For the fiscal year 1986 (April 1986–March 1987), Japanese direct investment was reported as $22.3 billion.

More and more Japanese high-technology firms, automobile makers, chemical firms, and machinery manufacturers have made direct investments in the U.S. and European markets. Several new characteristics of Japanese direct overseas investment have emerged. First, instead of relying upon joint ventures or seeking minority ownership, an increasing number of Japanese firms establish wholly owned subsidiaries or enter the market through acquisitions and mergers. Second, these firms are establishing not only production facilities but also research and development centers to gather technological information and to meet the needs of local markets more promptly and precisely. Third, they integrate overseas production facilities in different countries to meet the global strategies of the Japanese headquarters.

Some may conclude that these recent behavioral patterns of Japanese multinationals—the opening of production facilities in developed countries; the entry through merger and acquisition; the establishment of wholly owned subsidiaries; and the integration of overseas subsidiaries for global strategy—are similar to those of American and European multinationals.[4] Some scholars argue that this is a sign that Japanese firms have finally caught up with American and European multinationals in their global strategies.[5]

In contrast, I argue that the internationalization processes of Japanese firms reveal certain managerial perspectives, institutional arrangements, and cultural dynamics influenced by their past experiences and organizational arrangements in Japan. It is my contention that a social organization such as a multinational business firm is a product of collective human "praxis," created through the interconnected rubrics of micro- and macrodynamics of human reflexive actions. Managers reflect and act upon events, phenomena, and relationships. In acting and reacting they rely upon the meanings, metaphors, and affective consciousness created by their past experiences. Shared meanings help managers define, interpret, and comprehend reality, and these meanings are continuously re-created through constantly shifting relationships, communications, and actions. The end result of such activities is often a synergy of past and present, old and new. The development of a particular multinational corporate structure involves distinct internal and intraorganizational processes and styles of creative activities, symbolic interactions, and interpersonal communication among individual actors. Individual managers as agents of change create and re-create managerial ideology, organizational culture, and power structures with their own historical and cultural equipment.

This chapter will demonstrate that Japanese multinationals rely heavily on personnel management strategies for controlling foreign subsidiaries. They use human resource strategies that go above and beyond the conventional financial tools of capital allocation, profit retention, and dividend payment exercised by Western multinationals. I argue that the Japanese firms' approach to multinationalization derives from and is an extension of the relational dynamics of the interorganizational alliance between the parent firm and its subsidiaries in Japan.

Power Order of Japanese Keiretsu

To understand the relationship between the Japanese main office (honsha) and an overseas *kogaisha* (child company), one needs to understand the social order of the keiretsu. A keiretsu is a group of firms that are connected across industries through intercorporate stockholding and personnel transfer. The top one hundred Japanese industrial firms are closely affiliated with giant firms in other industrial sectors through a small percentage of mutual shareholdings. Together, this power center of Japanese business seeks to achieve international competitiveness and technological advancement.

Keiretsu is not a cartel, in which independent commercial enterprises together set prices, conditions of trade, and the like to limit competition in a particular industrial market. Instead, it is a corporate alliance across industrial sectors and markets, often tied through client-supplier business relationships. Competition in each market is fierce among firms with different keiretsu connections. Particularly powerful are six groups—Mitsubishi, Mitsui, Sumitomo, Fuyō, Sanwa, and Dai-Ichi Kangyō (Furukawa)— that link together batches of firms, banks, and trading houses with small cross-shareholdings. Another ten keiretsu combine suppliers and subsidiaries of one big firm (for example, Matsushita or Toyota) or bank. These sixteen groups account for a quarter of all Japanese firms' sales. They are also the most internationalized among Japanese firms, thus most relevant to the present study.

Clark (1979, 73–97) discussed basically three types of keiretsu: (1) former *zaibatsu* groups[6] such as the Mitsui, Sumitomo, and Mitsubishi groups, (2) bank-centered groups such as the Dai-Ichi Kangyō and Fuyō groups, and (3) manufacturer-centered groups such as the Hitachi, Matsushita, Toyota, and Toshiba groups. These categories are not necessarily mutually exclusive: a manufacturer-centered keiretsu may be a member of a former zaibatsu keiretsu, or a bank-centered group may include smaller manufacturer-centered groups.

Because of our interest in the relationship between the parent firm and its international subsidiary in the 1990s, this paper focuses upon manufacturing keiretsu networks such as the Sony, Nissan, Toyota, Matsushita, and Toshiba groups. They are based upon a large manufacturer surrounded by domestic and foreign subsidiaries and affiliates that are subcontractors of or vendors for the parent firm, manufacturing plants, sales offices, international joint ventures, and/or research and development (R&D) centers.

One needs to understand this institutional arrangement from a general political economic viewpoint. First, the main feature of the structure of the Japanese economy as a whole is the stratification of firms according to size. In general, the bigger a company, the better its quality in terms of technological advancement, productivity, financial strength, labor quality, and other conditions of competitiveness. Second, because of keiretsu alliances, a large percentage of a subsidiary firm's business is to provide parts and materials to the parent firm and other member firms. To this end, a special section or department is often established within the sales division of a subsidiary firm to undertake just such business transactions. The third important characteristic of manufacturing keiretsu is that the parent company is the leading company of a complex of legally independent companies, and the success of its corporate strategies depends largely on coordinating keiretsu activities.

Turning to the case study of Taihō Technology, we first notice that Taihō Kaisha belongs to the Heisei Group. The Heisei Group's domestic hierarchy is like a multilayered pyramid: the group involves more than one hundred member firms, each of which has its own subsidiaries. The subsidiaries of Taihō Kaisha provide components and materials to Taihō Kaisha and other Heisei Group member firms. A significant amount—42.4 percent —of Taihō Kaisha's cost of sales is due to buying from its subsidiaries.

The manufacturing keiretsu's distinct pattern of centrality transcends national boundaries. The intercorporate cohesion of keiretsu is maintained not only through daily business transactions but also through the tenzoku and shukkō personnel transfers from the center to the periphery.

Myth of Lifelong Employment

In the literature on economic organizations in Japan, there is still a tendency to assume that "permanent employment" means an undisturbed and upward career in one organization until retirement. In reality, however, lifelong job tenure is more a dream than a reasonable expectation for the great majority of Japanese adults (Hamada 1980; Plath 1983). Case studies such as those by Skinner (1983) and Noguchi (1990) remind us of a gap between organizational reality and such ideals of managerial ideology as permanent employment. Koike (1989) disputes the claim that the ideal of permanent employment is uniquely Japanese and notes that the relatively long years of service by blue-collar workers in Japan is a matter of degree, not an absolute employment practice. In fact, only 9.8 percent of Japanese male workers between the ages of fifty and fifty-four have worked for only one company since their graduation from school and entering the job market.

Most Japanese workers change organizations at least once in their life course. Among male university graduates working for large corporations, only about a third (34.1 percent) of those in their early fifties (50–54), more than a third (39.1 percent) of those in their late forties (45–49), and more than half (52.1 percent) of those in their early forties (40–44) have worked for only one company (Tachibanaki 1984, 82). Because of the aging of the workforce, the shortage of young workers, technological changes, and industrial structural shift, the chance of staying in one firm for life becomes increasingly unrealistic even to the elite core of Japanese employees, particularly middle-aged workers.

Personnel Transfer Systems: Tenzoku and Shukkō

Both tenzoku and shukkō serve to move personnel away from the head office to one of its affiliates or subsidiaries, including overseas subsidiaries. Although various official and business reasons can be given for such a transfer, there are two primary reasons for this practice: (1) to trim off redundant personnel at the managerial level and (2) to ensure intercorporate solidarity through human networks.

In tenzoku or "change of belonging," a person formally resigns from a company to be hired by its kogaisha. Tenzoku is used mostly for domestic personnel transfer and is rarely practiced for personnel transfer overseas, because very few Japanese would be willing to accept a permanent overseas assignment. It is, however, important to understand the practice of tenzoku to get a clear picture of the personnel dynamics of the keiretsu.

Tenzoku men are often managers who are moved to a subsidiary to (1) set up a new operation, (2) strengthen a particular aspect of the company, (3) provide a liaison between the parent company and the subsidiary, or (4) continue working after retirement from the parent company.

The official retirement age at Taihō Kaisha is currently age sixty, but if one becomes a junior director, he can stay until age sixty-five in the head office. One who becomes a board director stays an additional several years in the company. A manager who does not make directorship usually moves to a subsidiary to join its top management for several years. Over the last ten years, the average age of the Taihō Kaisha worker has risen from thirty-three to thirty-six and a half. To reduce "redundant" personnel at the higher end of the corporate hierarchy, Taihō Kaisha uses the tenzoku system rather than turning to more dramatic methods such as layoffs or forced resignations. The tenzoku practice of transferring to a smaller subsidiary is called *ama-kudari* (descent from heaven) (Skinner 1983, 56). It is the head office's defensive measure against the aging and stagnation of core personnel. So far, Taihō Kaisha's domestic subsidiaries have willingly accepted such transfers of management from the parent firm, partly because of their wish to strengthen managerial ties with the parent company, and partly because of their need for experienced managers, since most of Taihō Kaisha's subsidiaries are still relatively young.

The selection of managerial posts in subsidiaries is made through informal communication between the Affiliated Companies Division (ACD) of Taihō Kaisha and its subsidiaries. For the parent company, the ACD is a means to control the personnel and operations of subsidiaries. For subsidiaries, it is a way to open more communication channels and improve personal relationships with the top management of Taihō Kaisha.

Shukkō is a method for temporary transfer of personnel. It is widely practiced in Taihō Kaisha and also in many other Japanese companies, often for overseas assignment. Kaigai-shukkō-sha (overseas transferees) are in fact shukkō men whose destinations are more distant than those of domestic assignments. Shukkō is a dispatch of personnel to another firm within the industrial group for a limited time, from several months to several years. Assignment to posts in developing countries (i.e., a "hardship" assignment) is usually for no more than three years; assignments in developed countries are usually for five to seven years. Unlike tenzoku men, shukkō men have a chance to come back to the head office, although there are cases, especially in domestic assignments, when a shukkō man becomes a tenzoku man because of a change in the policy of Taihō Kaisha management or a change in economic circumstances.

The official reasons for shukkō are (1) to improve the management or technological expertise of a subsidiary through direct involvement, (2) to advise or guide the subsidiary's management more indirectly by dispatching managers, (3) to improve sales of Taihō Kaisha products by dispatching salesmen, and (4) to improve relationships with other companies or governmental agencies.

From the individual's life course view, the tenzoku and shukkō men need to modify, perhaps even revise, their occupational goals. They moved before, from one department to another within the original firm. This time the move is from one firm to another in the same keiretsu. The men try to console themselves, to justify their past political moves, and to rationalize the new outcome.

Historical Background: Taihō Technology, Inc.

Taihō Technology, Inc. is a wholly owned subsidiary of Taihō America, Inc., both of which are located in the United States. Taihō America, Inc., is in turn a subsidiary of Taihō Kaisha in Japan, which belongs to the Heisei Group.

Taihō Kaisha is a leading manufacturer of optical products and business machinery. In the 1970s Taihō Kaisha moved into a highly competitive segment of a consumer product market. Unfortunately, the firm encountered obstacles in the development and sale of its main product line, and it went into the red for the first time since its stock was listed in the late 1940s. This decline in earnings, together with the energy crisis, caused Taihō Kaisha to record a tremendous deficit for the first half of 1975. Although the firm recovered quickly, making up the deficit by a large margin during the second half, the temporary inability to pay a dividend was a great shock to corporate executives. At a closed-door meeting later in the year, a new corporate strategy was adopted, not merely to reorganize, but also to build morale. President Ryōhei Kuno (who was then managing director) proposed a six-year Premier Company Plan, to begin in the late 1970s. Under the plan, Taihō Kaisha had three years to become a leading corporation in Japan and another three to become a world leader.

The new plan was introduced to diversify product lines and also to enter into the highly competitive market of business machinery. Under the Premier Company Plan, a series of corporate objectives was outlined to strengthen the company's structure and increase its operational efficiency. The first task was to simplify Taihō Kaisha's complex production system of interlocking and interdependent factories. Before the new plan, a typical product was processed at plant A, transported to plant B for subassembly, and then taken to plant C for final assembly. A second related task was to create a new organizational framework based on product groups. A matrix management structure evolved out of the interaction between the product groups and the systems committees. During the succeeding decade, Taihō Kaisha, spurred by its relentless pursuit of research and development, dramatically emerged as a formidable world-class manufacturer. Many technical managers I interviewed entered the firm during this expansion/diversification/globalization period. Some managers were mid-career transfers that the company lured from its competitors as Taihō entered into this new business-machine field during the 1960s and 1970s. "Raiding" mid-career engineers and technical specialists from its competitors was an unusual practice for a Japanese firm at that time, and Taihō was criticized by its competitors for its aggressive human resources management policies. Today, headhunting for highly specialized workers is becoming increasingly common among high-technology firms that strive for global R&D dominance.

During the 1980s, tenzoku and shukkō were also practiced as parts of the firm's rationalization/reorganization measures. In 1985, for example, Taihō Kaisha had 970 shukkō men working for its affiliates and subsidiaries, both domestic and overseas. International competition, aging of the work force, and organizational restructuring brought changes that began to influence the employees' conventional image of Taihō Kaisha as a secure employer.

The corporate policy for rationalization reflected a wider trend in the Japanese labor market of the 1980s. For instance, top students who chose the thriving shipbuilding and aluminum firms of the 1950s and 1960s found themselves in the 1980s stuck in low-prestige, no-growth companies that had to release many employees. Although not that drastically, Taihō Kaisha began to transfer excess personnel to subsidiaries, while bringing in technical experts at mid-career. Today, new employees of Taihō Kaisha are aware that lifetime employment is no longer a certainty. Mr. Nakamori, a twenty-four-year-old Waseda University graduate who recently joined Taihō Technology, says, "A man who works for the firm for a long time may not get fired, but he may be shipped off to a subsidiary probably with a demotion in terms of status and salary. This is not lifelong employment. We know that lifelong employment is a myth."

Taihō Kaisha was expanding rapidly on a global scale during the 1980s. In the summer of 1985, a small group of Japanese managers, headed by plant manager Mr. Shimanaga Kōtarō, visited various prospective sites in the United States, where the company planned to establish a plant for manufacturing business machinery. After intensive studies and negotiations with state officials, at the end of the year 1985, Taihō Technology, Inc., was registered as a wholly owned subsidiary of Taihō America, Inc. In the years 1986–1990, the firm sent a total of 103 Japanese employees as kaigai-shukkō men to help build up Taihō Technology, Inc., in the United States.

To highlight the meanings of the overseas assignment and the general set of problems faced by managers who are asked to go abroad, we now turn to individual examples of kaigai-shukkō men.

Case 1: Mr. Aono Hiroaki, Chief Engineer of Taihō Technology, Inc.

Mr. Aono is a quiet, forty-five-year-old engineer of Taihō Technology, Inc. Born in Ibaragi prefecture, he was educated at a technical university in Tokyo, where he specialized in mechanical engineering. His goal when he entered Taihō Kaisha in the early 1970s was to follow his personal interest in developing optical equipment, of which Taihō was a leader in Japan. After working for several years at Taihō's Kasaoka Plant northeast of Tokyo as a junior engineer, Mr. Aono was appointed quality control engineer at the new Washinai manufacturing plant that was to produce business machines. His appointment coincided with the firm's decision to diversify its product line and to enter the high-tech market.

Although he had some reservations about leaving the Kasaoka Plant to move into a new technology area, Mr. Aono accepted the *jirei* (formally written order of job assignment) and, together with his wife and three children, moved into company housing in Washinai. Mr. Aono thought that he would stay at the Washinai Plant for many years, and he applied for and received a company loan to buy a house in a suburb of Washinai City. After three years of service, he began to immensely enjoy his task of quality control as he participated in several R&D projects that resulted in industrial patents. Mr. Aono's career goal was to become a chief engineer at Washinai and someday, plant manager.

When he was requested by Mr. Shimanaga, then the Washinai plant manager, to move to the United States to help set up Taihō Technology, Mr. Aono's reaction was mixed. After many anguished and sleepless nights, he finally accepted the offer from Mr. Shimanaga, who had been his mentor and who would head this new venture in the United States.

A few weeks after he agreed informally to take up this new assignment, Mr. Aono received an official brown envelope containing a white rice-paper letter from President Kuno. It indicated the company's wish to appoint him to a new technical manager's job at its newly established subsidiary in the United States. "When you receive jirei, it is like a *shōshū-rei-jō* [an imperial draft for military service]. There is no U-turn," says Mr. Aono.

Mr. Aono knew that the past success of Taihō Kaisha in this particular field had been due to its technical people's relentless R&D effort and to the constant incremental improvements in its production technology for quality and for cost effectiveness. Before his departure from Japan, Mr. Aono worried about the quality of American engineers and workers, whom he would hire in the United States and upon whose competence much of the firm's American venture and his future career would depend. According to Mr. Aono:

> Being away from the center of technological innovation at Washinai is very difficult for an engineer like me. Technology advances every day, and one needs to be constantly abreast of the latest innovations. Sitting in rural America, it is difficult to get all the information necessary to keep myself up to date with rapid technological progress. I would like to maintain myself as a first-class engineer, and yet I am getting behind my colleagues at Washinai.

When I moved out of Taihō Kaisha to help set up this
project, my former position was quickly filled by a younger
competent engineer. I will do my best to make this project successful, but I sometimes fear that I will not be able to go back to
the same production department at Washinai after this.

Soon after his new assignment was formally announced,
many *osenbetsu* (farewell gifts) were personally delivered to his
home by both superiors and junior colleagues in Japan. Mrs.
Aono diligently compiled a list of the gift givers and recorded the
monetary value of each gift. This would give her some ideas as to
what *ochūgen* and *oseibo* (seasonal gifts) she should send to these
Japanese people from the United States.

On May 15, 1986, Mr. and Mrs. Aono were at the Tokyo
International Airport in Narita waiting to board a Japan Airlines
(JAL) flight departing for the United States. Inside the JAL's
waiting lounge for business-class passengers, Mr. Aono was surrounded by several of his colleagues. On each of their suit collars
shone a small, golden company emblem. Technical Director
Takahashi was one of those who came to see Mr. Aono and his
family off.

The Aonos decided to take only their two younger children with them to the United States; they left their sixteen-year-
old son, Kazuo, with Mrs. Aono's aging parents in Japan. They
would not risk uprooting Kazuo, who was at a crucial age in preparing for the entrance examinations to top Japanese universities,
from the Japanese education race at this moment. They hoped to
find a good school in the United States for eleven-year-old Yoshio
and eight-year-old Akiko. Mrs. Aono had visited the Tokyo headquarters of Kaigai Shijo-Kyōiku-Kyōkai (Association for the Education of Sons and Daughters of Overseas Executives) to make
certain that there was a Japanese language school in the area to
which they were moving. She wrote to Mrs. Shiroyama, wife of
the director of general affairs of Taihō Technology, Inc., and
received personal advice about enrolling her children in an American public school. Mrs. Aono knew that there would be many
things to do once they arrived in the United States, and her husband would be very busy there.

Mr. and Mrs. Aono hoped that this overseas assignment
would be short, maybe a couple of years. But deep down, they

worried that kaigai-shukkō terms in developed countries such as the United States were getting longer and longer.

The Aonos have been in the United States for a few years now, and they are getting used to American ways of life. Still, they would like to go back to Japan as soon as possible. At home, Mrs. Aono continues to cook Japanese dishes. Every Saturday she drives her children to the Japanese language and math school. She maintains the gift-giving rituals with wives of managers at the Washinai Plant, using special "care-packages" services developed by Japanese airline companies and courier service firms.

The Aonos telephone their son Kazuo in Japan every week. Mrs. Aono has been back to Japan at her own expense twice, just to check on Kazuo's well-being. The firm pays for the family's home leave only after three years of foreign assignment.

Mr. Aono continues to telephone his friends at the Washinai Plant regularly. He wants to be familiar with the plant's latest technological innovations. He does not want to be left out of the inner circle of master engineers and researchers who have created and maintained Taihō's technological supremacy over its Japanese, American, and European competitors. Mr. Aono says,

> As for my career, I am already outside and have less contact with my former bosses in daily business interactions. I am now off the track of my career advancement. I hope to go back to the right track as soon as possible.
>
> I don't know whether the company can find a suitable position for me at Washinai after I finish this project. While I am away for several years, many capable technical managers will move up the ladder. I will miss a lot by stepping outside the company.

Because there are fewer and fewer higher positions in the company, junior managers certainly feel the competition among them to achieve the next position, although they rarely talk about it publicly. A deep source of frustration is the diminishing chance of becoming a top manager at the Japanese headquarters. There is already an increase in the number of persons at the top of the non-managerial sector, employees who do not hold the title of *fuku-sanji,* which is the lowest managerial title, and who work as deputy section chiefs. Additionally, a rapid increase in the number of employees with a university degree is causing a problem in the labor management of Taihō Kaisha. If the management of Taihō Kaisha tries to maintain its long-held tradition of using the seniority wage and promotion system, they must increase the number of managerial positions to meet the supply, particularly of those who entered the firm before the energy crisis of 1973, when the company was hiring more university graduates annually. Since 1974 the length of time to be promoted to director, always slow, has been stretched an additional 2.8 years.

Because of the relative shortage of managerial positions, competition among middle-level managers is intensifying. The competition for high positions among middle managers is fierce: at stake is not only rank and responsibility but their whole livelihood and self-esteem as long as they work for the company. The middle-level managers strive to reach the position of director, board director, and president.

In general, middle managers with twelve to twenty years of service who are highly ambitious prefer to stay in corporate headquarters because they consider their chances of promotion much higher at headquarters than in the field. If the management asks them to go abroad as shukkō men, they prefer to come back to the headquarters as soon as possible. Being away from headquarters means the possibility of becoming an outsider in the company hierarchy.

Announcements of promotion and personnel changes come regularly in spring. Every year, before the formal decision making, there is anxious scrambling of personnel negotiations behind the scenes for obtaining advantageous posts, for job rotations to avoid being stuck in a dead-end track, and for getting on the right path leading to top managerial positions. Long absence from the head office can mean difficulties in maintaining and manipulating such time-consuming, interdependent, and diffuse relationships at the power center. A manager's career success often depends upon his constant interaction with friends, mentors, rivals, and key personnel in the company whose interests, empathic concerns, and beliefs are in constant flux.

It is at this stage that junior managers start to follow certain top-level executives as their mentors, forming factions within the corporate power structure. Factions are usually based on close personal relationships between a mentor and a follower bound by mutual interests. If one must be away, it is the task of his mentor to keep his name alive in the head office and to advise him of the politics of headquarters.

It is not uncommon that followers of a particular clique suffer socially and economically if their mentor's rival obtains a high-level position. Every manager has his favorite story to tell about an overseas assignee whose mentor's sudden career death has derailed his own prospects. While he is helplessly trapped in a foreign subsidiary, the opposing factional leader promotes his followers to elite positions. Those who have lost political battles or those who do not have strong connections with the head office may be passed from one overseas position to another for a very long time without being summoned back to Tokyo. This type of manager is called *tarai-mawashi,* a term derived from the gift-giving practice in which a gift for which the receiver (and anyone else, for that matter) would have no conceivable use is simply passed on to another to meet the obligation of giving and returning irrespective of the individual's taste.[7]

One such manager, Mr. Shiroyama, whose case we examine next, sarcastically calls the overseas transfer system *shima-nagashi* (transfer to a desert island; a term signifying a medieval form of punishment). The hidden fear of losing jobs or of being transferred to advisory functions is particularly strong among middle-aged managers who have been trained to be generalists, rather than technical experts, and who have no particular skills to sell outside the company.

Case 2: Mr. Shiroyama Kaoru, Director of Finance and Administration of Taihō Technology, Inc.

Mr. Shiroyama is director of finance and administration at Taihō Technology, Inc. Although he is a member of the powerful seven-man corporate board at the pinnacle of this subsidiary in the United States, Mr. Shiroyama considers his career life in Taihō Kaisha bittersweet.

Mr. Shiroyama entered the firm in the 1950s, when Taihō Kaisha was a much smaller, more regional firm with fewer product lines. His mentor in the headquarters was a finance manager whose path he diligently followed for ten years. Unfortunately for Mr. Shiroyama, this mentor/director eventually was pushed out of the main office to a subsidiary.

In March 1962, Mr. Shiroyama married Etsuko, who was working as a salesclerk at a large retail store in Tokyo. With warm blessings from colleagues, superiors, relatives, and friends, they held a formal Japanese wedding ceremony. Etsuko was beautifully dressed in a traditional Japanese bridal costume. The couple went on a week-long honeymoon in March 1962.

On the Monday morning that Mr. Shiroyama went back to the Department of Finance to resume his work, he was called to the desk of the division director and handed a jirei. The company wanted him to go to the New York sales office as an accounting specialist within the month. The director added that Mrs. Shiroyama could join him in New York after six months. When her husband broke the news that evening, Etusko stood speechless in a living room filled with brand-new furniture that her parents had purchased as bridal gifts *(hanayome-dōgu)*. "What are we going to do with these large pieces of Japanese-style furniture? They won't fit into a tiny apartment in New York!" was the first thought that occurred to Etsuko's temporarily confused mind.

Mr. Shiroyama recalled that he had held an informal talk with his superiors about possible future overseas assignments several months before the couple's marriage. He could not believe that the actual decision could have been made so suddenly. He sorely missed his ex-mentor. If Mr. Shiroyama's mentor had still been at headquarters, the transfer could not have happened. In addition, Mr. Shiroyama, after working for ten years, had begun to gather his own *kogai-no buka* (subordinates I have raised myself) under his leadership at the Tokyo headquarters. Now he had to leave them, just as his own mentor had left him.

In May 1962, Mr. Shiroyama departed for the United States as tanshin-funin, leaving his bride behind. In New York, he struggled to learn American ways of doing business and the different operational and accounting methods of the sales office. Six months later, Etsuko, who spoke no English at all, arrived at New York's John F. Kennedy airport. The Shiroyamas moved to a larger apartment in Queens borough, on Long Island. Three years later their first son was born. Then, in the spring of 1965, instead of being sent back to Tokyo as they had expected, Mr. Shiroyama was transferred to Taihō Technology's Los Angeles office, ostensibly to streamline their accounting procedures. Their daughter was born in Los Angeles a year later. Mrs. Shiroyama learned to drive on Los Angeles freeways. The children were enrolled in an American public school. Soon the two children began to speak more English than Japanese, even at home. After five years in Los Angeles, to his and his family's dismay, Mr. Shiroyama was again transferred back to the New York office. Mr. Shiroyama spent a total of ten years in the United States before he was at last moved back to the Tokyo headquarters.

It was a very difficult move for both himself and his family. First they settled in *shataku* (company housing) in Kanagawa, but the children had difficulties in adjusting to the Japanese primary school system. Japanese school children taunted their poor Japanese language abilities and cultural differences. After a year, Mr. Shiroyama bought a house and moved out of the shataku community. At work, Mr. Shiroyama soon found that the Tokyo headquarters operated quite differently from overseas sales offices. While overseas, Mr. Shiroyama had been free to perform tasks independently, and he could personally discuss important business matters with top directors flown from Tokyo for short visits. At the Japanese headquarters, however, Mr. Shiroyama had to deal with bureaucratic procedures for corporate reporting. As a "newcomer" section chief in the accounting division, he had to relearn how to conduct group-oriented decision making. His ten-years' absence from the power center put him in a disadvantageous position because he lacked personal connections to conduct informal negotiations before attending formal meetings. Crucial pieces of information, disseminated through personal grapevines, frequently bypassed him. Political power had also shifted to the hands of certain production-oriented factions. Mr. Shiroyama became painfully aware that he was treated as a second-rate citizen within the Tokyo headquarters. He was bitterly disappointed when his colleagues and seniors ignored his suggestions for procedural improvement of financial reporting.

One early summer morning, Mr. Shiroyama telephoned his former boss, the president of Taihō America, Inc., at his home in Long Island, New York, and asked if there was an opening for him in the United States. Mr. Shiroyama told his former boss that he was not happy at headquarters, that he did not see much chance of promotion there, and that his family would be happier in the United States. Three years later, the company launched the Taihō Technology project, and Mr. Shiroyama received another

jirei, this time moving him into Taihō Technology, Inc., a manufacturing plant of Taihō America, Inc.

In "celebrating" Mr. Shiroyama's new assignment, colleagues at the department gave him a farewell party. Vice-Presi-
dent Sekiguchi attended the party and gave a speech on how
important Mr. Shiroyama's past service to Taihō Kaisha had
been, how much Taihō needed a truly international man like Mr.
Shiroyama, how significant his new post in the United States was,
and how his new assignment would bring benefits to the subsidiary and Taihō Kaisha. The speech ended with good wishes for his
go-kentō (strenuous efforts to make it successful). His colleagues
toasted "kanpai!" (bottoms-up/cheers !), lifting beer glasses. Vice-
President Sekiguchi assured Mr. Shiroyama that he and the home
office people would do their best to assist Mr. Shiroyama's new
venture. Mr. Shiroyama bowed deeply to Mr. Sekiguchi and said,
"Dōzo, yoroshiku-onegaishimasu" (I humbly ask your help).

Overseas Japanese Managers and Internationalization of the Head Office

Emphasis on human resources development has been a
fundamental part of Taihō Kaisha's corporate philosophy and pre-
dates the inauguration of Taihō Technology, Inc. The corporate
mission statement of Taihō Kaisha, enunciated by Taihō's
founder, Kitauchi Yasuhiko, and entitled "Four Taihō Principles," comprises the following:

1. Threefold Self: Seek self-motivation, self-respect, and
self-reliance.
2. Meritocracy: Maximize our human resources through
the merit system.
3. Industrial Familism Policy: Cooperate to deepen
mutual trust and understanding with a harmonious spirit.
4. Emphasis on Health: Make a healthy body and a
healthy mind the basis for personal development.

President Kuno of Taihō Kaisha in Japan announced in
the early 1980s: "We must move away from the kind of hardware
thinking that relies heavily on products toward something like

software thinking, which emphasizes the structure of operations and people." Thus corporate strategies for globalization and heavy investment of human resources in overseas subsidiaries are changing the perspective of the head office concerning the status of "internationalists" within the firm.

In the 1970s, Japanese manufacturing companies were more export-oriented. They relied upon *sōgō-shōsha* (general trading firms) to handle their exports and developed their own "internationalists" who spoke foreign languages in the *kaigai-bu* (overseas division). These internationalists were mostly good salesmen or cultural liaison officers. They were distinct from the rest of the corporate community and did not have high status in production-oriented manufacturing companies. With some notable exceptions, the career path in the international field was not considered an "elite" course (White 1988). In many large manufacturing firms, they were often considered a kind of lower-level clerk whose specialty was the English language (they were often called *eigo-ya-san* [Mr. English]) and as such they were excluded from the mainstream of the corporate power structure. Unlike many American firms where top executive positions have been dominated by MBAs, the top management of Japanese manufacturing firms have been predominantly those with science and engineering backgrounds.

In the 1990s, however, this notion is changing because of the growing importance of overseas manufacturing bases. Interfaces and contacts with things foreign among corporate divisions have multiplied as more and more overseas production facilities require the technological expertise, production know-how, and management skills of the head office. The firm today needs skills beyond sales and linguistic abilities to handle international businesses. Because of the "internal internationalization" of the head office, an increasing number of shukkō men feel that strategically important and thus selective foreign assignments can actually enhance their career opportunities.[8]

Unlike the "English specialists" of the 1970s, new kaigai-shukkō-sha are from the core of Japanese manufacturing firms (White 1988, 114). They are plant managers, production engineers, quality control experts, product design researchers, computer scientists, biochemists, electronics engineers, and international corporate law and taxation experts. In the 1990s, cross-cultural interactions permeate deeper into the Japanese manufacturers' organizational structure.

Case 3: Mr. Shimanaga Kōtarō, President of Taihō Technology, Inc.

Mr. Shimanaga is a short, stout man, aged fifty-five, with a shock of gray hair over a well-tanned, broad forehead. Mr. Shimanaga considers himself an anomaly in Japanese companies, where the typical worker joins at university graduation and stays until retirement. Mr. Shimanaga, a chemical engineer, prefers "pursuing my professional field and doing research I like" to lifetime employment. When he joined Taihō Kaisha in 1966, he already had excellent career track records at two other firms. Taihō Kaisha hired him into its new line of business, where he rapidly climbed the corporate ladder as head of the product division and eventually became Washinai plant manager. He earned 160 patents for new technology, and in 1983 he was named a director of Taihō Kaisha in Japan.

In 1985, Mr. Shimanaga became president of Taihō Technology, Inc., and moved to the United States with two of his trusted subordinates to establish an overseas manufacturing plant. Today, Taihō Technology, Inc., employs 1,232 people, both American and Japanese. Facilities expansion has raised Taihō Technology's capital investment in this rural region of the United States to more than $140 million. During these years, sales of business machinery shipped from this plant have exploded from zero to $400 million.

The 160-acre-plant grounds are landscaped with ornamental trees and shrubs, and adorned with a Japanese-style pond with red foot bridges. Municipal workers have attentively thinned the woods in such a manner that drivers on a nearby interstate highway can admire the clean and functional beauty of the plant in the midst of green woods. On the upper side of a white building facing the interstate, red letters indicate the corporate logo in elegant clarity.

Today, after several years of the spectacular growth of Taihō Technology, Inc., Mr. Shimanaga is the picture of total confidence. He believes that the Heisei Group is metamorphosing into a transnational keiretsu. In its global expansion in coming years, the group will need internationalists who have had hands-on experience in running a manufacturing operation overseas. They will need men with "hard skills" plus international experience. Mr. Shimanaga thinks he is such a person. When asked about the *kurō* (hardships) of overseas assignment, he laughs and says that business to him is a game.

The only low point in his life in the United States came at the very beginning of this project in early 1986 when he was one of a few Japanese executives working at a temporary office near the plant construction site. While inspecting the site by himself, Mr. Shimanaga got lost and wandered around for hours in the woods and marshy terrain. When he finally got his bearings, his shoes were muddy and briars snagged his suit. A strong sense of gloom settled over him as he stared at a murky ditch on the property. He felt overwhelmed by the challenge of building a state-of-the-art manufacturing plant on this heap of mud visited only by raccoons, rabbits, and other wild animals. Mr. Shimanaga reveals this "amusing anecdote" to emphasize the subsequent success of Taihō Technology, Inc.

Backed by his growing confidence in this manufacturing operation in the United States, Mr. Shimanaga foresees going head-to-head with Taihō Kaisha's Washinai plant in Japan, the world's largest factory for this line of products. Brushing off other giant business-machine competitors, Mr. Shimanaga states that his overriding goal is nothing less than "to surpass the Washinai plant in every aspect—sales, production, quality, everything." He plans that products manufactured at this American factory will be exported back to Japan in a few years, and then his next target will be Europe. Mr. Shimanaga thinks he will be the man to push the Heisei Group's globalization.

Mr. Shimanaga enjoys discussing science, technology, and community work with his American friends. A very personable man with a deep, strong voice, he is at ease entertaining his American clients at an elegant Western-style dining club, although he loves to relax with a Budweiser by himself. He favors American hors d'oeuvres for company receptions.

Mr. Shimanaga decided to come to the United States as

tanshin-funin. His children are all grown up, and Mrs. Shimanaga is living with her aging parents in his home in Japan. Unlike the lonely image of the term, Mr. Shimanaga enjoys the challenge of his new task and loves to devote his entire energy to his work at Taihō Technology, Inc. Tanshin-funin is fine with him because there is not much time left for family life anyway. Mr. Shimanaga says, "The person who benefits most from my overseas assignment is my wife in Japan, who does not need to look after me, on top of taking care of her aging parents. The best husband is the one who is healthy, who brings home paychecks regularly, and who is absent." Mr. Shimanaga shops for weekly groceries at a nearby supermarket every Sunday afternoon, and he sometimes cooks supper in the modern kitchen of his contemporary three-bedroom house in an exclusive residential community with two private swimming pools and two golf courses.

Mr. Shimanaga uses his tanshin-funin excuse to visit Japan frequently to keep personal connections with key members of the head office. He takes every opportunity to make himself visible in the Tokyo power center; he spends a lot of time on the airplane crossing the Pacific, contemplating his next career move. Indeed, after several years of shukkō to Taihō Technology, Inc., Mr. Shimanaga intends to go home as a new corporate elite, wrapped in glory (as the Japanese proverb says).

Together with the corporate strategic shift from export orientation to overseas manufacturing, Taihō Technology transformed the overseas division (kaigai-bu) to the overseas operations division *(kaigai-jigyō-bu)*. The overseas operations division coordinates the activities of different divisions in a matrix manner for overseas operations. As the overseas operations division expands, the status and power of several key overseas subsidiaries are increasing in the overall structure of the group.

In this new phase of development, Japanese multinationals are repeating the past formula of domestic keiretsu formation. They dispatch many managers from the head office to newly established subsidiaries to ensure the continuity of corporate and intercorporate cultural transfer. Through such manpower management, men like Mr. Shimanaga will eventually bring back new information and experiences gained from overseas operations to enhance the overall internationalization of the Heisei Group.

Centrality, Continuity, and Hierarchy

A 1987 survey by the Ministry of International Trade and Industry shows that Japanese companies are far more likely to staff management positions abroad with shukkō personnel dispatched from the home office than are their foreign counterparts. Of the top officials at Japanese-owned subsidiaries abroad, 45.4 percent have been transferred from the home office against 17.3 percent for foreign-owned subsidiaries in Japan. The staffing ratio for section chiefs and department heads is 17.4 percent for Japanese firms and 1.6 percent for foreign firms in Japan.[9]

The Japanese personnel transfer system signifies a continuity between an employee's past career in the parent company and his new assignment. A tenzoku and shukkō man is no longer officially a Taihō Kaisha man, because subsidiaries are legally separate entities. However, he is still a member of the Heisei Group no matter how peripheral his new position becomes. The pattern of centrality and the hierarchical order of the keiretsu become obvious when one looks at the positions held by these kaigai-shukkō men after their transfers. Kaigai-shukkō men from the parent firm are given senior managerial positions one or two ranks higher than their previous positions. Mr. Shimanaga, president of Taihō Technology, Inc., previously held a position as a plant manager (director) in Washinai. Likewise, Mr. Aono, now a chief engineer and director of Taihō Technology, Inc., was a junior engineer at the Washinai plant. Mr. Shiroyama was a section chief in Tokyo before becoming a junior director of finance·and administration at Taihō Technology, Inc.

While managers of the Japanese parent company are usually better paid than subsidiary managers, salary is not the most important status differential. Foreign assignment allowances and other fringe benefits as well as the relatively higher purchasing power of one's income in a foreign country make kaigai-shukkō-sha enjoy a higher standard of living than those remaining in Japan. In addition, many expatriate managers belong to prestigious local golf clubs and entertain their guests lavishly at top restaurants and bars. They drive luxury automobiles, and they hire maid services for their newly rented three-to-four-bedroom houses, all of which are the envy of average Japanese "salary-

men" cramped in tiny apartments or company housing in the
Tokyo area. In spite of such material well-being, Japanese managers of kogaisha in general perceive themselves lower in status than
those who hold the same nominal positional titles at the head
offices. Power, authority, prestige, and other intangible rewards
are important factors in stratifying this interorganizational relationship.

Taihō Kaisha has an Affiliated Companies Division that
audits the subsidiaries' financial reports. Managers of the division
occasionally visit the top management of the affiliates and subsidiaries to check on and give advice about financial management,
production procedures, and personnel matters. The division
produces financial reports on the total group with the cooperation
of the accounting division.

The vertical relationship between the parent and child
firms is also manifested symbolically. For example, when Taihō
Kaisha's section chief Mr. Ayabe visits Taihō Technology, Inc., he
is treated by the subsidiary personnel as if he were a department
head, or a man whose position is a few ranks higher than his nominal title suggests. In a company limousine, Mr. Ayabe would sit in
the back with Mr. Aono, the chief engineer, while Taihō Technology's section chief would sit next to the chauffeur.

The head office possesses and often exercises decision-
making authority to control and influence the American subsidiary's internal decision making. Many important decisions need to
be confirmed by Tokyo, and fax messages (in the Japanese language) and international telephone calls go back and forth across
the Pacific Ocean. Corporate guidance and control are given in
terms of technical advice, quality control management, training
programs, manpower supply, financial support, material and
parts procurement, intercorporate business and, most of all, a
sense of common purpose.

Discussion

We have learned that Japanese multinationals rely heavily on kaigai-shukkō men to manage foreign subsidiary operations. The mechanism of human dynamics between the Japanese
headquarters and the foreign subsidiary is similar to those
between the main office and its subsidiaries within the keiretsu

group in Japan. To Taihō expatriate managers, keiretsu membership is like being part of a prestigious club where members share a
sense of belonging and common historical experience in a hierarchical order. It represents an interwoven nexus of business and
personal relationships where a boundary is drawn between insiders and outsiders and between seniors and juniors. With a strong
centrifugal force, it spins off personnel, functions, and divisions
from the core to the periphery, while concentrating power, status,
and prestige at the center.

Such mechanisms of intercorporate control differ from
conventional methods of Western multinationals' control in which
capitalistic principles bind each subsidiary operation primarily
through financial control. In such a case, at least in theory, neutral
(emotion-free), numerically presented financial data serve as the
basis for evaluating the performance of an overseas subsidiary
against specific targets.

In the Japanese keiretsu multinationalization, in contrast,
control extends beyond mere financial control, through personal
networks between the center and the subsidiary. The spirit of
"consultation" and "planning" among keiretsu members becomes very real, and perhaps more powerful than a mere contractual obligation. My interviews with Taihō Technology managers
revealed that an overwhelming majority do not regard their
shukkō jobs as based upon a contractual relationship. In fact,
unlike Western practices, they often do not even know the specific
terms of their overseas assignment.[10] A Japanese manager identi-
fies himself as a creative and sometimes manipulative agent influ-
encing and being influenced by human relationships involving his
mentors, colleagues, followers, rivals, enemies, heroes, confi-
dants, and key personnel in the company and the keiretsu group.
The Japanese managers presented here perceive organizational
reality through the symbolic and dialogical relationships between
the parent firm and its foreign subsidiary. They see themselves
placed in organic processes of symbolic interactions, of fissions
and fusions among factional members, of formal and informal
group dynamics, and of a constantly shifting nexus of dyad rela
tionships. From such a relational viewpoint, business is confined
to neither finance, technology, nor contract alone.

In the mind of a Japanese expatriate manager, all subsidiaries are working for the success of the global strategies of the par-

ent firm. Their continuous and strenuous efforts for the overseas subsidiary's success is based upon their ardent desire to go back "home" with a mark of distinction. The referees of their accomplishments are the organizational insiders, particularly those privileged enough to stay at its core. In this case objective financial data such as the firm's past performance against its international competitors are not considered as meaningful as is perceived level of performance vis-à-vis the domestic unit in Japan. At the individual level, the Japanese managers in this study evaluate their performance against the perceived task performance of the "significant others" at the Washinai plant or at the Tokyo headquarters. The strong work motivation of overseas managers situated at the periphery of the keiretsu formation seems to originate from their almost obsessive drive to catch up to and outperform the power center.

We have begun to comprehend several characteristics of Japanese multinational management: the heavy reliance on the shukkō transfers; the multiple and "subjective" meanings of kaigai-shukkō; the vertical relationship between the parent and child firms; the symbolic manipulation of the centrality of power; the cultural demarcation between organizational insiders and outsiders; and the duality of cooperation and competition between center and periphery. These consequential issues pose theoretical and empirical questions. They imply that Japanese multinational management may behave differently from their Western counterparts in other critical areas. Our future research must examine such issues as how Japanese overseas subsidiaries utilize locally hired managers; how they define, maintain, or change the cultural demarcation between organizational insiders and outsiders; and how they balance the issue of corporate centralization and decentralization in their decision making.

Notes

This research was made possible by the financial support of the Northeast Asia Council of the Association for Asian Studies, of the Virginia Foundation for the Humanities and Public Policy, and of the summer faculty research program of the College of William and Mary, Virginia.

1. Of the female respondents, 51.5 percent did not approve tan-shin-funin, while 40.4 percent thought it "cannot be helped." See Nihon Bōeki Shinkō-kai (JETRO) 1988, 58–59.

2. For studies on overseas children and their problems, see, for example, Kobayashi 1981; Minoura 1984; and White 1988. Monbu-shō (Ministry of Education) annually publishes a report on the issue entitled *Kaigai-shijo no genjō* (Present situation of overseas Japanese children).

3. For example, see Kojima 1985; Tsurumi 1976; Yoshihara 1979; and Yoshino 1976.

4. For example, see Ueno 1988. For discussion on the Japanese type of direct investment in the 1970s, see Kojima 1985.

5. For discussion on earlier European and American multinationals, see, for example, Vernon 1971 and Franko 1976.

6. *Zaibatsu* refers to a group of Japanese companies controlled and dominated by a family-owned holding company in Japan before World War II. Each *zaibatsu* had at its center a holding company, owned by the founder family. The holding company owned a large proportion of each of the dozen or so core companies, including the bank, the trading company, the trust company, and the insurance company. There was a great measure of centralized management.

7. For discussion on Japanese gift giving, see Befu 1968, 445–456.

8. The term *uchinaru kokusai-ka* (internal internationalization) is discussed by Yoshihara, Hayashi, and Yasumuro 1988.

9. The Ministry of International Trade and Industry (MITI) surveyed 1,043 Japanese corporations and their overseas affiliates in comparison to 1,052 foreign companies operating in Japan for the fiscal year 1986 (April 1, 1986–March 31, 1987).

10. Itami uses the term *jinhon-shugi* (human-capital-ism) instead of *shihon-shugi* (capital-ism) to illustrate the Japanese management principles. See Itami 1987. My research supports the concept of human-capitalism presented by Itami.

References

Befu, Harumi. 1968. "Gift-Giving in a Modernizing Japan." *Monumental Nipponica* 23:445–456.

Clark, Rodney. 1979. *The Japanese Company.* New Haven, Conn.: Yale University Press.

Franko, Lawrence G. 1976. *The European Multinationals.* New York: Harper & Row.

Hamada, Tomoko. 1980. "Winds of Change: Economic Realism and Japanese Labor Management." *Asian Survey* 20 (4): 397–406.

Itami Hiroyuki. 1987. *Jinhon-shugi kigyō* (Human-capitalistic enterprise). Tokyo: Chikuma-shobō.

Kobayashi Tetsuya. 1981. *Kaigai-shijo-kyōiku* (Overseas children's education). Tokyo: Yūhikaku.

Koike, Kazuo. 1989. *Japanese Workers' Skill.* London: Macmillan.

Kojima Kiyoshi. 1985. *Nihon no kaigai chokusetsu-tōshi* (Japanese overseas direct investment). Tokyo: Bunshin-do.

Ministry of International Trade and Industry (MITI) (Tsūshō Sangyōshō, Seikatsukyoku, Kokusai Kigyōka), ed. 1987. *Kaigai jigyō katsudō kihon chōsa, kaigai tōshi tōkei sōran* (Basic survey on overseas business activities, general statistical survey on overseas investment). Tokyo: Ōkurashō Insatsukyoku.

Minoura Yasuko. 1984. *Kodomo no ibunka-taiken* (Cross-cultural experiences of children). Tokyo: Shisaku-sha.

Nihon Bōeki Shinkō-kai (JETRO), ed. 1988. *Nippon 1988: Business Facts and Figures.* Tokyo: Nihon Bōeki Shinkō-kai.

Noguchi, Paul. 1990. *Delayed Departures, Overdue Arrivals: Industrial Familialism and the Japanese National Railways.* Honolulu: University of Hawaii Press.

Plath, David W., ed. 1983. *Work and Lifecourse in Japan.* Albany: State University of New York Press.

Skinner, Kenneth. 1983. "Aborted Careers in a Public Corporation." In *Work and Lifecourse in Japan,* edited by David W. Plath. Pp. 50–73. Albany: State University of New York Press.

Tachibanaki, Toshiaki. 1984. "Labour Mobility and Job Tenure." In *The Economic Analysis of the Japanese Firm,* edited by Masahiko Aoki. Pp. 81–89. New York: North-Holland.

Tsurumi, Yoshi. 1976. *The Japanese are Coming.* New York: Ballinger.

Ueno Akira. 1988. *Shin-kokusai-keiei-senryaku-ron* (New international management strategy). Tokyo: Yūhikaku.

Vernon, Raymond. 1971. *Sovereignty at Bay.* New York: Basic Books.

White, Merry. 1988. *The Japanese Overseas: Can They Go Home Again?* New York: Free Press.

Yoshihara Hideki. 1979. *Takokuseki-keiei-ron* (Multinational management). Tokyo: Hakuto-shobō.

Yoshihara Hideki, Hayashi Kichiro, and Yasumuro Kenichi. 1988. *Nihon-kigyō no gurōbaru keiei* (Global management of Japanese enterprise). Tokyo: Tōyō-keizaishinpō-sha.

Yoshino, Michael. 1976. *Japan's Multinational Enterprise.* Cambridge, Mass.: Harvard University Press.

CHAPTER 6

Doing and Undoing
"Female" and "Male" in Japan:
The Takarazuka Revue

Jennifer Robertson

This essay is an exploration of the production, reproduction, and refraction of representations of female and male in twentieth-century Japan, using as a framework the Takarazuka Revue (Takarazuka kagekidan), an all-female theater founded in 1913 and very active today. The Takarasiennes *(takarajiennu),* as the Revue's actors are called—after Parisiennes, in recognition of the early influence of the French revue—include *otokoyaku,* who specialize in signifying "male" gender, and *musumeyaku,* who specialize in signifying "female" gender. Founded by Kobayashi Ichizō (1873–1957), the Hankyū railroad and department store tycoon, the Revue boasts two huge theaters in Takarazuka and Tokyo[1]; it regularly goes on regional and international tours and appears on television and radio broadcasts. It remains one of the most widely recognized, watched, and written about of the so-called theaters for the masses *(taishū engeki)* created in the early twentieth century.

The overall aim of this essay is to deepen our understanding of, on the one hand, Japanese female sexualities in particular, and on the other, the nature of the gender ideology informing and informed by different modes of social organization, including theatrical revues and the state-sanctioned "family system." The key resources mobilized for this task are the ongoing debates among the Revue's directors and performers, their fans, the mass media, and the state[2] about the significance and symbolism of the Takarazuka Revue. Any interpretation of the popularity of the Revue today must take into account its historical beginnings and unprecedented impact on the status quo. Therefore, a substantial part of my description and analysis focuses on pre- and interwar developments in the Revue and the society at large. Information about and insights into the circumstances of the Revue in the postwar period are included.

Strategic Definitions

The idea of gender and the relationship among sex, gender, and sexuality are socio-historical constructions, products of multiple, competing discourses[3] conducted over the course of, on one level, a culture's history, and on another level, an individual's lifetime (De Lauretis 1987; Foucault 1980; Kessler and McKenna 1985; Silverman 1985; Vance 1985). These discourses have the effect of forming and re-forming the configuration of social relations; for example, they can both reinforce and subvert conventional gender roles and sexual identity.

> The construction of gender goes on today through the various technologies of gender (e.g., cinema) and institutional discourses (e.g., theory) with power to control the field of social meaning and thus produce, promote, and "implant" representations of gender. But the terms of a different construction of gender also exist, in the margins of hegemonic discourses. Posed from outside the heterosexual social contract, and inscribed in micropolitical practices, these terms can also have a part in the construction of gender, and the effects are rather at the "local" level of resistances, in subjectivity and self-representation. (De Lauretis 1987, 18)

Regardless of their popular conflation, there is a major difference between "sex roles" and "gender roles." The former refer to the various capabilities of female and male genitalia, such as menstruation and seminal ejaculation; the latter pertain to socio-cultural and historical conventions of deportment and costume attributed to females and males (see Kessler and McKenna 1985, 1–12). "Sexuality" may overlap with sex and gender, but it remains a separate domain of desire and erotic pleasure (Vance 1985, 9). Sex, gender, and sexuality may be related, but they are not the same thing. The degree of their relationship, or the lack thereof, is negotiable, and it is negotiated constantly. In Japan, as among Anglo-Americans,[4] a person's gender initially is assigned and (hetero)sexuality assumed at birth on the basis of genital type, but this is neither an immutable assignment nor an unproblematic assumption. Although two sexes and two genders are recognized, "female" gender (femininity) and "male" gender (masculinity) are not ultimately regarded as the exclusive province of female- and male-sexed bodies. Sex, gender, and sexuality may be popularly perceived as irreducibly joined, but this remains a situational, not a permanently fixed, condition.[5]

In Japanese, linguistic distinctions between sex and gender are created through suffixes. Generally speaking, *"sei"* is used to denote sex, as in *josei* for female and *dansei* for male. Since the *"dan"* in dansei can refer both to male sex and "male" gender, the suffix "sei," with its allusions to fundamental parts (e.g., genitalia), is necessary to specifically denote sex. Gender is denoted by the suffix *"rashii,"* with its allusion to appearance and likeness (*Kōjien* 1978, 1,214, 2,300; Fukutomi 1985). A femalelike or "female"-gendered person is *onnarashii,* a malelike person, *otokorashii.*[6] The emphasis here is on the person's likeness to a gender stereotype. When attention is drawn to an individual's resemblance to a particular female or male, the term often used is *joseiteki* (like a/that female) or *danseiteki* (like a/that male). An individual can resemble a particular female or male precisely because both parties approximate a more generic gender stereotype. The difference between onnarashii/otokorashii and joseiteki/danseiteki is significant, although the two terms are often used interchangeably in popular parlance. Further complicating matters is the use of the terms *onna* and *otoko* to refer to both sex and gender, the difference evident only in the context used.

Upon their acceptance to the Takarazuka Music Academy, founded in 1919 and from which all the Revue's actors must graduate, the Takarasiennes are *assigned* their "secondary" genders, for, as in real life, there are no gender-role auditions. Unlike "primary" gender, which is assigned at birth on the basis of an infant's genitalia, secondary gender is based on both physical (but not genital) and socio-psychological criteria—height, physique, voice, facial shape, personality, and, to a certain extent, personal preference. Secondary gender attributes or markers are premised on contrastive gender stereotypes themselves; for example, "males" ideally should be taller than "females," have a more rectangular face, a higher bridged nose, darker skin, straighter shoulders, narrower hips, and a lower voice than "females" and should exude *kosei* (charisma), which is disparaged in "females." The assignment of gender involves the selection and exaggeration of physical differences between females and males and reinforces socially prescribed and culturally inscribed behavioral differences between women and men.

Since its founding in 1919, several years after the Revue itself was established, the academy has solicited applications from females between fifteen and twenty-four years of age. Today, most of the applicants are nineteen years old and, as required, are either junior high or high school graduates or are enrolled in a high school. Academy officials continue to claim that the young women are from "good families," and although detailed information about their socioeconomic status is kept confidential, it is widely understood that "good" translates as "affluent." Students and academy officials alike acknowledge that without the generous support of their parents, the aspiring Takarasiennes would be unable to attend the private singing and dance lessons necessary to keep them competitive. According to data provided by the principal's office, 75 percent of the students recruited between 1983 and 1987 reside in Tokyo, Osaka, and Hyōgo prefectures. Graduation from the two-year academy marks a Takarasienne's public debut as a gender specialist and enables her to perform on stage as a bona fide member of one of the four troupes comprising the Revue.

The four troupes are Flower *(hana)*, Moon *(tsuki)*, Snow *(yuki)*, and Star *(hoshi)*. The Flower and Moon troupes, established in 1921, are the oldest. The Snow Troupe was formed in 1924, the Star Troupe in 1933. Each troupe possesses a distinctive character: the Flower Troupe is known for its florid but elegant style, the Moon Troupe for its exquisite charm, the Snow Troupe for its restrained grace, and the Star Troupe for its showiness (Hashimoto 1984, 48; Takagi 1976, 65–67). Dividing the actors into troupes facilitated organizing the growing number of applicants (from twenty at the outset to seventy-seven in 1933). Each troupe is overseen by a (male) member of the Revue administration appointed to that post. The internal hierarchy consists of a troupe manager *(kumichō)* and a vice-manager *(fukukumichō)* drawn from the ranks of the senior actors and several chairpersons *(zachō)*, including the leading romantic "male" *(nimaime)*,[7] the leading musumeyaku, the leading comic "male" *(sanmaime)*, and the leading "male" and "female" supporting actors *(wakiyaku)*. Since each troupe has a leading otokoyaku and musumeyaku, more fans and their diverse tastes are more likely to be satisfied than if only one leading couple represented the Revue as a whole.

The Takarazuka Music Academy presently provides a two-year curriculum of Japanese and Western performing arts training. Of the 734 applicants in 1985, 42 (or one in 17.5) were accepted. The annual tuition averages nearly 300,000 yen, and the students must buy their own gray, military-style uniforms. (The switch from *hakama,* Japanese formal wear, to Western, military-style outfits was made in 1939.) To help secure highly visible roles in the Revue proper, the students must also take private dance, voice, and acting lessons—paid for by their parents.

Most of the students live with one or two roommates in the Sumire (Violet) dormitories,[8] where the administration seeks to socialize the young women into a life of discipline and vertical relationships. All residents are required to clean the dorms, but the first-year or junior *(kōhai)* students are also responsible for cleaning the classrooms under the watchful eyes of the second-year or senior *(senpai)* students. (The *senpai-kōhai* relationships formed at this time are maintained throughout and even beyond the young women's tenure in the Takarazuka Revue.) A strict curfew (10:00 P.M.) is maintained, and first-year students are not allowed to venture outside the campus itself. Males are strictly forbidden on the premises with the exception of fathers and brothers, who, like all guests, are limited to the lobby (Ueda 1986, 118–119). Although the attrition rate is not publicized, a number of students drop out midway through the Spartan regimen. Many of the young women continue to live in the dormitory after they join the Revue proper, although some—leading Takarasiennes in particular—are able to maintain their own apartments.

Varieties of Gender(ed) Experience

Why an all-female theater? In his autobiography, *Takarazuka manpitsu* (Takarazuka jottings), Kobayashi (1960) notes that he was partly motivated to create an all-female revue as a novel solution to his financial woes. Two years earlier, he had opened and then quickly closed a luxury indoor swimming pool in the village of Takarazuka, west of Osaka in Hyōgo prefecture. The pool

was part of the Victorian-Moorish hot springs spa called Paradise
—renamed Familyland in 1960. Ostensibly, it had failed to attract
guests for two reasons. Not only had Kobayashi overlooked the
proscription of mixed bathing, but he had neglected to install
devices to heat the water. Converting the indoor pool into a theater "made good business sense," and the Revue was promoted as
"wholesome family entertainment."

The Takarazuka Revue was among the modern theaters
that marked the return of females to a major public stage after
being banned from public (Kabuki) performances in 1629 by the
Confucian-oriented Tokugawa Shogunate.[9] At the time the Revue
was founded, actresses (*joyū*)[10] were still publicly denounced as
"defiled women" who led profligate lives. It seems that Kobayashi
founded the Takarazuka Music Academy not only to train students in the Western and Japanese theatrical arts, but also to reassure parents that their daughters were under the constant supervision of academy officials whose responsibility it was to prevent the
young women from falling into a decadent lifestyle.

In this connection, Kobayashi envisioned Paradise as
both a place to resocialize otherwise "unfeminine" women and a
commercially viable complement of the all-male Kabuki theater—
complementary, perhaps, but not equally privileged or prestigious, for reasons related to Japanese paternalism in general and
to Kobayashi's choice of nomenclature in particular. Kabuki *onnagata,* as the name implies, are regarded as exemplary models *(kata)*
of "female" *(onna)* gender for females offstage to approximate.
(The terms *otokoyaku* and *musumeyaku* are not used in the Kabuki
theater.) *Yaku,* unlike kata, connotes serviceability and dutiful-
ness. An otokoyaku thus is an actor whose theatrical (and patriarchal) duty is to showcase "male" gender; she is not, however, promoted as a model for males offstage to approximate.

Moreover, Kobayashi resorted to the terminology of kinship in naming the Takarazuka "female" gender-specialist musumeyaku, or "daughter role," instead of *onnayaku,* or " 'female'
role." The conflation of gender and kinship attribution in the
vocabulary of the Takarazuka Revue alludes to the principle that
gender and kinship are mutually constructed. "[N]either can be
treated as analytically prior to the other, because they are realized
together in particular cultural, economic, and political systems"
(Collier and Yanagisako 1987, 7).

Kobayashi's choice of nomenclature was informed by the "good wife, wise mother" *(ryōsai kenbo)* model of female subjectivity and "female" gender codified in the Meiji Civil Code (operative from 1898 to 1947), together with the primacy of the patriarchal, conjugal household. Females acting on their own behalf outside the household were regarded by the state as socially disruptive and dangerously anomalous—social disorder was a "woman problem" (Nolte 1983, 3). Note, in this connection, that "good husband, wise father" was never employed as a trope for social order, nor was social disorder ever linked to a "man problem." The public vocation of the actor, however, reversed the usual association of females with the private domain, and consequently, distinctions between "private" and "public" were neither incumbent upon nor possible for Takarasiennes.

> One result of this is that although [the actor] is aware of the dominant role governing the society of which her small dramatic world is a part, her experience permits her to fuse the value-systems, and to bring the . . . private interpersonal sphere of women in the home into the light of public scrutiny. (Blair 1981, 205)

The fusion was manipulated in a number of ways. Whereas Kobayashi sought to use the actor as a vehicle for introducing the artistry *(geijutsu)* of the theater into the home (Kobayashi 1960, 106), some Takarasiennes and their fans used the theater as a starting point for an opposing strategy, including the rejection of gender roles associated with the patriarchal household and the construction of an "alternative" style or mode of sexuality.

Kobayashi tempered the revolutionary potential of the actor by relegating the "female" gender specialists to the status of "daughter," with its attendant connotations of filial piety, youthfulness, pedigree, virginity, and unmarried status. These were precisely the characteristics that Kobayashi sought in the young recruits and that marked the makings of a "good wife, wise mother." To clinch the filial and paternal symbolism, he encouraged all Takarasiennes to call him "father" *(otōsan)*. Gender assignment notwithstanding, all the actors thereby were "daughters." Many Takarasiennes and their fans eventually appropriated kinship terminology effectively to subvert the "father's" filial symbolism and assert their own.

The deployment of kinship terminology in the Takarazuka Revue recalls the parent (father)-child *(oyabun-kobun)* type of group formation, whereby a patriarch controls a tightly knit, hierarchical following of "children," in this case, daughters. The relationship between individual Takarasiennes denoted by kinship terminology is based both on age or seniority, as "elder sister" *(onēsan* or *ane)* and "younger sister" *(imōto),* and on gender, as "older brother" *(aniki)* and "younger sister," without regard, necessarily, to age or seniority. As I discuss subsequently, both sets of kinship terms were applied by Takarasiennes and their fans to identify both homosocial and homosexual relations between females.

The representational inequality between the Kabuki onnagata and the Takarazuka otokoyaku is paralleled by the inequality between the otokoyaku and the musumeyaku. The naïve and compliant "daughter" represents not only femininity, but also the female subject in a patriarchal society who is excluded from participating in discourses about "female" gender and sexuality. Kobayashi, on the other hand, as the privileged father, invested much energy in advocating arranged marriages for retired Takarasiennes, in keeping with the state-sanctioned "good wife, wise mother" model of "female" gender (Kobayashi 1960, 27, 29, 34, 91). The otokoyaku, Kobayashi argued, participates not in the construction of alternative "female" gender roles, but in the glorification of "male" gender. He proclaimed that "the otokoyaku is not male but is more suave, more affectionate, more courageous, more charming, more handsome, and more fascinating than a real male" (ibid. 38). One of the subtexts to his statement is that "real" (anatomically correct) males *need not* be suave, charming, and so forth in the real world, where patriarchal privilege compensates for aesthetic deficiencies. Another subtext is that "male" and "female" gender account for processes of representation, not for the historical realities of males and females.

The construction of gender in the Revue continues to be informed by the Stanislavski System of acting, according to which actors base a performance upon inner emotional experiences and improvisation. The Stanislavski System, named after its Russian inventor, Konstantin Stanislavski (1863–1938), subscribes to the principle that the quality of an actor's performance depends not only upon the creation of the inner life of a role but also upon the physical embodiment of it. . . . An actor must . . . answer the question, "What would I do *if* I were in . . . [X's] position?" This "magic *if,*" . . . transforms the character's aim into the actor's. (Moore 1988, 52, 25)

Kobayashi theorized that by performing as "males," females learned to understand and appreciate the masculine psyche. He also believed that performing as otokoyaku rendered females more stable, reliable, secure, trustworthy *(shikkari)* and rational *(riseiteki),* although this logic was not translated into an argument for the assumption by women of jobs in business or government (Kobayashi 1960, 32). Consequently, when they eventually retired from the stage and married—which Kobayashi urged them to do—they would be better able to perform as "good wives, wise mothers," knowing exactly what their husbands expected of them (ibid. 38, 91; Ueda 1974, 139). Significantly, even after graduating from the academy and joining the Revue proper, a Takarasienne is still called "student" *(seito),* for as Kobayashi believed, the wedding ceremony marks the start of her real career, whereupon a woman becomes a full-fledged actor, and the conjugal household her stage.

Enter the *Shōjo*

A number of Takarasiennes, nevertheless, interpreted and appropriated their secondary genders in such a way as to resist and subvert Kobayashi's designs. To show how they did this, it is necessary to review from another angle the origins of the Revue and its popular reception.

Originally called the Takarazuka Choir (Takarazuka shōkatai), Kobayashi changed the name within five months to the Takarazuka Girls' Opera Training Association (Takarazuka shōjo kageki yōseikai). This name change, specifically with the addition of the term *shōjo,* set the enduring public image of the Takarazuka theater, even though shōjo was removed in a final name change in 1940. Literally speaking, shōjo means a "not-quite female" female. To become a fully female adult in Japan involves marriage and motherhood. Shōjo then, denotes both heterosexually inexperienced females between puberty and marriage and that period of time itself *(shōjoki)* (Kawahara 1921, 112).[11]

The state's emphasis on universal—if segregated and sexist—education, together with the notion that a brief stint in the burgeoning industrial and commercial workforce was a desirable thing for females, effectively increased the number of years between puberty and marriage (see Murakami 1983). Tenure in the Takarazuka Revue further lengthened the shōjo period, a point made in a newspaper article on a leading Takarasienne that bore the headline "Still a shōjo at 36!" *(Shin nippō,* April 2, 1940). This was not intended as a compliment. Takarasiennes by definition were unmarried, but the reporter here was drawing attention to the disturbing lack of correspondence between chronological age and shōjo existence.

Occupants of the shōjo category of "female" gender included the "new working women" *(shinshokugyō fujin)* and her jaunty counterpart, the "modern girl" *(modan gāru,* or *moga),*[12] herself the antithesis of the "good wife, wise mother." An article on department store clerks in a series on the "soul of the working woman" published in the *Osaka mainichi* (May 29, 1923), noted that instead of marriage, clerks expressed a desire to join the Takarazuka Revue, which, moreover, proved to be the most popular form of entertainment for "working women." The large number of teenagers who flocked to Takarazuka soon after its founding attested the popularity of the Revue and prompted a ban on all junior high school students from attending Takarazuka performances *(Kageki* 1, 1918, 5–6). Throughout the pre- and interwar periods, the Revue continued to attract "rebellious" teens, female and male, who ran away from home to be closer to their idols *(Osaka asahi,* July 17, 1923). Young heterosexual and homosexual couples alike selected Takarazuka as an appropriately romantic setting for their "love suicides" *(shinjū) (Osaka mainichi,* July 12, 1932). Throughout the 1920s and 1930s, the Revue attracted boys and men along with girls and women, although the most zealous (and problematic) fans were female. Since, roughly, the 1950s through the present day, audiences overwhelmingly are composed of females, from teenagers to senior citizens, representing a broad range of class, regional, and professional affiliations. The editors of official and private fan magazines and the directors of private fan clubs have told me that contrary to popular thought, the majority of female fans today are between thirty and fifty years of age, and that the majority of those over thirty are also married.

Kobayashi envisioned Takarazuka as a world of "dreams and romance"; the name "Paradise" emphasized symbolically its idealism and "dream world" *(yume no sekai)* ambience. He was inspired by a new genre of literature, shōjo fiction *(shosetsu)*, most tenaciously associated with Yoshiya Nobuko (1904–1973), an influential, prolific author and a lesbian. Her widely read stories framed female couples in a dreamy, sweetly erotic light. Unlike her fiction, Yoshiya's own life was patently political, even subversive, in that she openly rejected marriage, motherhood, and the "compulsory heterosexuality" of the Civil Code (Komazaka 1975; Ōzawa 1985; Tanabe 1986; Wada 1987, 78–79; Yoshitake 1986). Kobayashi shared Yoshiya's romantic vision, but colored it heterosexual: his dream world was one in which gallant males were sustained by adoring females. Contrary to Kobayashi's original intentions, however, Takarasiennes inverted the image of the shōjo and in the process inspired an enduring style for a Japanese lesbian subculture, namely, "butch-femme."

Refracted Gender Roles

The following expressions were used in reference to female couples in early twentieth-century Japan and continue to be used today: the generic *dōseiai,* or "same-sex love," and more popularly, "S" or "Class S" *(kurasu esu)*. The "S" stands for sex, sister, or shōjo, or all three combined. Class S continues to conjure up the image of two schoolgirls, often a junior-senior pair, with a crush on each other, an altogether typical and accepted feature of the shōjo period of the female life cycle (Mochizuki 1959; Norbeck and Befu 1958, 109). Parents and society at large continue to frown on women's casual and premarital heterosexual relations, the prevention of which is the main reason for the persistence of Takarazuka's strict "females only" policy.

Among Takarasiennes, one slang expression used since the 1920s in reference to female couples has been *deben,* from *demae bentō,* or "take-out lunch box." The basic idea is that intimacy between two cloistered females is analogous to a lunch of "rice" *(gohan)* and "dishes eaten along with the rice" *(okazu)* (Kasahara

1981, 44). Apparently, the "male" partner is identified with rice, a crop saturated with gendered meaning (*Kageki* 44, 1923, 14; see Robertson 1984).

Takarasiennes and their fans also have used the kinship terms aniki and imōto, as well as the stage terms otokoyaku and musumeyaku to denote the parties in a "butch-femme" couple. *Tachi,* written in the *katakana* syllabary, with the likely meaning of "one who wields the 'sword'," is another term for the "butch" woman. The corresponding term for the "femme" woman is *neko,* literally "cat" but also a historical nickname for unlicensed geisha, which "could be written with characters implying the possibility of pussy from these cats" (Dalby 1985, 57; see also Hattori 1975, 53; Mizukawa 1987; Togawa 1975, 62). Tachi may also be an abbreviated reference to *tachiyaku,* the theatrical term for "leading man."

The leading otokoyaku and musumeyaku of each troupe are paired as a "golden combination" *(gōruden konbi)* for the duration of their careers. This dyadic structure alludes to the monogamy and fidelity underlying the idealized heterosexual relations promoted by the state since the Meiji period. In addition, the "butch" has been called garçon and *onabe* (literally, a [shallow] pot), a term coined (probably in the early 1900s) as the "gender" opposite of *okama* (pot), the term for a male homosexual (Mizukawa 1987; *Osaka mainichi,* February 10, 1932). The term "lesbian" *(rezubian),* although used since the early 1900s, was not adopted by women to name a politicized female identity—as opposed to sexual practices per se—until the 1970s (see Hirozawa 1987a and 1987b).

Girls' schools, including the Takarazuka Music Academy and the Revue, and their (unmarried) female instructors and students were singled out by sexologists and social critics writing in the early twentieth century as the sites and agents of homosexuality among females (e.g., Sugita 1929 and 1935; Tamura 1913; Ushijima 1943).[13] In 1910, one of the first articles on this subject was published in a leading women's newspaper, the *Fujo shinbun.* Distinctions were drawn between two types of homosexual relationships between females: dōseiai and *ome no kankei* (male-female relations).[14] It is clear from the article that what the editorial staff meant by "same *sex*" was actually "same *gender*," and that *ome* referred to a "butch-femme"–like couple, that is, same sex, different gender. A dōseiai relationship was characterized as a passionate but supposedly platonic friendship and was regarded as typical among girls and women from all walks of life, but especially among girls' school students and graduates, female educators, female civil servants, and actresses (in Fukushima 1984, 561; see also Tamura 1913 and Yasuda 1935). Such relationships were also referred to as S or Class S. In contrast, ome relationships were described as

> a strange phenomenon difficult to diagnose on the basis of modern psychology and physiology.[15] . . . One of the couple has malelike *(danseiteki)* characteristics and dominates the [femalelike] other. . . . Unlike the [dōseiai couple], friends whose spiritual bond took a passionate turn, the ome couple have developed a strange, carnal relationship *(niku no sesshoku)* . . . stemming from their carnal depravity *(nikuteki daraku).* . . . The malelike female is technically proficient at manipulating women. . . . Doctors have yet to put their hoes to this uncultivated land *(mikaikonchi).* (Fukushima 1984, 562)

This article and others like it (e.g., Tamura 1913; Yasuda 1935) made it clear that even an overheated dōseiai (ie., homogender) relationship was not pathological in the way that an ome (i.e., heterogender) relationship was, the latter being not only sexual, but also a heretical refraction of the heterosexual norm codified in the Meiji Civil Code. The most objective writers, not surprisingly, referred to an ome couple as *fūfu* (husband and wife), a marital metaphor that safely contained (and conveniently erased) the difference embodied by the two women.

The *Fujo shinbun* attributed lesbian practices of the Class S variety to environmental conditions: abusive stepmothers, exploitative employers, constant hardship, others' callousness, false accusations, and unrequited love (Fukushima 1984, 561). The article introduced recent "medical" findings in surmising that females were more prone than males to homosexuality. It was postulated that the "natural" passivity *(muteikōshugi)* of females made them susceptible to neurasthenia *(shinkeishitsu)* which, in turn, occasioned a pessimism manifested in the guise of homosexuality.[16] Ome relationships, however, seemed to stymie the sexologists and worry the social critics of the day, since unmarried women in particular were stereotyped as blissfully unaware of sexual desire, and females in general were certainly not supposed to play an active role in sex. "Moral depravity" fostered by Westernization seemed to be the only viable "explanation" for ome relationships among urban women, at least until the appearance of Takarazuka otokoyaku prompted critics to come up with new ideas to account for the increasingly visible masculine female.

Overall, it seems that much more print space was devoted to defending the typicality and relative "normality" of dōseiai relationships among shōjo and insisting on their—ideally, at least—platonic character. Educators and mothers were advised to encourage the development of passionate female friendships— "for without passion society is cold and indifferent"—but to squelch the flames of "overheated passion," lest "morality, common sense, and life itself be burned up" (Fukushima 1984, 562–563).

Apart from eyecatching headlines and titles, proportionately little attention was paid to the ome relationship itself, although the "origins" of the "abnormal and anomalous" *(hentaiteki)* masculine partner generated several speculations. The author of a 1930 newspaper article on the Takarazuka Revue, for example, went so far as to assert that the emergence of ome-type relationships was the "direct result of females playing 'male' roles" and suggested that the Revue was the medium through which Class S couples were transformed into ome couples. This was an evolutionary thesis absent from the *Fujo shinbun* article published twenty years earlier (*Osaka nichinichi,* July 21, 1930; see also Yoshiwara 1935, 187, for essentially the same argument). The headline of the article sums up the gist of the author's argument: "From Class S to feverish yearning for otokoyaku." Other critics blamed Western movies and theatrical practices for arousing in Japanese women the desire to deport like men.

Sex, Lies, and Newspapers

The erotic potential of the Takarazuka otokoyaku was recognized within a decade of the Revue's founding. One of the first books on the lifestyle of the Takarasiennes included a chapter on love letters from female fans that the author regarded as examples of "abnormal psychology" *(hentai seiri)* (Kawahara 1921,

113). Eight years later, in 1929, the mass media began to sensationalize the link between the Takarazuka Revue and lesbian practices. The *Shin nippō,* a leading daily newspaper, ran a series on Takarazuka called "Abnormal Sensations" *(hentaiteki kankaku).* The male author worried that otokoyaku would begin to feel natural doing "male" gender. Their private lives, he fretted, would soon "become an extension of the stage" (March 16, 1929).

His worst fears came true when, less than a year later, the leading dailies exposed the "same-sex" love affair between Nara Miyako, a leading otokoyaku, and Mizutani Yaeko, the leading woman of the Shinpa (New School) theater. He and other critics seemed particularly disturbed by the realization that the Takarazuka otokoyaku, like the moga, could effectively undermine a gender role (the "good wife, wise mother") premised on the strict alignment of sex, gender, and sexuality and on women's dependence on and subordination to men.

The brouhaha that erupted over the Nara-Mizutani affair was part of the larger socio-cultural discourse on the problematic relationship between eros and modernism. The revue "Parisette," staged in 1930, ushered in Takarazuka's overtly modern and erotic phase (*Kyoto,* November 20, 1930). From this production onward, Takarasiennes ceased to apply the traditional stage makeup, *oshiroi* (whiteface). Modernism warranted a transition from denaturalized flesh to its naturalization. The whiteface had disguised the fact that the mask worn by Takarasiennes was their gender specialty, which, as it turned out, did not so much hide as reveal their sex, gender, and sexuality.

The naturalization of "male" females continued with otokoyaku Kadota Ashiko's sudden decision to cut off her hair in the spring of 1932. As reported in the press, Kadota was irked by the unnaturalness of having to stuff her regulation-long hair under every type of headgear except wigs, for the all-male management had deemed that wigs would give otokoyaku an overly natural appearance. Takarazuka fans and moga, on the other hand, had sported short hair at least a decade ahead of their idols (*Osaka asahi,* July 17, 1923).

Hair is redolent of symbolism throughout Japanese history. Prior to the moga, short hair announced a woman's withdrawal from secular and sexual affairs. The moga turned hair symbolism on its head, and short hair became the hallmark of the extroverted, maverick, and in the eyes of the state, dangerous woman. Otokoyaku gave short hair yet another layer of symbolic meaning: "butch" sexuality. The Takarazuka management eventually sought to divest short hair of its radical symbolism by assuming authority over haircuts. Since at least the postwar period, and probably before, a student assigned to "male" gender is required to cut her hair short by the end of her first semester at the academy. Until ordered to do otherwise, all junior students are required to wear their hair in shoulder-length braids.

So many of Kadota's otokoyaku colleagues followed suit that a worried Kobayashi offered them money and "gifts from Tokyo" in exchange for growing out their hair (*Nichinichi,* April 24, 1932). Critics, meanwhile, had a field day with the new bobbed look. Newspaper articles referred disparagingly to the haircuts as "male heads" *(otoko no atama)* and noted that many otokoyaku were also using the term *boku,* a self-referent that signifies "male" gender.

Kobayashi was unsettled by the muckraking reports on the revue theater in general and Takarazuka in particular, which he felt would create public misunderstandings about Paradise. In a 1935 editorial in *Kageki,* an official fan magazine, he worried about how the otokoyaku had become a "symbol of abnormal love" and asserted that "nothing must compromise" [the Revue's] reputation or worry the parents of [Takarazuka Music Academy] students." Two years earlier, in 1933, Kobayashi had coined a motto for the academy and Revue—"Purely, Righteously, Beautifully" *(kiyoku, tadashiku, utsukushiku)*—in an apparent public relations move to emphasize the honorable aspirations of the Takarasiennes (Sakada 1983, 317–318).

The heated discourse on eros, modernism, and the Takarazuka Revue recalls Dick Hebdige's observations about the relationship between dominant discourses and subcultural style: "In most cases, it is the subculture's stylistic innovations which first attract the media's attention" and which, when that style is confused with deviance, "can provide the catalyst for a moral panic" (1985, 93).

Setting Things Straight

All the adverse publicity motivated Kobayashi to remove the now problematic term *shōjo* in the final name change of 1940 for two ostensible reasons: to acknowledge the more eroticized ("adult") content of the modernizing theater and to prepare for the short-lived inclusion of a male chorus. Kobayashi's controversial plan to recruit male vocalists was a strategic move to denaturalize otokoyaku style and to deflect allegations of lesbian relationships among Takarasiennes and their fans. The invisible but audible presence of anatomically correct males would set things straight.

Political factors exacerbated the "moral panic" over "male" females. The period of the late 1930s and early 1940s was one of intensified militarization and increasing state control over females' minds and bodies (see Nolte 1983; and Nolte and Hastings 1991). Pronatal policies and a cult of sanctified motherhood took precedence over the mobilization of female laborers, despite the steady depletion through conscription of the male workforce (Havens 1975; Miyake 1991). Kobayashi, who from July 1940 to April 1941 served (in the second Konoe cabinet) as minister of commerce and industry, colluded with government censors to produce patriotic musicals that exalted the image of the "good wife, wise mother," an image further reified at that time as *Nippon fujin* (Japanese Woman) (*Osaka chōhō*, September 7, 1940; Kamura 1984, 96–98). Typical of the musicals staged during this period of militarization and state censorship was "Illustrious Women of Japan" (*Nippon meifu den*, 1941), a nationalistic extravanganza dedicated to heroines, mothers of heroes, and "women of chastity."

Despite Kobayashi's efforts, however, Takarazuka otokoyaku were singled out and denounced as the "acme of offensiveness" *(shūaku no kiwami)*, and in August 1939, the Osaka prefectural government outlawed otokoyaku from public performances in that prefecture, signaling the beginning of a generalized castigation of the Revue (*Osaka asahi*, May 15, 1939; *Osaka nichinichi*, August 20, 1939). All Takarasiennes were chastised in the mass media for their "abnormal and ostentatious" lifestyle, and government censors ordered the uniforms of Takarazuka Music Academy students changed from the original hakama to the militarylike uniform worn today (*Kokumin*, September 6, 1940; *Osaka asahi*, August 20, 1939). Takarasiennes were not permitted to answer fan mail, much less socialize with their admirers (*Osaka nichinichi*, August 19, 1940).

Redressing Gender

During the interwar years, the state's domineering voice drowned out competing voices in the debate over the relationship among sex, gender, and sexuality. In 1946, about eight months after Takarazuka productions had been suspended by the wartime government, the Revue reopened with the permission of the SCAP (Supreme Commander Allied Powers).

In the prewar period, otokoyaku sought to appropriate and naturalize "male" gender and were, along with the Revue as a whole, castigated severely. One aspect of the postwar revival of Takarazuka has been the efforts of musumeyaku to make "female" gender more than just a foil for masculine privilege. Significantly, in fan magazines published independently, and occasionally in those published by the Revue, Takarasiennes and their female fans refer to the actor not as musumeyaku ("daughter"-role player), but as onnayaku ("female"-role player), thereby claiming a nomenclatural parity with the otokoyaku. This act of (re)naming is a reminder that the "sex-gender system . . . is both a sociocultural construct and a semiotic apparatus, a system of representation which assigns meaning (identity, value, prestige, . . . status in the social hierarchy, etc.) to individuals within the society" (De Lauretis 1987, 5). The actors began to stress their female being over their status as daughters, and, accordingly, demanded more definitive roles.

The all-male directorship responded to these demands by creating highly visible, dynamic, and often overtly sensuous "female" characters, such as Scarlett O'Hara in "Gone with the Wind" and Jacqueline Carstone in "Me and My Girl." In a move that undercut musumeyaku intentions, however, the directors assigned these new roles to otokoyaku. Musumeyaku, contrarily, almost never have been reassigned to "male" roles: the transposition of gender is not a reciprocal operation (cf. Kamura 1984, 185). As several musumeyaku have remarked, "Japanese society is a male's world, and Takarazuka is an otokoyaku's world" (*Takarazuka gurafu* 1, 1967, 54).

It is also important to note that the plays whose charismatic women characters are performed by otokoyaku are Euro-American plays. Earlier I noted how, in the early twentieth century, the Paris-inspired revue and Western films were deemed accountable for the "masculinization" of Japanese females. In this case, however, the directors felt that the requisite innocence and naïveté of the musumeyaku would be irreparably compromised by roles that called for (hetero)sexually literate characters. Although all Takarasiennes by definition are unmarried and ostensibly (hetero)sexually inexperienced, otokoyaku, by virtue of their more resilient "male" gender, are perceived as less likely to be corrupted by charismatic "female" roles.

Many otokoyaku, along with disfranchised musumeyaku, have protested the directors' gender-switching antics, and many otokoyaku claimed to have experienced, as a result of playing "female" roles, a sense of conflict or resistance *(teikō)* and a loss of confidence (*Takarazuka gurafu* 1, 1967, 71; 5, 1968, 70–71; 4, 1971, 49; 7, 1974, 68; 7, 1977, 38). Gō Chigusa, an otokoyaku who retired in 1972, remarked that on the rare occasion she was assigned "female" gender, her fans complained bitterly of their resultant dis-ease *(kimochi warui),* that eerie feeling when the familiar suddenly is defamiliarized (ibid., 1, 1967, 71).

Some young women, such as Minakaze Mai, who enrolled in the academy specifically to do "male" gender, were assigned instead to do "female" gender. Minakaze's short height (5 feet, 2 inches) put her in the category of "female" gender specialist. To resolve the conflict between her offstage desires and her onstage role, she "stopped wearing blue-jeans" and "always exerts [herself] to the fullest to be a musumeyaku, even in [her] private life"[17] (*Nihonkai,* April 18, 1987). Minakaze is not alone in originally believing that females encountered less resistance doing "female" gender. She now agrees with several of her colleagues that locating "the 'female' within the female poses a perplexing problem"[18] (*Hankyū* 6, 1987). Similarly, after ten years of performing only "male" roles, otokoyaku Matsu Akira, who retired in 1982, was unable to perform a "female" role: "Even though I am a female, the thing called 'female' just won't emerge at all"[19] (*Takarazuka gurafu* 7, 1974, 68). Whether in terms of "resistance" or "emergence," the Takarasiennes have drawn attention to the incompatibility between their experiences as females and the dominant construction of "female" gender.

Kobayashi's assertion that "Takarazuka involves studying the male"[20] is only partially correct (Kobayashi 1948, 29). "Female" gender is also taught and studied; this, in fact, is the

ultimate objective of the academy. Takarasiennes who are assigned a (secondary) gender contrary to their personal preference
represent all Japanese females who are socialized into gender roles
not of their own making. And like the musumeyaku in particular,
girls and women are suspended between the depiction and definition of "female" gender and its achievement or approximation—
ironically, a limbo many young women have sought to avoid by
enrolling in the academy.[21]

Nevertheless, the Revue offers Takarasiennes an alternative to, or at least a respite from, the gender role of "good wife,
wise mother." One actor declared that for her, to become an otokoyaku was tantamount to "realizing her personal ideals"[22]
(*Takarazuka gurafu* 7, 1986, 45). Another enrolled in the Takarazuka Music Academy specifically because "despite her female
body, she could assume a masculine persona"[23] (ibid., 12, 1969,
39). She made a point of referring to herself as boku (ibid., 6,
1966, 42). As otokoyaku, the actors have access to, and provide
fans with vicarious access to, a wide range of occupations limited
to males—general, matador, impresario, and gangster, for example. Many "male"-gender specialists have noted that had they not
joined Takarazuka, they would have pursued—as if employment
opportunities were equal—careers such as import-export trader,
airplane pilot, train engineer, and lumber yard manager, among
others. My recent field research on fans suggests that for female
fans especially, the Takarazuka otokoyaku represents an exemplary female who can successfully negotiate both genders, and
their attendant roles and domains, without (theoretically) being
constrained by either.

Conclusion

From its establishment in 1913, the social organization of
the Takarazuka Revue has reflected and refracted "female" and
"male" gender roles and has been inspired by, and has inspired,
modes of sexuality, from the "good wife, wise mother" to "butch-
femme." The Revue continues both to idealize heterosexuality
and inform a lesbian subcultural style.

The history of the gender discourse generated by the
Takarazuka Revue alone indicates that a lesbian subculture has
been not so much absent from Japanese society—although many

indigenous forces have sought to eliminate it—as it has been ignored by most (published) contemporary Japanologists, despite much historical literature on this subject, although not necessarily from a feminist point of view (see Robertson, forthcoming). Apart from those who fear being stigmatized or ostracized for undertaking serious research on Japanese sexualities, those who do pursue this line of study may encounter, depending on their own sex, gender, and sexuality, a socio-historically motivated silence surrounding the issue of female sexualities in particular. The persistence of the dominant ideology that, shōjo notwithstanding, females are objects of male desire and not the subjects of their own desire, effectively inhibits both naming that desire and discussing the topic of modes of female sexualities in Japan (see articles in *Bessatsu takarajima* 64, 1987; *Onna erosu* 16, 1981; and *Shinchihei* 6, 1987).

One of the most tenacious of the mistaken assumptions that needs to be dismantled if any progress is to be made on the subject of sexuality is the equation of marriage with (hetero)sexuality. An examination of the Meiji Civil Code alone should alert researchers to the role of the state in regulating gender and sexuality and in making marriage and motherhood virtually compulsory for women. For women (but not men), sex was to be limited to procreation and practiced under the auspices of marriage, which, along with motherhood, continues to mark both adulthood and gender- and sex-role maturity, demonstrating the relative staying power of state-sanctioned conventions—for the time being, at least. Many Japanese women continue to marry neither for love nor as an expression of their sexuality, but rather, as is common knowledge, to survive economically. Few women can afford the financial strain of being unmarried and independent given the prevalence of sexism and ageism in the workplace (see Atsumi 1988; Shida and Yuda 1987, 114). In this connection, many female fans are attracted to the Takarazuka otokoyaku because she represents an exemplary female who can negotiate successfully both genders and their attendant roles and domains without—theoretically, at least—being constrained by either.

Competing discourses on the construction and performance of gender have informed and shaped—and have been shaped by—the Takarazuka Revue. The history of the all-female theater shows that Takarasiennes have, and on occasion have exercised, the potential to challenge the socio-cultural status quo represented by the "good wife, wise mother" model of "female" gender. However, whatever consciousness the actors have of their political (i.e., feminist), and also subversive or revolutionary potential, has also been compromised, at least publicly, by their need to survive within an organization, a vocation (show business), and a society where male privilege has been the rule. However many dreams the Takarasiennes spin for their fans, Japanese society is the bigger—and far from dreamy—stage.

Notes

Fieldwork and archival research in Japan (Tokyo and Takarazuka) during 1987–1990 was funded by the following: Fulbright Research Scholar Grant; University of California, San Diego (UCSD) Affirmative Action Faculty Career Development Grant; UCSD Japanese Studies Program Travel Grant; Japan Foundation Professional Fellowship; Northeast Asia Council of the Association for Asian Studies Grant; and Social Science Research Council Research Grant. I am grateful for the generous assistance in 1987 of Mr. Hashimoto Masao, Director, Takarazuka Revue, and also the management, administration, and actors of the Takarazuka Revue and the Takarazuka Music Academy. Heartfelt thanks to the late N. Serena Tennekoon for her invaluable help in preparing this manuscript.

Earlier versions and parts of this paper were presented in 1988 at the Association for Asian Studies Annual Meeting and Yale University; in 1989 at the University of Oklahoma, the University of California, Irvine, and the American Anthropological Association Annual Meeting; and in 1990 at UCSD, the University of Michigan, American Ethnological Society Annual Meeting, Harvard University, and the University of California, Santa Barbara. This essay is a substantially reworked incarnation of my article in *Genders* 5 (1989): 188–207.

1. The Tokyo Takarazuka theater opened on New Year's Day, 1934. The Takarazuka grand theater, with its three thousand seats, is still one of the largest theaters in Japan.

2. By "the state," I do not simply mean an "organ of coercion" or a "bureaucratic lineage," but rather a "repertoire of activities and institutions" that shape and are shaped by socio-historical circumstances and experiences (Corrigan and Sayer 1985, 2–3). Although for the sake of convenience I refer to the state as a thing-in-itself, namely, "the state," I regard the state as "an ideological project," an "exercise in legitima-

tion" (P. Abrams in ibid. 8). As Durkheim understood, "the state" is "parasitic upon the wider *conscience collective,* which it conversely regulates. . . . The *conscience collective* itself is not free-floating either. Forms of social consciousness are anchored in historical experiences, and the material relations upon which they rest" (ibid. 5–6).

3. Following Scott, I use *discourse* to mean "not a language or a text but a historically, socially, and institutionally specific structure of statements, terms, categories, and beliefs. . . . Discourse is thus contained or expressed in organizations and institutions as well as in words." (1988, 35).

4. While this method of gender assignment is most typical of but not limited to Anglo-Americans, the lack of specific information on the assignment and assumption of "female" or "male" gender among non-Anglos makes me reluctant to generalize for all Americans. The unrepresentativeness of Anglo gender categories for non-Anglos is addressed cogently by Alonso and Koreck (1989) in the context of the autoimmune deficiency syndrome (AIDS) and the construction of "Hispanic" sexualities. To generalize a "Japanese" notion of gender admittedly is problematic, given the various ethnic groups comprising that surficially "homogenous" society, although "Japanese" is undoubtedly a more inclusive signifier than is "American."

5. There is a growing ethnographic literature (books and journals) on the situationality and fluidity of the relationship among sex, gender, and sexuality.

6. The *jo* in *josei* may also be read as *onna,* and *dan* as *otoko*. *Mesu* (female) and *osu* (male) are terms used exclusively for plants and animals and are applied to humans as rather crude put-downs, as in the case of *ome (osu-mesu),* a slang expression for lesbian ("butch-femme") couples.

7. *Nimaime,* literally "second sheet," derives from the Edo-period practice of listing on Kabuki programs the name of the romantic lead after that of the lead actor.

8. The violet is the Revue flower.

9. Although a female, the legendary dancer Okuni from Izumo, is credited with having initiated Kabuki at the start of the seventeenth century, females have been banned from that stage since 1629. Apparently, the newly installed Shogunate was disturbed by the general disorder, including unlicensed prostitution, following the performances, when patrons quarreled with each other for access to their favorite dancers. Replacing the females with boys did not solve the problem, for the male patrons were also attracted to their own sex. Eventually, the prohibition of females, and later boys, prompted the emergence of the *onnagata,* adult males who specialize in "female" gender.

10. Theater critics proclaimed the newly coined *joyū,* with its

connotations of superiority and excellence *(yū)*, preferable to the older term *onnayakusha*, with its historical connotations of itinerant actresses who were associated with unlicensed prostitution (Asagawa 1921, 112). As I explain, Kobayashi used the word *yaku* in a different sense to underscore the dutylike role of the "male" and "female" gender specialists.

11. *Shōjo* also implies homosexual experience, and significantly, some male chauvinists and some lesbian feminists have appropriated the term. The former use it to disparage lesbians, convinced that "lesbian" names not a mode of sexuality, but an "unadult" (i.e., "virgin") female (Ōzawa 1985, 25). The latter use the term *chōshōjo* (ultra shōjo) in reference to adult females who eschew heterosexism and believe in the power of sisterhood (Takano 1987).

12. For further information on the *moga* and the "new working woman" in English, see Silverberg (1991), Nolte (1983), and Nolte and Hastings (1991).

13. *Dōseiai*, literally "same-sex love," was the Japanese term used among early twentieth-century sexologists for "homosexuality," just as *iseiai*, literally "different-sex love," was the translation of "heterosexuality" (e.g., Kure 1920). These terms, in addition to others, were not limited to use in specialized medical journals, but appeared in a wide range of print media, including women's newspapers and journals and works of fiction, and thus were familiar to a broad spectrum of literate persons.

The Meiji government ruled in 1872 that primary education, if sex-segregated, was compulsory for girls and boys alike, although home economics constituted the bulk of education for girls. Public and private secondary schools for girls and young women, called "higher schools," were established countrywide in the early 1900s, and by 1907, 40,273 female students were enrolled in 133 higher schools (Pflugfelder 1989, 7). For a comparative perspective, see Vicinus' work on English boarding school friendships (1989).

14. Although *dōseiai* is a generic term for "same-sex love" or homosexual relationships, it is defined more specifically in this particular article as an essentially platonic if passionate relationship.

An 1818 reference to ome refers not to a same-sex couple but to an androgyne, in this case a female who passed as a man (Tomioka 1938, 102).

15. This is in reference to the fact that the "male" partner was not physically androgynous, but had a "normal" female body.

16. *Shinkeishitsu* originated around the turn of the century as a category of socio-sexual dis-ease, with special relevance to urban middle-class women (who represented about 30 percent of the female population).

17. *Watakushi seikatsu de mo musumeyaku ni narikirō to kyōryoku shite iru.*

18. *Onna no naka no onnatte muzukashii no yo.*

19. *Onna de arinagara, zenzen onna to yū mono ga denai.*

20. *Takarazuka ga dansei no kyōiku shite-iru.*

21. The number of applicants in the postwar period ranges from 579 (57 admitted) in 1946 to 734 (42 admitted) in 1985, and from a low of 175 (70 admitted) in 1959 to a high of 1,052 (49 admitted) in 1978 (Ueda 1986, 25). The 1978 peak reflects the tremendous popularity of the newly revived musical "The Rose of Versailles" (1974–1976), attended by more than 1.4 million people (Hashimoto 1984, 89).

22. *Jibun no risō o takuseru mono desu.*

23. *Takarazuka de wa onna no hito demo otoko no kakkō ga dekiru to yū no de haitta.*

References

BOOKS AND ARTICLES

Alonso A., and M. T. Koreck. 1989. "Silences: 'Hispanics,' AIDS, and Sexual Practices." *Differences* 1 (1) (Winter 1989): 101–124.

Asagawa Y. 1921. "Joyū to onnayakusha" (Actresses and female actors). *Josei Nihonjin* 4:112–113.

Atsumi, R. 1988. "Dilemmas and Accommodations of Married Japanese Women in White-Collar Employment." *Bulletin of Concerned Asian Scholars* 20 (3): 54–62.

Blair, J. 1981. "Private Parts in Public Places: The Case of Actresses." In *Women and Space: Ground Rules and Social Maps,* edited by S. Ardener. Pp. 205–228. New York: St. Martin's Press.

Collier, J. F., and S. Yanagisako. 1987. "Toward a Unified Analysis of Gender and Kinship." In *Gender and Kinship: Essays Toward a Unified Analysis,* edited by J. F. Collier and S. Yanagisako. Pp. 14–50. Stanford, Calif.: Stanford University Press.

Corrigan, P., and D. Sayer. 1985. *The Great Arch: English State Formation as Cultural Revolution.* London: Basil Blackwell.

Dalby, L. 1985. *Geisha.* New York: Vintage Books.

De Lauretis, T. 1987. *Technologies of Gender: Essays on Theory, Film, and Fiction.* Bloomington: Indiana University Press.

Foucault, M. 1980. *The History of Sexuality.* Vol. 1: *An Introduction.* New York: Vintage Books.

Fukushima S. 1984 (1935). *Fujinkai "sanjūgonen"* (Thirty years of *Women's World*). Tokyo: Fuji Shuppansha.

Fukutomi M. 1985. " 'Rashisa' no shinrigaku" (The psychology of "gender"). In *Kōndansha gendai shinsho*, p. 797. Tokyo: Kodansha.

Hashimoto M. 1984. *Takarazuka kageki no 70 nen* (Seventy years of the Takarazuka Revue). Takarazuka: Takarazuka Kagekidan.

Hattori Y. 1975. *Hengeron: Kabuki no seishinshi* (Treatise on transformation: The spiritual history of Kabuki). Tokyo: Heibonsha.

Havens, T. 1975. "Women and War in Japan, 1937–45." *American Historical Review* 80 (4): 913–934.

Hebdige, D. 1985 (1979). *Subculture: The Meaning of Style*. New York: Methuen.

Hirozawa Y. 1987a. "Iseiai chōsei to iu fuashizumu" (The fascism of compulsory heterosexuality). *Shinchihei* 6 (150): 34–39.

———. 1987b. "Yūasa Yoshiko hōmonki" (Interview with Yūasa Yoshiko). *Bessatsu takarajima* 64:67–73.

Kamura K. 1984. *Itoshi no Takarazuka e* (To beloved Takarazuka). Kobe: Kobe Shinbun Shuppan Sentā.

Kasahara M. 1981. *Takarazuka episodo 350* (350 Takarazuka episodes). Tokyo: Rippu Shobo.

Kawahara Y. 1921. *Takarazuka kageki shōjo no seikatsu* (The lifestyle of Takarasienne). Osaka: Ikubunkan Shoten.

Kessler, S., and W. McKenna. 1985 (1978). *Gender: An Ethnomethodological Approach*. Chicago: University of Chicago Press.

Kobayashi I. 1948. "Omoitsuki" (Suggestions). *Kageki* 271:29.

———. 1960. *Takarazuka manpitsu* (Takarazuka jottings). Tokyo: Jitsugyō no Nihonsha.

Kōjien. 1978. 2d enl. ed., 3d printing. Tokyo: Iwanami Shoten.

Komazaka Y. 1975. "Yoshiya Nobuko: Onnatachi e no manazashi" (Yoshiya Nobuko: Her way of looking at women). *Shisō no Kagaku* 51 (9): 55–64.

Kure H. 1920. "Dōsei no ai" (Same-sex love). *Fujin gahō* 10:24–27.

Miyake, Y. 1991. "Doubling Expectations: Motherhood and Women's Factory Work Under State Management in Japan in the 1930s and 1940s." In *Recreating Japanese Women*, edited by G. Bernstein. Pp. 267–295. Berkeley, Los Angeles, and Oxford: University of California Press.

Mizukawa Y. 1987. "Tachi: Kono kōdoku na ikimono" (Butch: This lonely creature). *Bessatsu takarajima* 64:18–23.

Mochizuki, M. 1959. "Cultural Aspects of Japanese Girl's Opera." In *Japanese Popular Culture*, edited by H. Kato. Pp. 165–174. Tokyo: Charles E. Tuttle.

Moore, S. 1988. *The Stanislavski System: The Professional Training of an Actor*. London and New York: Penguin Books.

Murakami N. 1983. *Taishōki no shokugyō fujin* (Working women of the Taisho period). Tokyo: Domesu Shuppan.

Nolte, S. 1983. "Women, the State, and Repression in Imperial Japan." *Women in International Development Working Paper*, no. 33. Lansing, Mich.: Michigan State University.

Nolte, S., and S. Hastings. 1991. "The 'New Japanese Woman': The Home Ministry's Redefinition of Public and Private, 1890–1910." In *Recreating Japanese Women*, edited by G. Bernstein. Pp. 151–174. Berkeley, Los Angeles, and Oxford: University of California Press.

Norbeck, E., and H. Befu. 1958. "Informal Fictive Kinship in Japan." *American Anthropologist* 60:102–117.

Ōzawa H. 1985. "Yoshiya Nobuko no genten to natta shōjo shosetsu" (Yoshiya Nobuko's first *shōjo* novel). *Shōjoza* 1:24–25.

Pflugfelder, G. 1989. " 'Smashing' in Cross-Cultural Perspective: Japan and the United States." Stanford University. Manuscript.

Robertson, J. 1984. "Sexy Rice: Plant Gender, Farm Manuals, and Grass-Roots Nativism." *Monumenta Nipponica* 39 (3): 233–260.

———. 1989. "Gender-Bending in Paradise: Doing 'Female' and 'Male' in Japan. *Genders* 5:50–69.

———. Forthcoming. "The Politics of Androgyny in Japan: Sexuality and Subversion in the Theatre and Beyond." *American Ethnologist*.

Sakada T. 1983. *Waga Kobayashi Ichizō* (Our Kobayashi Ichizō). Tokyo: Kawade Shobo.

Scott, J. 1988. "Deconstructing Equality-Versus-Difference: Or, the Uses of Post-Structuralist Theory for Feminism." *Feminist Studies* 14 (1): 33–50.

Shida A. and Yuda N. 1987. "Shufu no Tomo" (Housewife's companion). In *Fujin zasshi kara mita 1930 nendai* (The 1930s from the perspective of women's journals), edited by Watashi tachi no rekishi o tsuzuru kai. Pp. 48–121. Tokyo: Dōjidaisha.

Silverberg, M. 1991. "The Modern Girl as Militant." In *Recreating Japanese Women*, edited by G. Bernstein. Pp. 88–107. Berkeley, Los Angeles, and Oxford: University of California Press.

Silverman, K. 1985. "Histoire d'O: The Construction of a Female Subject." In *Pleasure and Danger: Exploring Female Sexuality*, edited by C. Vance. Pp. 320–349. Boston: Routledge and Kegan Paul.

Sugita M. 1929. "Seihonnō ni hisomu zangyakusei" (The latent cruelty within original instinct). *Kaizō* 4:70–80.

———. 1935. "Shōjo kageki netsu no shindan" (An analysis of the girls' opera craze). *Fujin kōron* 4:274–278.

Takagi S. 1976. *Takarazuka no wakaru hon* (Takarazuka guidebook). Tokyo: Kōsaidō.

Takano M. 1987. "Chōshōjo to fueminizumu no kyōhan kankei ni" (The conspiratorial partnership between ultra-*shōjo* and feminism). *Kuriteiiku* 6:53–63.

Tamura T. 1913. "Dōsei no koi" (Same-sex love). *Chūō kōron* 1:165–168.

Tanabe S. 1986. "Kaisetsu: Taoyaka ni yasashiki sebone no hito" (Commentary: The person with soft and graceful mettle). In *Nyonin Yoshiya Nobuko* (The woman Yoshiya Nobuko), edited by T. Yoshitake. Pp. 317–324. Bunshun Bunko 427–2. Tokyo: Bungeishunjū.

Togawa S. 1975. "Dokyumento: Rezubian" (Document: Lesbian). *Yangu redei*, January 1, pp. 67–62.

Tomioka M. 1938. "Dansei josō to josei dansō." *Kaizō* 10:98–105.

Ueda Y. 1974. *Takarazuka sutā: Sono engi to bigaku.* (Takarazuka stars: Their acting and aesthetics). Tokyo: Yomiuri Shinbunsha.

———. 1986. *Takarazuka ongaku gakkō* (The Takarazuka Music Academy). Tokyo: Yomiuri Raifu.

Ushijima Y. 1943. *Joshi no shinri* (Female psychology). Tokyo: Ganshodō.

Vance, C. 1985. "Pleasure and Danger: Toward a Politics of Sexuality." In *Pleasure and Danger: Exploring Female Sexuality,* edited by C. Vance. Pp. 1–27. Boston: Routledge and Kegan Paul.

Vicinus, M. 1989. "Distance and Desire: English Boarding School Friendships, 1870–1920." In *Hidden from History: Reclaiming the Gay and Lesbian Past,* edited by M. Vicinus, M. Duberman, and G. Chauncey. Pp. 212–229. New York: New American Library.

Wada T. 1987. "Nihon no senpai rezubiantachi" (Japan's lesbian elders). *Bessatsu takarajima* 64:74–79.

Yasuda T. 1935. "Dōseiai no rekishikan" (The historical consciousness of same-sex love). *Chūō kōron* 3:146–152.

Yoshida G. "Musume no ren'ai, dōseiai to haha" (Mothers and their daughters' [heterosexual] love and same-sex love). *Fujin kōron* 3:156–160.

Yoshitake T. 1986. *Nyonin Yoshiya Nobuko* (The woman Yoshiya Nobuko). Bunshun Bunko 427–2. Tokyo: Bungeishunjū.

Yoshiwara R. 1935. "Gekkyū shōchōki ni aru musume o motsu okasama e" (To mothers with pubertal daughters). *Fujin kōron* 3:184–187.

JOURNALS AND MAGAZINES

Bessatsu takarajima	*Onna erosu*
Hankyū	*Shinchihei*
Kageki	*Takarazuka gurafu*
Nihonkai	

Newspapers

Kokumin　　　　　*Osaka chōhō*
Kyōto　　　　　　*Osaka mainichi*
Nichinichi　　　　*Osaka nichinichi*
Nihonkai　　　　　*Shin nippō*
Osaka asahi

CHAPTER 7

Death by Defeatism and Other Fables: The Social Dynamics of the Rengō Sekigun Purge

Patricia G. Steinhoff

Deep in the Japanese alps in the winter of 1972, a small Japanese revolutionary group called Rengō Sekigun (United Red Army) beat, stabbed, and tortured twelve of its own members to death. The raw, face-to-face brutality of the purge lends itself readily to pseudo-explanations that portray the perpetrators as monsters, fundamentally different from normal people. Yet the real horror of the Rengō Sekigun purge is that its bizarre outcomes resulted from very ordinary social processes enacted by quite normal individuals.

The Rengō Sekigun purge was a dynamic social process, comprising not only the acts and ideological justifications the participants created and carried out together, but also the assumptions and habits they brought to the situation as well-socialized members of Japanese society. By reconstructing the dynamics of the purge from survivors' accounts, this study examines these underlying social processes and patterns.[1]

The Problem of Unification

Rengō Sekigun was an ill-fated attempt to fuse two extreme left student groups. Sekigun (Red Army) was famous for its headline-grabbing activities, which included an aborted attack on the prime minister's residence in 1969; a successful airplane hijacking to North Korea in 1970; and a series of bank, payroll, and post office robberies undertaken in 1971 to finance the group's revolutionary activities. These activities made Sekigun the object of very intense police pressure and soon decimated its ranks. Sekigun's original leaders all had been arrested or had gone into exile by mid-1970, to be succeeded by Mori Tsuneo. Sekigun's dramatic ideology characterized the group as part of an international revolutionary vanguard linked to similar groups throughout the world. It attracted bright students from good universities who were often the children of middle-class intellectuals in regional cities.

Kakusa, the abbreviated name of the Japan Communist Party Revolutionary Left Wing (Nihon Kyōsantō Kakumei Saha),[2] was more Maoist than Sekigun as well as more nationalistically anti-American. Kakusa recruited mainly from technical colleges in Yokohama and Nagoya and attracted more students from working-class backgrounds. It also had a strong feminist position, which attracted many women. Its original leaders had been arrested or drifted away, and leadership had devolved onto a small working group headed by a woman, Nagata Hiroko. Kakusa's leaders were also underground, following an abortive attack on a police box in December 1970 and a successful gunshop robbery in early 1971.

By mid-1971, Sekigun and Kakusa each had a small, underground core army but also drew on the services of a more public support group with a different name.[3] While competing for recognition as the boldest and most militant revolutionary group in Japan, the two little bands were drawn together by practical considerations. Kakusa had obtained a cache of guns and ammunition through its gunshop robbery but was desperately short of living expenses for its underground members. Sekigun had acquired quite a bit of money through its series of robberies but had been unable to obtain sufficient weapons for the revolutionary activities it hoped to carry out.

Kakusa had moved into an abandoned cabin in the Japanese alps in Gumma prefecture and invited a number of support group members to join them. Sekigun's Mori was not interested in abandoning the city entirely, but his army had shrunk to a handful of desperados on the run. He saw Kakusa's weapons and manpower as valuable resources. By the fall of 1971, the leaders of the two groups had agreed to a merger of their armies, which later was to expand into a merged party with a new name, Rengō Sekigun. They initiated the merger in December with a joint training exercise at a remote mountain cabin Sekigun had found.

Group Structure and Leadership

The merger of two groups is always a delicate and uncertain venture in Japan. Japanese groups tend to have a hierarchical structure with relatively strong vertical ties, counterbalanced by rituals and ideology that emphasize membership in the group as a whole. Fusion of two such groups can sometimes be accomplished by creating a unified hierarchy among the leaders while leaving the leaders' ties with lower-level members intact.

In Rengō Sekigun the hierarchy among the leaders was clear from the outset. Sekigun leader Mori Tsuneo became the head of the new group, with Kakusa's woman leader Nagata Hiroko just below him, followed by a small circle of their closest associates who served as the central committee of the new organization. This arrangement did not reflect the number of followers each brought to the new group, since Sekigun was far outnumbered by Kakusa.

Mori headed the merger because he was superior to Nagata in a critical skill: he excelled at manipulating revolutionary theory to create novel ideological interpretations of the immediate situation. In the upper reaches of the Japanese student left, where major issues of policy and power are played out as ideological debates, this skill is highly valued. Indeed, the main function of the leader is to provide continuous ideological justification for the group's activities.

Nagata had impressive public speaking skills and could write theoretical statements when necessary, but she was much more comfortable using her energies to follow someone else's ideological direction. Although Mori treated Nagata politely as a co-leader and after his arrest wrote as if they had been equal, his intention from the beginning was to take over Kakusa. Mori respected Nagata for her straightforward toughness and tenacity, but he was not able to share power.

Unification Ritual

Mori needed new rituals and ideology to bring the group together. He was also concerned about the disparity of experience among the members. His Sekigun group consisted of several "soldiers" who had been underground for months and two or three members who had worked primarily with the legal front organization on support activities. Kakusa's situation was similar. Its core group had been underground a long time, but an even larger number of its remaining members were women and even children without any underground experience.

The problem of the disparity of revolutionary experience among members, as well as the gap between the two organizations, was revealed vividly during the joint training exercise, when Nagata openly criticized the one woman in the Sekigun contingent, Toyama Mieko, for her feminine demeanor. Kakusa took the position that women's liberation required women to be revolutionaries first and women second, so Nagata was shocked by Toyama's display of traditional femininity. But Sekigun had never dealt with feminist issues, and Toyama was naïve about the rigors of underground life. She responded to Nagata's critical blast with silence, the standard polite Japanese response to anything one objects to or cannot deal with comfortably. That response only further infuriated Nagata.

Nagata used the consciousness-raising technique familiar to American women's groups of that era to convey her message. She criticized Toyama's attitudes and behavior directly in a group meeting, with the expectation that Toyama would become aware of her problem and try to overcome it. The practice was common within Kakusa, but unheard of in Sekigun. Moreover, it was a serious breach of etiquette for Nagata to attack directly a lower-ranking member of the other group. Toyama had no idea how to respond, nor did anyone else in Sekigun, while the Kakusa members understood Nagata's criticism and were equally surprised at Toyama's inability to answer it.

Mori was protective of Toyama and Sekigun, but fascinated by Nagata's method. From it he fashioned the ingenious ideological creation that was to lead Rengō Sekigun down the path of destruction.

Communization: Ideology and Process

After withdrawing to confer briefly with his Sekigun colleagues in the kitchen, Mori returned to the joint training group session to announce the new process of *kyōsanshugika,* which translates as "communist transformation," or "communization." The term had been used earlier in Sekigun's theoretical writings, in a call for the "communization of revolutionary soldiers," but there had been no method for bringing it about (Mori 1984, 10).

Mori argued that before the new group was ready to carry out any revolutionary activities, the internal preparation of its members had to be addressed, and each individual had to "become communized." Although the precise content of kyōsanshugika was never specified, the idea was to examine one's own bourgeois attitudes and behavior and eliminate them to become a better-prepared revolutionary soldier. The method for accomplishing kyōsanshugika was to be collective examination of each person's weaknesses, followed by individual effort to overcome them.

Even before the Rengō Sekigun merger, Mori had been trying to get individual members of Sekigun to reflect on their personal failings and overcome them, but he had only dealt directly with the individual. His method had been to demand that the person think about his particular problem and then make an oral self-criticism before Mori, at which time a penalty such as denial of alcohol and cigarettes for a month might be prescribed for disciplinary purposes.

For serious offenses against the organization, formal self-criticism was a well-established practice throughout the student movement, a legacy of an earlier period of affiliation with the Japan Communist Party. Characteristically, Mori fused the practice of self-criticism *jikohihan* with the term for a different activity, *sōkatsu,* which is a collective critical examination of the current problem of the organization, resulting in a summary interpretation with clear implications for the next course of action (Steinhoff 1984; 1989). Even before Rengō Sekigun, Mori had sometimes blurred the linguistic distinction and demanded a sōkatsu from an individual when he meant a self-criticism, rather than an interpretation of the group's situation with policy implications.

This time, Mori applied his idiosyncratic use of the term *sōkatsu* to his new demand that each person face a group criticism session, then reevaluate his or her thinking and behavior accordingly. The "method" of kyōsanshugika was to make one's personal sōkatsu. The proposal was accepted enthusiastically, even though the meaning of his jargon was a bit fuzzy. The group members had gathered with the sincere intention of becoming revolutionaries, and they expected to be challenged and changed in the process.

In this initial phase, three elements combined to make kyōsanshugika a potentially deadly ideology. The first element was the method of group consciousness raising, which unleashes powerful group dynamics that only trained leadership can control. The second was the ambiguity of both the desired end state of kyōsanshugika and the individual changes necessary to achieve it. The third was the requirement that no one could leave the mountain camp until he or she had achieved kyōsanshugika.

Consciousness-Raising

Although Mori was introducing a new practice into Rengō Sekigun, the technique is widely used in American group psychotherapy sessions, from which it has spread to various sorts of self-help and personal development groups. The purpose of the technique is to help build a stronger personality, but the first step is to tear down unproductive defenses by making the person acutely aware of them in a group criticism session.

Such groups are generally run by a trained leader who is aware of the tendency for criticism sessions to become dangerously harsh and has learned techniques for controlling the course of the discussion. When consciousness-raising or group criticism sessions occur without a clear authority figure in the United States, the group is generally egalitarian enough that reservations about the process itself can be expressed, thus deflecting the tendency to be excessively critical. There have been enough excesses, however, that the practice is regarded as questionable for amateurs to use.

Rengō Sekigun had neither trained leadership nor group egalitarianism to check the tendency for excess. Nagata's practice had been essentially an individual blast of criticism, followed up later with compensating warmth. Her method was not a deliberately orchestrated group enterprise. Although both leaders had considerable experience in leadership of group discussions, Mori had initiated a new form of group criticism that he was not prepared to control. Yet because of the clear hierarchy of authority in the group, as well as the traditional Japanese practice of decision making by consensus, it was unlikely that any other group member would take the initiative to control excesses, especially if that meant confronting the leader or opposing the group's mood.

Ambiguity

The concept of kyōsanshugika was so vague that survivors of the Rengō Sekigun purge often claim not to have understood it. They certainly grasped the emotional appeal of the general idea of self-transformation; the problem was that neither the end-state of the transformation nor the changes one would have to make were spelled out clearly. The all-encompassing nature of the transformation from bourgeois Japanese college student to revolutionary soldier made virtually any aspect of the individual's past or present thought and behavior a potential character flaw.

In a consciousness-raising session, the more enlightened participants help the less enlightened to reevaluate themselves. This reevaluation cannot be accomplished simply by imposing an external behavioral requirement upon the subject. Since the key is *self*-consciousness, the individual has to discover the problem to correct it. This process has parallels in Western psychotherapy and in indigenous Japanese psychotherapies such as Morita therapy and Naikan therapy.

The process requires sincere individuals to search their minds and memories for possible solutions and report their progress periodically for evaluation. In kyōsanshugika, the person searched for bourgeois thoughts and behaviors to be corrected. The report thus became a confession of errant thoughts and acts, but since the confessors did not have a clear idea of what their sins were, they were likely to dredge up all sorts of minor skeletons out of their mental closets and offer them as problems a sincere revolutionary should overcome.

Initially, Mori insisted that the individual make his or her own confession, or sōkatsu, without assistance from others in defining the problem. He employed a rather simplistic psychology drawn from the traditional Buddhist evils such as greed, envy, and self-indulgence and apparently expected to hear a confession of specific lapses attributed to these weaknesses of personal character. In Mori's view, the individual could overcome these failings by toughening up. Hence he relied increasingly on demeanor as an indicator of whether the person was developing a fighting spirit. The others did not necessarily share these assumptions about cause and effect and thus could not comprehend what should be confessed, how it should be interpreted, and when it had been overcome.

To compound the confusion, the Kakusa group was more concerned with sexual thoughts and behavior because of its explicit ideology of revolution as the precurser of women's liberation and because its male and female members had been living together in close quarters for some time. Sekigun had already been put on notice by Kakusa that its bourgeois attitudes toward women were a serious problem. This was also one of the few areas where the participants were likely to have anything substantial to confess.

Thus it is not surprising that in the spirit of kyōsanshugika members earnestly confessed to minor sexual thoughts and acts, which were magnified into serious problems of backward bourgeois mentality through the process of group criticism. These confessions of trivia did not help clarify the process of transformation into a revolutionary communist soldier. Rather, they aroused doubts in the minds of those who had not yet confessed to thoughts and actions on a similar level of insignificance.

The situation was ripe for what Lofland (1969) has called deviant labeling. There were many vague indicators of a newly emerging form of deviance (in this case the inability to "make one's sōkatsu" and achieve communization), only a few of which were sufficient to make the diagnosis. The criteria were so obscure and difficult to interpret that only a special expert (Mori) could make the identification properly. Mori's labeling was idiosyncratic and inscrutable, however, and only added to the confusion. Mori himself shared in the general uncertainty and vague sense of guilt that the process aroused, and thus he could not channel the collective energy into a clear image of how one could become communized.

No Exit

The third critical element was Mori's decree that no one could leave the mountain camp until he or she had achieved kyōsanshugika. This no-exit provision was intended as a protection against defectors who might compromise the group's location. The rule applied only to persons who came under suspicion and were explicitly told to make a sōkatsu. Other members were frequently sent out in small groups for two or three days at a time on official group business. Mori's demand was apparently not viewed as a particularly stringent requirement, since in the initial flush of enthusiasm, most members assumed that they could readily achieve kyōsanshugika, and even those who had already become objects of criticism expected that their sincere efforts to change would be rewarded. It was not until later that the no-exit rule took on more sinister implications.

Deadly Escalation

Without question, Mori's creation of kyōsanshugika established the critical element for the Rengō Sekigun purge. Yet kyōsanshugika was at that point still a relatively innocent game from which the participants could well have emerged unharmed. The next phase of the Rengō Sekigun purge was characterized by small increments of innovation and accident that unintentionally transformed it into a ritual of death. As the events became more extreme, Mori elaborated the ideology of kyōsanshugika with interpretations that made objection and resistance increasingly difficult.

Acts of Self-Improvement

Through a series of separate incidents in December 1971, the process of communization began to incorporate physical acts for discipline and self-improvement. At first these were simple admonitions to engage in self-reflection while carrying out some constructive activity. At the end of the joint training exercise, for example, three Sekigun members were ordered to reflect on their sōkatsu while doing extra rifle-firing drill. Mori issued these disciplinary prescriptions ad hoc, carefully tailoring them to the particular problem of the individual.

Moral discipline of this sort is found in the child-rearing practices of societies throughout the world. It is also widely associated with religious, military, and athletic training. The notion that ascetic practices and humbling physical discipline produce spiritual rewards is also thoroughly engrained in Japanese culture. Indeed, this assumption was embodied in the concept of kyōsanshugika from the beginning. Hence no one questioned the appropriateness of such demands, even if the recipients did grumble a bit. Then, in a series of small increments, the acts of self-improvement escalated into violence and torture.

Leaving six Sekigun members behind at the Sekigun cabin, Mori and the others went to Kakusa's larger and better appointed cabin to continue discussing the details of the new organization. For a variety of reasons, Mori soon identified Kakusa members Katō Yoshitaka and Kojima Kazuko as persons in need of communization, and they were made the targets of a group criticism session. At Nagata's suggestion, Katō and Kojima were then put together at a table with writing materials and told to develop their sōkatsu. Mori soon was dissatisfied with their progress and ordered them separated, then increased the restrictions to include sitting in formal Japanese posture on the knees, denial of food, and restricted communication. Katō and Kojima still tried to act as members of the group despite the restrictions, and other Kakusa members also initially tried to normalize the situation. The treatment of Katō and Kojima made the other members uncomfortable, but it was ordered by the leaders and rationalized ideologically by the unwillingness of Katō and Kojima to make progress toward the elusive state of communization. At the same time, the other members were ordered to cooperate in the disciplinary measures and exhorted to help the pair hurry up and achieve communization so the restrictions could be lifted.

Mori became increasingly frustrated by the slow progress Katō and Kojima were making and expressed a desire for a boxing match between Katō and another Kakusa member as a means of enlightening Katō. Then, in the middle of the following night, Kojima suddenly announced that Katō had molested her while they were sleeping next to each other. The announcement outraged Nagata and provided the opportunity for Mori to order a beating of both Katō and Kojima.[4]

The two leaders were not so much concerned about the sexual behavior itself as with the fact that people who were supposed to be concentrating on self-improvement for group good were distracted by private emotions. A very basic principle of Japanese group dynamics is the demand that group needs supersede individual emotions and private relationships. Hence any attention that Katō and Kojima devoted to each other was regarded as inappropriate lack of attention to the serious matters of collective group concern.

In addition, the issue here, as with Toyama's problem earlier, was not simply the behavior and thoughts of individuals.

It was bound up with the past rivalry between the two groups and the concern of each leader that his or her own followers not be shown up by the other group. Each leader felt public responsibility for the behavior of his or her subordinates. The effect was to make the leader exert greater pressure on the follower to change, because the little drama was being played out before an audience of members and leaders of the other group. Nagata, ashamed that her group's members would appear less revolutionary to Mori (interview with Nagata, May 1986), out of guilt expressed enthusiastic support for whatever measures he proposed.

The beatings elicited further sexual confessions from both Katō and Kojima, who probably thought what they said represented progress toward a proper sōkatsu. Mori, however, regarded this as additional evidence of their inability to understand kyōsanshugika. The other members had mixed reactions. On the one hand, they could legitimately feel outraged at Katō, who had confessed to aggressive sexual relations with Kojima and others. On the other hand, they did not necessarily approve of the violence. It was apparent to all, however, that beatings elicited confessions that milder restrictions had not brought to light.

Mori clearly interpreted the beatings not as punishment for wrong acts, but rather as a method for forcing a person to face his own weaknesses in order to overcome them. That new information came out, even if it was not what he had hoped for, reinforced his conviction that he had found an effective method for bringing about kyōsanshugika. He expressed considerable satisfaction with the outcome, describing it as a "new level" that the group had achieved in the process of communization. He elaborated the new level by ordering that Katō and Kojima be tied up to the cabin's support posts and be denied food and toilet privileges indefinitely. The justification for these actions was that such punishment would help Katō and Kojima concentrate totally on their sōkatsu.

Neither Sekigun nor Kakusa advocated nonviolence as an ideological principle. Their rhetoric was violent and their imagery military. Consequently, there was no principled basis on which to resist the introduction of physical violence into the process of communization. The decisions to introduce violence were made by a leader whose authority had been accepted by the group on the basis of his ability to make ideological interpretations. Each escalation of violence was accompanied by an ideological elaboration consistent with the basic theory of communization.

Participatory Violence

Although some people were completely caught up in the rhetoric of communization, others regarded the escalating violence apprehensively and hung back. Nagata responded by urging reluctant observers to participate, both as an expression of collective sentiment and as a means of strengthening their own resolve. True to form, Mori quickly transformed Nagata's spontaneous cheerleading into an ideological principle: participation in the violence employed to make someone else achieve sōkatsu was an essential aspect of achieving one's own communization.

From the beginning, kyōsanshugika had been conceived as a cooperative group enterprise in which one person's open criticism aided a fellow member to achieve a breakthrough in understanding. Normal Japanese group procedure involves both periods of voluntary and spontaneous comment by individuals and periods when each person in turn makes an obligatory expression of agreement with the emerging group consensus. These decision-making procedures were generally followed when Mori initially introduced the idea of kyōsanshugika and again when it was put into operation against specific individuals.

The procedures are as routine as taking a vote in an American group, but they carry somewhat different expectations about participation. With a voting procedure the person who loses is expected to go along with the majority but remains free to express opposition and to criticize the majority's decision. Emotional commmitment to a decision one disagrees with is not required.

By contrast, in Japanese consensus procedures, there is a general expectation that people should abandon their private objections once the group has agreed. They are expected to participate fully in the group's action, even if they originally disagreed with it. A group leader has to be sensitive to any signs of reluctance, because a consensus requires the assent of all members. The more significant the issue, the more important it becomes that all members participate fully and not just nominally. The new principle put members into a double bind that is very familiar in Japanese society, precisely because of the strong group pressure for displays of cooperative participation.

The psychological dynamic behind Mori's elaboration of the ideology of communization to encompass participatory violence is well understood. Festinger and his associates (1956) found that when individuals in a small group are faced with cognitive dissonance between their ideology and external reality, they will reinterpret the external reality to make it ideologically consistent. Individuals uneasy about the escalating violence in Rengō Sekigun were quickly put on notice that any expression of hesitance indicated their own backwardness. To continue to resist participation in violence, a Rengō Sekigun member would have had to reject the very reason for being in the mountains and simultaneously accept a self-definition of being too weak to overcome the fear of violence and achieve communist transformation. The alternative was to throw oneself into participatory violence, complying outwardly with the demand for cooperation and hoping that it would achieve the desired result of helping one's own communist transformation. Indeed, to resolve the dissonance one had to believe all the more firmly that this was the only way to overcome one's fear of violence and achieve communization.

Death by Defeatism

Mori's evolving ideology soon faced a critical confrontation with reality. Two days after the beatings of Katō and Kojima, another member, Ozaki Atsuo, came under suspicion. After an initial period of criticism and mild restrictions, Mori decided that Ozaki needed to engage in a boxing match to toughen him up into a real revolutionary fighter. The small and physically weak Ozaki was matched with the much taller and stronger Sakaguchi Hiroshi (Nagata's husband) and forced to keep fighting by the intervention of Mori and another man.

Over the next two days, Ozaki was left tied upright to a door post and beaten intermittently. At one point, Ozaki thanked Mori for beating him, a tactic Mori and Nagata angrily viewed as an attempt at *amae,* or seeking someone's favor by creating a relationship of dependency. Although amae is a culturally valued traditional relationship pattern, student radicals of the 1960s generally rejected it as a deterrent to the development of strong individual character. Labeling Ozaki's behavior as amae thus further marked him as weak and lacking in revolutionary character.

On New Year's eve Mori checked Ozaki and reported that he was not showing any signs of making a sōkatsu, meaning that in his seriously weakened state he was not showing the fighting spirit that Mori saw as the key indicator of progress toward communization. On Mori's instructions Ozaki was beaten again while still tied to the post, this time with the blows deliberately concentrated on his stomach. He was then left alone again.

A while later, the central committee discovered that Ozaki was dead. Ozaki's death was genuinely unexpected, which seems almost incredible since several members of the group had some medical or paramedical training. Nagata was a licensed pharmacist, and some of the other Kakusa women were nurses. All had participated in beating him, but in their zeal to achieve his communist transformation and their own, no one was able to acknowledge the seriousness of the damage they had inflicted on him. Nagata and the other members of the central committee were singularly unable to explain how he had died so suddenly, when he had "appeared okay" during a routine check only a short time earlier.

They waited tensely while Mori conferred briefly with Yamada, the other Sekigun member of the central committee present. Then Mori announced that Ozaki had suffered *haibokushi,* or death by defeatism. He had died of shock, Mori explained, because he realized that he was unable to achieve kyōsanshugika. The association of Mori's invention, death by defeatism, with the medical condition of shock was adequate to appease the scientific orientation of the members. More important, Mori had once again created an ideological interpretation that neatly resolved the cognitive dissonance.

Because of the earlier requirement of participatory violence, every person present had actively beaten Ozaki, even when it was apparent that he was badly injured and unable to resist. They had done it to protect themselves, but in the name of ideology that said they were also doing it for his sake. Now he was dead. If their beating had caused his death, then they were murderers, and their collective efforts to achieve kyōsanshugika had led them astray. Mori declared that on the contrary, Ozaki had died not from their actions, but from his own failures. He had *chosen* defeat and death because he had not been strong enough to achieve the state of communist transformation, despite their help.

The argument follows the crude logic of blaming the victim, a common process by which people dissociate themselves from the consequences of their behavior. Yet in the context of the developing theory of kyōsanshugika, this interpretation of Ozaki's death carried additional psychological force. If one accepted the death-by-defeatism interpretation, one not only avoided responsibility for Ozaki's death, but also accepted responsibility in advance for one's own potential death by defeatism. This logic reinforced each person's motivation to continue the process of violent kyōsanshugika, despite its having suddenly been elevated to a matter of life and death. The only alternative to participation in the process had been closed off by the no-exit rule, which specified that a person could not leave the camp until he or she had achieved kyōsanshugika. Hence, the one way to avoid death by defeatism was to do better than Ozaki had, to succeed where he had failed.

The unexpected death of Ozaki could have provided an opportunity for the group to reevaluate its situation and deescalate the course of violence. Rengō Sekigun might have pulled back from the brink if it had been unable to account for Ozaki's death satisfactorily. In the group's own jargon, the sōkatsu of his death might have led to a reevaluation of participatory violence and a fresh orientation. Had that happened, the members undoubtedly would have greeted the deescalation of violence with relief. That did not happen because Mori offered a different ideological interpretation of the event, one that had powerful immediate appeal because it allayed everyone's guilt. Mori's interpretation set the course for further disaster, because it obliterated any other limit to the acceptability of violence.

Group Process and the Spiral of Violence

Ozaki's death and Mori's interpretation of it as death by defeatism marked the point of no return for the Rengō Sekigun participants. They plunged into a spiral of accusation, violence, and death from which they were unable to extricate themselves. A fundamental course had been set, and the major opportunities to reverse it had passed by. Over the next several weeks the purge consumed eleven more victims.[5]

An understanding of the Rengō Sekigun purge requires not only an explanation of the dynamics that precipitated it, but also an analysis of how it was perpetuated over such a long series of victims. This question leads to a deeper examination of the internal structure of the organization and to the related question of how the relationships among members were altered by the social processes of the purge.

The dynamics that propelled the group during this period revolved around two axes of conflict: the interaction between leaders and followers and that between perpetrators and victims. Both relationships embodied complex mixtures of antagonism and interdependence.

Leadership and Group Structure

Mori had achieved formal authority over the group through legitimate means: the assent of Nagata, the concurrence of the two central committees of Sekigun and Kakusa, and a formal consensus procedure by the combined membership. Formal authority carries a great deal of weight in Japanese society, regardless of the leader's actual performance. Groups will go to great lengths to support a very weak leader or will submit to an erratic one without even considering the possibility of changing leaders. Mori, however, was also a very strong leader.

By the time of Ozaki's death, Mori had achieved undisputed authority over Rengō Sekigun. Violence escalated rapidly under his leadership, with virtually no objection. This process is particularly noteworthy because most of the transformation took place at the Kakusa camp during a time when Mori and one or two other Sekigun members were overwhelmingly outnumbered by Kakusa members. Moreover, the first three persons against whom the violence was directed were Kakusa members.

A style of leadership had developed in which Mori's small central committee met in almost continual session in a room apart from the ordinary members. All new information was reported directly to the central committee, and all instructions and explanations emanated from it. After the central committee had agreed with one of Mori's interpretations, Nagata would often be delegated to explain it to the rest of the membership. Thus the Kakusa members received Mori's ideas through their own legitimate leader, Nagata, after those ideas had already been accepted by the first layer of subleaders.

Despite the bureaucratization of authority in Rengō Sekigun, the whole group was still small enough for full membership meetings and consensus-style participation to be held virtually every night. Study of survivors' sequential accounts reveals that initially these large meetings entailed lively, spontaneous participation by the members. The ritualized form of the whole group meeting remained consensual and participatory over the next several weeks, but the content and tone changed profoundly. Gradually meetings came to consist of unilateral speeches by the leaders to announce and explain policy decisions they had already made, followed by a demand for responses from the group members. The level of members' participation diminished as the atmosphere became more tense, and members learned that whatever they said could become the basis for severe criticism.

After the first few deaths, members complied passively with the formal requirements of the consensus procedure, but they no longer dared to express any spontaneous thoughts. The only break in this pattern occurred in mid-January, when central committee member Teraoka Kōichi came under attack. At that time, after considerable prompting, the ordinary members participated energetically in the criticism and vented on Teraoka their frustrations with the entire central committee (Uegaki 1984, 310–312). Afterwards, the group reverted once again to listless, fearful compliance.

Mori's dominance over the group derived both from his personal style and from his ability to create ideological interpretations of the evolving situation. Regardless of how absurd they sound to outsiders, Mori's ideological creations had an uncanny ability to speak to the deepest psychological needs of the Rengō Sekigun participants. How did he manage to touch the right psychological nerves to make his interpretations so compelling in the Rengō Sekigun context?

In his prison confession, written in an isolation cell just two months after the Rengō Sekigun purge, Mori tried to explain his motivations at the time of the events and his reinterpretations since his arrest. It is apparent from this document that Mori was not aware of the powerful emotional implications of his ideological creations when he uttered them, but upon reflection after his arrest, he was able to see the dynamic they had unleashed.

In the critical case of death by defeatism as an explanation of Ozaki's sudden death, it is clear that Mori crystallized his own fears that the beatings had killed Ozaki and that the shock of learning about it might kill Katō and Kojima into the concept of death by defeatism. The rationalization met his own private needs and performed the same magic for the rest of the group. Mori's ideology was potent precisely because it was the self-delusion that helped him overcome the same problems that would trouble his followers. Emotionally, he was in the same state as his followers, but he was a more creative rationalizer.

Followership by Fear and Doubt

As Max Weber pointed out early in this century, the central question about authority is why people acquiesce to it. It is not sufficient to understand how Mori led; one must also explain why others followed more or less willingly. Rengō Sekigun followers did have serious doubts about the course of events, but they rarely had any opportunities to raise them, for three reasons.

First, followers soon lost confidence in their own ability to judge. The increasing confusion of the situation elevated Mori to the position of being the only person who could make a definitive interpretation. Each time Mori produced an unexpected judgment, the others lost faith in their own ability to interpret reality. Such disorientation is a characteristic feature of the process of deviant labeling (Lofland 1969), but it was no doubt exacerbated by the general tendency in Japanese culture for individuals to rely heavily on external validation rather than make firm judgments based on their perceptions.

Second, expressing one's reservations about the course of events at the Rengō Sekigun camp soon became physically dangerous. Expressions of doubt were immediately defined as symptoms of weakness or backwardness in achieving the organization's goals. They were turned back on the doubter and rendered the person vulnerable to attack.

Third, Japanese group process is not conducive to the direct expression of opposition to the leader or the group as a whole. Most ordinary group members would not have felt there was any way to express such opposition, even if they did not feel physically threatened. Only persons with a certain amount of independent standing in the group would have the temerity to cross a strong leader. Moreover, the normal cultural means of expressing opposition are indirect and ambiguous. Even when a person thinks he is expressing strong opposition, it is easy for others to ignore, misconstrue, or override the objection.

These factors operated together to weaken the major potential opportunities for resistance: subleaders' participation in central committee discussion, the introduction of newcomers into the surreal world of Rengō Sekigun, and opportunities for escape.

Opposition in the Central Committee

While Mori alone was interpreting events as the ideological leader, the followers' acceptance of those interpretations came in two stages. First, they had to be accepted by the other members of the central committee, where there was still some opportunity for disagreement. Then they were offered to the larger membership as collective decisions. Only members of the central committee, indeed only certain members within that circle, could conceivably have dissented openly from the leader's position. The person whose opposition would have carried the most weight was Nagata, but she was the person most completely under the spell of Mori's ideas and personality. Two other central committee members did try to object.

In the central committee discussion immediately after the third death, Sekigun subleader Yamada Takashi angrily asked Mori to think about the fact that thrusting death in people's faces didn't seem to turn them into revolutionaries. Yamada, who was senior to Mori in Sekigun in length of membership if not rank, was probably the only person besides Nagata who could have mounted such a direct challenge.

Even though no one else voiced support for Yamada's view, Mori was obliged to respond; he promptly elaborated kyōsanshugika into a version of the traditional zen-based samurai ethic of overcoming all physical limitations through a higher union of spirit and body. His comments bore striking parallels to the military ethic of wartime Japan, which led many zealous military officers to contend that the spiritual power of the Japanese military could overcome the material superiority of its enemies.

Yamada yielded immediately to this interpretation. Thus not only was one potential opportunity to reevaluate the violence quickly smothered, but in the process the ideology was elaborated to suggest that true revolutionaries could overcome all conceivable levels of torture without succumbing to death. While justifying the deaths, this elaboration was bound to arouse further doubts in the minds of all the members about their own ability to achieve what they were demanding of others.

The only other person who might have succeeded in challenging the proceedings was Sakaguchi. Because he was a high-ranking member of Kakusa with strong revolutionary credentials and the husband of Nagata Hiroko, Sakaguchi had considerable standing in the central committee. Unlike Nagata, he was suspicious of Mori and was not fully convinced by his ideas.

Sakaguchi's very Japanese communication style, however, made it extremely difficult for him to convey his doubts effectively. Silence was Sakaguchi's primary means of expressing disagreement, but in the context of the Rengō Sekigun central committee, his silence was easily overlooked or misread as assent. His initial attempts to express his dissatisfaction were simply ignored. Accustomed to sycophants and uncomfortable with direct criticism, Mori did not take note of Sakaguchi's silence. Nagata, who did know how to read Sakaguchi's cues, was too taken by Mori's theories to pay attention (Nagata 1982–1983, vol. 2).

Sakaguchi's initial doubts were expressed ambiguously in part because he was also experiencing the same double bind as the others. He, too, was vulnerable to the concept of death by defeatism as a way of denying personal guilt over the death of his associates (Sakaguchi 1972).

At a somewhat later point in the purge, after five people had died, Sakaguchi could not keep his feelings to himself any longer. He announced angrily that he was sick of it all and did not want to be in the central committee any longer. The others were shocked. They argued that everything they were doing was necessary, and they finally convinced him that he could not leave the central committee (Bandō 1984, 187–188).

Sakaguchi again had expressed himself in a traditional Japanese way, by threatening to withdraw. Expressing a desire to withdraw from a group is generally understood in Japanese society as a demand for greater personal attention from other group members. The other central committee members made the characteristic response to such a message: they protested that he could not withdraw and persuaded him to remain. They treated Sakaguchi's gesture as an emotional message about participation, skirting his objection to the substance of what the group was doing.

These two challenges to the group's direction were both

made within the confines of the central committee, more or less out of earshot of the remaining membership. Neither Yamada nor Sakaguchi would have dreamed of challenging Mori in a full meeting; it was the purpose of central committee meetings to develop a consensus to be presented to the whole group, and the central committee did not break ranks in public.

The Socialization of Newcomers

The power of the evolving group dynamic of Rengō Sekigun is illustrated clearly by its ability to ensnare newcomers, who had not participated in the initial elaboration of ideology and practice into violence. When new arrivals were introduced to the tense atmosphere and bizarre activities at the Kakusa camp, they stifled their initial apprehensions by reiterating their deep personal commitment to become better revolutionaries, whatever might be demanded of them. If unexpectedly high and repellent demands were made while they were still struggling to understand the new rhetoric, the newcomers quickly accepted the group's interpretation that they were lagging behind and tried all the harder to overcome their perceived weakness.

Shortly after Ozaki's death, several of the remaining Sekigun members were brought to the Kakusa camp from their own cabin, arriving in time to participate in the meeting at which the death-by-defeatism interpretation was advanced. This group included the three Sekigun members already under some suspicion in Mori's eyes, Toyama, Namekata, and Shindō. Mori saw clearly their fear and discomfort at the conditions in the Kakusa camp, but he interpreted this as evidence of their backwardness and need for sōkatsu (Mori 1984, 48–49).

Within twenty-four hours, Shindō had already fallen victim to violent kyōsanshugika and had died in much the same fashion as Ozaki. Toyama and Namekata had initially expressed reluctance to beat Shindō but had been urged to participate in the violence against him as part of their own treatment.

The following day Kojima died after several days of starvation and exposure. As was by then the practice, the whole group was convened to hear the leaders' explanation of Kojima's death and to express their reactions as part of the consensus procedure. As a result of Yamada's challenge within the central committee, this meeting became the occasion for an increased demand that members demonstrate their strength of will in the face of the death and violence around them and overcome their fear of death. The demand was experienced most acutely by the newcomers from the Sekigun camp. Toyama and Namekata were singled out for criticism because they had been reluctant to participate in the violence directed at their comrade Shindō. When it was Toyama's turn to comment, she affirmed vigorously that she wanted to become a revolutionary and then indiscreetly added that she did not want to die. Mori immediately saw this response as evidence of Toyama's failure to achieve a satisfactory level of communization.

After the group discussion of Kojima's death was completed, Nagata asked Toyama if she thought burying Kojima's corpse would help her overcome her fear of death. Toyama jumped at the chance to prove herself through some concrete action. Namekata, the other Sekigun newcomer under suspicion, volunteered to help. It was past midnight, but all the members except the highest-ranking leaders went outside in the snow to watch Toyama and Namekata carry Kojima's frozen body out from under the cabin, dig the grave, and strip the corpse for burial. In the midst of these macabre activities, Toyama suddenly began hitting Kojima's corpse. Shortly afterward all the members present were ordered to join in hitting Kojima's face to change her supposedly defiant death expression (Uegaki 1984, 286–287). In this manner new arrivals were quickly initiated into the surrealistic atmosphere of Rengō Sekigun and found themselves escalating the level of violence in order to catch up to the others.

Commitment and Escape Opportunities

The Rengō Sekigun purge gained much of its momentum because it occurred in a closed system, a total society in which participants fed on their own rhetoric and emotions without any external reality to serve as a corrective. In fact, however, the system was not completely closed. Members were sent off regularly in groups of two or three to conduct the organization's business. The people who were sent off on errands were by definition regarded as reliable and were not directly subject to the no-exit rule. It was still broadly understood, however, that a person who came to Rengō Sekigun was not free to leave. Any departure on one's own volition was thus an escape. Official excursions on organization business potentially offered an opportunity for escape, but very few people took advantage of it.

Some members did not escape while they were away from the camp because they remained under the group's surveillance. The teams sent on errands were carefully constructed by Mori to combine persons who did not know one another well and therefore could not trust one another well enough to express thoughts contrary to official ideology.

Surveillance alone does not explain the lack of escapees from Rengō Sekigun. Some people had opportunities to escape but did not take advantage of them. Relatives, lovers, and close friends were never sent off together, and it was unlikely that one would escape and leave the other behind. Some members really had no other alternative to Rengō Sekigun. Wanted by the police and with no money or resources, they were safer in Rengō Sekigun than if they tried to strike out on their own.

Yet to a remarkable degree, the participants in Rengō Sekigun also retained a sense of commitment to the organization and its members despite what was happening at the camp. In many cases, it did not even occur to members that they might escape, so long as Rengō Sekigun and its leadership remained the clear focus around which their lives revolved. If they had been entrusted with organizational funds to buy supplies or had been given a particular mission to carry out, they perceived that as their primary obligation. They felt that they could not take money that belonged to the group and that they had to report the results of their mission back to the organization. There was often no clear point at which they had discharged their responsibilities and could entertain the possibility of leaving.

This powerful sense of responsibility to the group is not unique to Rengō Sekigun. It is a characteristic that virtually every commentator on Japanese society points out. Members of Japanese society do seem to feel a greater sense of obligation to their group than Americans in a similar situation would.

In sum, underlying the bizarre specifics of the purge were a variety of characteristic features of Japanese social organization that reduced the likelihood of challenges to authority, encouraged newcomers to demonstrate their commitment, and limited the inclination to escape.

Victims and Perpetrators

While the purge bound its members together through their guilty practices and the collective ideology that masked them, those same practices required a shifting polarization of members into the categories of victims and perpetrators. Since each new victim was pulled from the ranks of the perpetrators of violence, there was no natural basis for distinguishing the two categories. Yet to insulate themselves from the threat of fully acknowledging the inhumanity of their behavior, group members had to create a separation. They began to reject the victims to create distance, even as they tried to maintain the bizarre fiction that the violent attacks were really comradely assistance. It was not hard to reject the victims, who were tied in abnormal positions, imprisoned in their own excrement, and disfigured by severe beatings. The more wretched and inhuman the victims became, the easier it was to inflict further violence upon them. The process of internal polarization involved three critical aspects: the physical and symbolic separation of victims from the group, the psychological mechanism of blaming the victim, and the process of taking the victim role.

Symbolic Separation

From the time of the first two deaths, persons who were confined for long periods supposedly making their sōkatsu were tied to exterior building support poles or tree trunks and left outside in temperatures below freezing. The practice of placing victims outside had deep symbolic meaning for both the victims and the other members. Placing a child outside is a traditional punishment in Japan, signifying total rejection and isolation from the warmth and security of the family. (The child is not tied, just put outside the house with some rejecting remarks.) The child's typical response is a frantic effort to get back into the house, coupled with heartfelt apologies and promises to do whatever the parent wants.

In the Rengō Sekigun case, putting victims outside clearly sent a message of rejection—along with the sheer physical torture of being tied to a post in freezing weather. It helped the remaining members separate themselves emotionally from the victims, even though they continued to regard their occasional checks on the victims as solicitous acts of kindness toward friends. Mori did not want the isolated victims to beg and plead to be restored to favor, but rather to display stoicism and a fighting spirit sufficient to overcome all privations. Yet the underlying message was that persons ostracized in this way should strive mightily to comply with the group's demands so they could be restored to the warmth of the group's inner environment.

Brutality and Blaming the Victim

In reality, the victims were weakened physically by denial of food, excessive exposure to cold, and repeated brutal beatings. Their inability to escape produced a sense of resignation, punctuated by occasional flashes of defiance. They were supposed to be "making a sōkatsu," but they were completely confused about how to comply, let alone whether they could or should. They showed signs of disorientation from extreme hunger and pain that were interpreted by Mori and then the others as evidence of inappropriate behavior on the part of someone making a sōkatsu. Facial expressions resulting from disorientation or even death were taken as evidence of deliberate defiance. Their weakness, resignation, resistance, and confusion were all viewed as indicators of incorrect demeanor which provoked further anger and rejection by the other members. New elements were continually added to the repertoire of torture. When people began to confess fantasies of escape, their legs were smashed with pieces of firewood to prevent the possibility. The two members who received death sentences were stabbed with knives and icepicks and finally strangled to death.

How could people behave so brutally toward their friends? Forced to participate in violence in the name of "comradely assistance," they transformed their anguish into frustration and anger toward their victim-comrades. Why, they wondered, were the victims unable to change their behavior and attitudes sufficiently so that the violence could stop? Unable to question the authority who ordered them to perform acts of violence against friends or the theory that justified their actions, they could question only the friends themselves. It was relatively easy at that point for their own fear, doubt, and confusion to be channeled into an anger that could be vented safely, even satiated, through physical violence against a dehumanized victim. Through such inverted emotional logic, the victims came to deserve their beatings and to "cause" their own deaths.

This behavior is a universal social phenomenon that goes far beyond Japanese society. A vast literature on scapegoating and blaming the victim has traced it in events large and small throughout the world. The reverse side of this universal process is taking the role of the victim.

Becoming a Victim

As the process of victimization cut more deeply into the ranks of strong, long-term members, Mori shifted attention from personal weakness to the style of leadership needed to advance the party. At group meetings, members were all asked to evaluate their own problems; these sessions provided an opportunity for sudden criticism of persons who until that moment had been regarded as strong, reliable members. Though the people who now became targets of criticism had better initial defenses than their predecessors, they also found themselves taking on the victim role and willingly playing out its rituals.

Uegaki Yasuhiro, the only Rengō Sekigun member who experienced a substantial degree of overt pressure to make a personal sōkatsu and lived to tell about it, has described the ambiguities of the process of becoming a victim at length in his autobiography. Uegaki's experience reveals that the mental process of becoming a victim was the mirror image of becoming a perpetrator of violence. Initially, victim and perpetrator were the same: group members trusting both their fellow members and the group's leadership, participating willingly in collective rituals. Gradually, the rituals polarized group members into two roles: accuser and victim.

Uegaki was never beaten or tied up, yet he had already begun to separate himself from those who criticized him. The criticism made him feel unfairly harassed, alienated, and resentful. These emotions in turn permitted him to differentiate his view of events from the official view. In contrast to the perpetrator, who had to suppress his private thoughts by reiterating the official explanation in order to avoid condemning his own behavior, the victim's grievances and isolation encouraged him to respond more naturally and objectively. Eventually, these discrepancies came out in his demeanor and interaction. He could no longer work cheerfully and wholeheartedly; depression slowed his movement and changed his expression. His honest responses sometimes revealed a lack of faith, and occasionally he even talked back to his critics. To the others, all of these behaviors were signs justifying further polarization and escalation of pressure against the victim. In Uegaki's case the process was very gradual, because both sides were really trying hard to prevent the polarization. Yet Uegaki feels as keenly as the other survivors that he would have become a victim if the purge had continued.

Endings

By late January the kyōsanshugika process was so completely out of control that it threatened to consume everyone. No one who had been ordered to make a sōkatsu had been able to do so to Mori's satisfaction, so there was still no model for success. At the same time, so much guilt had been aroused that no one could feel his own position was unassailable. There was no way to distinguish today's perpetrator of violence from tomorrow's victim. Eleven people had died, and one remained tied up in the snow, severely injured and awaiting inevitable death. There had been five victims from Sekigun and seven from Kakusa, eight men and four women. Sekigun had only four men left; Kakusa had seven men and six women. Three family groups had been divided by death.

The spiral of violence was finally broken in mid-February by a combination of factors. Like the original escalation of violence, the deescalation was also an ambiguous process: a gradual crumbling of authority and resolve rather than a clear decision to stop. Both the commitment of members to stay in the group and the ability of the leaders to direct the group and control the members changed rapidly once the situation began to unravel.

In early February, Mori and Nagata suddenly went off to Tokyo on business, leaving Sakaguchi in charge. Without the strong presence of Mori and Nagata, Rengō Sekigun lost some of its compelling ability to hold members in a reign of terror. One by one, members sent off on errands began to slip away. Although none of the members who left the group went to the police, the dragnet was closing on Rengō Sekigun. From November 1971, nine of the ten most wanted criminals in Japan were Sekigun and

Kakusa members, and seven of those on the list were with Rengō Sekigun. The police had lost their trail when they went into the mountains but by the beginning of February 1972 had picked it up again.

The growing danger of discovery kept the remaining Rengō Sekigun members on the move. A few days later the group learned from radio news broadcasts that Mori and Nagata had been arrested on their return to a campsite that the rest of the group had hastily abandoned just the day before. The remaining members eluded the police by hiking for two nights and a day over the top of the Japanese alps into Karuizawa, a popular resort on the other side of the mountains. One group was arrested almost immediately in the Karuizawa train station; the last five members, with the police in pursuit, barricaded themselves in the Asama Sansō mountain lodge. There, with the caretaker's wife as hostage, they held off several thousand riot police for ten days, until the police demolished the side of the building with a wrecking crane and took out the five fugitives and their hostage, unharmed. The purge only came to light after the siege had ended, as police tried to find out where the remaining members were.

Like any social event, the Rengō Sekigun purge was a complex combination of the unique inventions of its participants, social practices characteristic in their society, and universal social processes. It is all too easy to concentrate on the individuals who carried out the purge and their unique inventions and to overlook the broader social processes and patterns involved.

The Rengō Sekigun purge belongs to a large class of events, occurring throughout the world, in which groups of people inflict terrible brutality on their fellow human beings, masking their behavior through ingenious ideological constructions. Groups cling to such ideologies in spite of external evidence to the contrary (cognitive dissonance), and they may elaborate the ideology to blame the victims for their fate. The processes of scapegoating, deviant labeling, and becoming a victim are the same, whether the event is the holocaust, the My Lai massacre, the mistreatment of racial minorities, or the tiny Rengō Sekigun purge. To that extent, the purge could have happened anywhere, and it could have been committed by anybody.

This analysis has also examined the role of certain features of Japanese social organization in the dynamics of the purge: deference to formal authority and unwillingness to challenge it;

consensus decision-making procedures that carry high expectations of subsequent participation; indirect and ambiguous means of expressing dissent; and high levels of commitment and loyalty to the group.

Under normal circumstances, these social assumptions and practices keep Japanese society humming along smoothly and efficiently and reduce overt conflict within groups. Rengō Sekigun was like any other small Japanese group in its casual, unstudied use of these social practices. But within Rengō Sekigun there was a social conflict, as direct and severe as it is possible for a conflict among two dozen people to be. The members not only criticized each other verbally, they brutally beat, stabbed, and tortured one another until nearly half the group was dead.

The personal dynamics among the individual members of the group and the universal social-psychological processes to which we are all vulnerable might have sparked such an internal conflict in any society, but the characteristics of Japanese social organization gave it added momentum. The everyday features of Japanese social organization were used to initiate the purge, and they greatly exacerbated the conflict once it had begun. Indeed, they made it virtually impossible for the members to stop the process, even when their lives depended on it.

Notes

Research for this study was conducted with support from the Fulbright program and the Japan Endowment Fund, a gift of the government of Japan to the University of Hawaii. Takeshi Ishida kindly arranged for my affiliation with the Institute of Social Science at Tokyo University. My deepest thanks to these agencies and to the scholars, officials, and Rengō Sekigun participants and their associates who have assisted me.

1. The primary sources include six autobiographical books, numerous published statements and articles, the voluminous records of two group trials plus lengthy appeals, and interviews with survivors including a continuing series of prison interviews and correspondence with three central participants.

2. Despite the name, it had no official connection with the Japan Communist Party. Some of its members had previously been part of the pro-China "left-wing" faction that split from the JCP in 1966.

3. The parallel to Kakumei Sensen, Sekigun's support group, was Kakusa's Keihin Ampo Kyōtō.

4. Kojima was included in the beating because Nagata and Mori blamed her for having slept next to Katō and also because Mori thought Kojima was trying to present herself as a martyred heroine.

5. All except two followed the standard pattern of a demand for sōkatsu and escalating violence against a victim who finally weakened and died "from defeatism." The two exceptions began in the same manner but suddenly turned into kangaroo courts that collectively pronounced a death sentence on the victims and then carried it out.

References

Bandō Kunio. 1984. *Nagata Hiroko san e no tegami* (Letters to Nagata Hiroko). Tokyo: Sairyūsha.

Festinger, Leon. 1956. *When Prophecy Fails*. Minneapolis: University of Minnesota Press.

Lofland, John. 1969. *Deviance and Identity*. Englewood Cliffs, N.J.: Prentice-Hall.

Mori Tsuneo. 1984. *Jūgekisen to shukusei* (The shooting war and the purge). Tokyo: Shinchōsha.

Nagata Hiroko. 1982–1983. *Jūroku no bohyō* (Sixteen tombstones). 2 vols. Tokyo: Sairyūsha.

———. 1983. *Nagatoku: onna jiritsu o motomete* (Long unraveling: Searching for woman's self-reliance). Tokyo: Kōdansha.

Sakaguchi Hiroshi. 1972. "Shuki" [Notes]. In *Jinmin dokusai ni mukete* (Facing the dictatorship of the people), edited by Kanagawa-ken Iinkai. Tokyo: Nihon Kyōsantō (Kakumei saha).

Steinhoff, Patricia G. 1984. "Student Conflict." In *Conflict in Japan*, edited by Ellis Krauss, Thomas Rohlen, and Patricia G. Steinhoff. Honolulu: University of Hawaii Press.

———. 1988. "Tenkō and Thought Control." In *The Japanese and the World*, edited by Haruhiro Fukui and Gail Bernstein. London: Macmillan.

———. 1989. "Hijackers, Bombers, and Bank Robbers: Managerial Style in the Japanese Red Amy." *Journal of Asian Studies* 48 (4): 724–740.

———. 1991. *Nihon Sekigunha: shakaigakuteki monogatari* (Japan Red Army faction: a sociological story). Tokyo: Kawade Shobō Shinsha.

Uegaki Yasuhiro. 1984. *Heishitachi no Rengō Sekigun* (The Comrades' United Red Army). Tokyo: Sairyūsha.

Yomiuri Shinbun Osaka Honsha Shakaibu. 1972. *Rengō Sekigun* (United Red Army). Tokyo: Shiō Shuppansha.

Contributors

Theodore C. Bestor, associate professor of anthropology and a member of the East Asian Institute at Columbia University, has a Ph.D. from Stanford University. Most notable among his numerous publications is the prize-winning book, *Neighborhood Tokyo*. His latest work is *Tokyo's Marketplace: Custom and Trade in the Tsukiji Market*.

Diana Lynn Bethel, program associate at the Center for Japanese Studies at the University of Hawaii, is completing an anthropological dissertation on a Japanese institution for the elderly. Her publications include "Alienation and Reconnection in a Home for the Elderly."

Mary C. Brinton received her Ph.D. from the University of Washington and is now associate professor of sociology at the University of Chicago. Among her publications are "Gender Stratification in Contemporary Urban Japan," and *Women and the Economic Miracle: Gender and Work in Postwar Japan*.

Tomoko Hamada, who has a Ph.D. from the University of California, Berkeley, is associate professor of anthropology at the College of William and Mary. She is the author of *American Enterprise in Japan*, among other publications, and editor of *Asians and Asian Americans in Virginia*.

Takie Sugiyama Lebra, professor of anthropology at the University of Hawaii, holds a doctorate from the University of Pittsburgh. Among her latest publications are "Resurrecting Ancestral Charisma: Aristocratic Descendants in Contemporary Japan" and *Above the Clouds: Status Culture of the Modern Japanese Nobility*.

Jennifer Robertson, associate professor of anthropology and women's studies at the University of Michigan, has a Ph.D. from Cornell University. In addition to many articles, including "The Shingaku Woman: Straight from the Heart," she has authored *Natives and Newcomers: Making and Remaking a Japanese City* and is completing *Same Sex, Different Gender: The Cultural Politics of the Revue Theater in Japan*.

Robert J. Smith, past president of the Association for Asian Studies, is Goldwin Smith Professor of Anthropology and Asian Studies, Cornell University, where he received his Ph.D. His many influential books include *Japanese Society: Tradition, Self, and the*

Social Order and, with Ella Lury Wiswell, *The Women of Suye Mura.*

Patricia G. Steinhoff, who received her doctorate from Harvard University, is professor of sociology, and director of the Center for Japanese Studies at the University of Hawaii. She is author of, among other publications, "Hijackers, Bombers and Bank Robbers: Managerial Style in the Japanese Red Army" and *Tenkō: Ideology and Societal Integration in Prewar Japan.*

Index

Adoption: among the kazoku, 54
Age, 9–10, 12; and division and conflict in political leadership, 36–37; grades in, 115–116, 132. *See also* Hierarchy(ies): by age; Life course: age-(in)congruity and
Aging, 79; institutionalized, 8; of population, 110. *See also* Elderly
Aidagara, 9
Amae, 1; as weakness of revolutionary character, 207
Amaterasu of the palace shrine, 76n.12
Ancestors: the dead and, 12, 16, 129; national, 15; symbols and rites of, 16
Aniki, 172, 176
Anomaly: concubines as, 67; in the segregation rule, 66
Aotani Institution for the Elderly, The, 111. *See also* Elderly
Architecture, residential, 54, 62
Ariga, Kizaemon, 17
Aristocracy: the British, 75; modern, 6; reorganized, 51; Tokyo resettlement of, 54. See also *Kazoku* (the nobility)
Ariyoshi, Sawako, 110
Arrow, Kenneth, 91
Asagawa, Y., 188n.10
Atsumi, R., 185
Authority, 24, 113, 131; acquiescence/ deference to, 212–213, 222
Azumi, Koya, 91

Ba, 5
Bachnik, Jane, 16
Bandō, Kunio, 214
Banquet: neighborhood festival and, 33–34; seating arrangement at, 33–34

Beardsley, Richard K., ix
Befu, Harumi, 16, 17, 114, 163n.7
Benedict, Ruth, 110
Bestor, Theodore, 6, 8, 14, 45
Bethel, Diana, 7
Body(ies), natural and public, 70
Bon Odori, 31
Boundary(ies): claimed by the mikoshi, 35; of communities, 25–26; of domestic space, 62; insider/outsider, 26, 132, 149–150, 162; of *kami/shimo*, 63; of *omote/oku*, 63, 64; of public and private domains, 117–118, 131, 171; redrawn, 30. See also *Omote/Ura*; Space; Space/Time; *Uchi/Soto*
Bourdieu, Pierre, 73
Brinton, Mary, 10, 11, 14, 79, 80, 91, 92
Brown, L. Keith, 17
Buddhism: Buddhist altar, 12, 129–130; and memorial tablets *(ihai)*, 129; and temples, 75n.9. *See also* Ancestors
Bunke. See Dōzoku
Business: multinational, 8; in the neighborhood, 26, 27, 28. See also *Keiretsu; Kogaisha;* Overseas investment

Campbell, Ruth, 110
Career: predictability of, 11; changes in, 142, 145, 156. *See also* Employment; Labor market; Life course
Chaperonage, 59
Cherlin, Andrew, 101
Child(ren): and childbirth, 99–100, 101; overseas, 163n.2. *See also* Education; Life course
Chō, 6. *See also* Neighborhood(s)

Chōkai, 6, 29, 31, 32, 36, 37, 39;
    defined as a quasi-administrative
    neighborhood association, 26. *See
    also* Neighborhood(s)
Christmas cake, 80, 93, 100n.1
"Civilization and Enlightenment," 62,
    74n.3. *See also* Westernization of the
    elite
Clark, Rodney, 91, 140
Class(es): marginal, 25, 43; old mid-
    dle, new middle, 25–26, 28; of
    residential geography, 55; social,
    6; upper, 54; upper-middle, 57, 60.
    See also Aristocracy; Elite; Hier-
    archy; Kazoku (the nobility); Nobil-
    ity
Cognitive dissonance, 207, 222
Cohn, Bernard, 24
Coleman, Samuel, 99
Collier, J. F., 170
Commoners, 51
Communist Party (Japan), 196, 199,
    223n.2
Community: creation of, 29; develop-
    ment of, 131; events in, 32; face-to-
    face, 23, 27; factions of, 24; mar-
    ginal members of, 25; mutual aid in,
    27; symbolic expressions of, 23; as
    symbol of communal survival, 30.
    See also Neighborhood(s)
Communization. See *Kyōsanshugika*
Competition between neighborhoods,
    35–36, 39. See also *Mikoshi*
Concubine(s), 67
Confinement, spatial, 56
Conflict, 24–25, 223; with construction
    laborers, 42–43; between genera-
    tions in local politics, 36–41;
    between the neighborhood and
    government, 29; within the neigh-
    borhood, 31, 36; between the old
    and new middle classes, 43–44
Consensus procedures, 206, 210–211,
    215, 223
Constitution of 1889, 51
Cornell, John, 17
Corrigan, P., 186n.2
Court nobles, 51

Daimyō, 51; *kazoku,* 51, 53; the post-
    Meiji economic condition of, 74;
    yashiki, 56
Dalby, L., 176
Dansei(-teki), 167
Davidoff, Leonore, 75
Death, 12; by defeatism, 207–209,
    211–212, 215; elements of, 200–203;
    end of, 221–222; at institution for
    elderly, 128–130. *See also* Ancestors;
    Funerals; *Kyōsanshugika*
Deben, 175. *See also* Lesbian(ism)
De Lauretis, T., 166, 182
Denjōbito, 63. See also *Jige*
Divorce, 14, 96–97
Domesticity: as a source of power, 75
Dore, Ronald, 1, 6
Dōseiai, 175, 176–177, 188n.13. *See also*
    Lesbian(ism)
Double occupancy, 68–70
Douglas, Mary, 70
Dōzoku, 17; main house/branch house
    (honke/bunke), 16–17
Dyarchy, 49, 70–73; reproduction of,
    73; of symbolic hegemony and
    politico-economic domination, 72

Edo, 24; Castle, 51. *See also* Tokyo
Education: and age-congruity, 90;
    child's, 11, 137, 148, 149, 153; and
    educators as stakeholders, 100;
    enrollment in, 87; and irreversibility
    of leaving school, 90; and labor
    market, 86–87, 90–93; as prepara-
    tion for marriage, 86, 87; the system
    of, 85; and women's life course, 85,
    86–90. *See also* Life course
Elderly, 12; birthday parties and, 116–
    117; coresidence and, 110, 112;
    homes/institutions for, 110–111;
    institutionalization of, 110; and
    marriage, 125–126; social integra-
    tion and, 121; social networks
    among, 116, 118; social stigma of
    institutionalization and, 112, 131;
    social units at institution for, 117–
    118; work tasks of, 121–122. See also
    Obasuteyama

Elias, Norbert, 70
Elite: hereditary, 49, 52, 69, 73; the ascribed, 71; the former, 56; the private, kinship base of, 69
Emperor, 51; the Heisei, 15; the hidden, 76; the Shōwa, 15, 73, 76–77; as a single sovereign, 52; surrogacy for, 71. *See also* Imperial House; Royalty
Employment: changes in over life course, 142; life(long/time), 141–142, 145–146. *See also* Education; Labor market; Life course
Enka, 116
Enryo, 1
Enthronement, the Heisei emperor's, 15
Equal Employment Opportunity Law, 101. *See also* Gender
Evans, Robert, Jr., 90

Factions: in companies, 150–151, 161; leadership in, 25; in local politics, 36, 37. *See also* Community; Conflict
Family(ies), 7, 8; business, 17; discourses of, 132; and intimacy, 113, 120. *See also* Household(s)
Featherman, David, 81
Feinberg, Richard, 49, 69
Feminism/feminists, 3, 18n.5, 185, 186, 196, 198, 202. *See also* Lesbian(ism)
Festinger, Leon, 207
Festival(s), 27; assignments in, 32; folk-dance in, 31; neighborhood's annual, 24; of shitamachi, 56; as symbolic of status distinctions, 33–34. See also *Matsuri*
Filial piety: Confucian ethic of, 110, 112; elderly and, 109. *See also* Elderly
Foreigner(s), 62; encounter with, 8
Foucault, M., 166
Fūfu, 177. *See also* Lesbian(ism); *Ome (no kankei)*
Fujimura-Fanselow, Kumiko, 86
Fukazawa, Shichirō, 110
Fuku-sanji, 149
Fukushima, S., 177, 178

Funerals: communal help at, 27; funerary donation for, 129; the Shōwa emperor's, 15. *See also* Death

Gakushuin, 54; attendance in, 59; subculture of, 57
Gaman, 123
Geertz, Clifford, 3
Geijutsu, 171
Gender, 7, 11–12: and conflicts with assigned, 183–184; discourses of, 184–185; distinction between sex and gender (roles), 166–167; hierarchy in, 15; ideology of, 165; male/female, 10, 184, 187n.4; negotiation of, 184; role division by, 14, 33; secondary, 167, 173; socio-historical construction of, 166–167; stereotypes of, 167; as taught, 183. *See also* Lesbian(ism); Sex/Sexuality
Generations: continuity and discontinuity in, 12, 14, 16; and division of labor, 33
Genkan, 114
Geta bako, 117, 118
Giddens, Anthony, 5, 49, 72
Giri, 1
Go-kentō, 154
"Good wife, wise mother," 171, 173, 179, 181, 186; as state-sanctioned gender model, 172; Takarazuka Revue as alternative to, 184. *See also* Gender; Sex/Sexuality; Takarazuka (Music) Academy
Government(s), 27; branch office of the ward, 29, 31; and *Chōkai*, 27; municipal, ward, or *ku*, 25, 29, 30, 58; officials as outsiders, 26; and Shintō, 32; Tokyo metropolitan, 30
Gōruden konbi, 176

Hachiarai, 33, 34. *See also* Banquet
Haibokushi, 208. *See also* Death: by defeatism; *Kyōsanshugika*
Hair, symbolism of, 179–180. See also *Moga*
Hakama, 169, 181
Hamabata, Matthews, 16

Hamada, Tomoko, 8, 10, 11, 141
Hamlet, 25
Hanayome-dōgu, 152
Hanpei, 52
Haring, Douglas G., ix
Hashimoto, Masanori, 91, 189n.21
Hattori, Y., 176
Havens, T., 181
Hayden, Ilse, 70
Heimin, 51. *See also* Commoners
Heisei Group, 135. See also *Keiretsu*
Heisei (the period), 14
Hendry, Joy, 18n.3
Hentai seiri, 178–179
Hierarchy(ies): by age,113, 114–115,
  119–120, 132; within groups, 197;
  and health status, 126; (inter-)
  corporate, 135; internal, of Takara-
  zuka troupes, 168–169; lateral, 69;
  multilayered, 8; reversal of, 72, 76;
  seating of, 33; spatial representation
  of, 49; tri-dimensional, 62–68
Hogan, Dennis, 81, 87
Home: for the elderly, 7–8. *See also*
  Family(ies); Household; Residence
Honke/Bunke. See *Dōzoku*
Honsha, 135, 139. *See also* Business;
  Internationalization/Multinationali-
  zation
Household(s), 7, 26, 32; the head of,
  68, 69. See also *Dōzoku; Ie*
House of Peers, 52
Hsu, Francis, 17
Human resource management. *See*
  Personnel management

Identity: residents' sentiments toward,
  30
Ie, 132, ancestors of, 15; the legally
  obsolescent, 50; perpetuation of, 17;
  society of, 16; succession of, 16; the
  survival of the, 15
Iemoto, 17, 18n.6; aristocratic, 72
Ihai. See Buddhism: Buddhist altar
Imamura, Shōhei, 110
Imōto, 172, 176
Imperial House: the kazoku's duty to,
  52; the landownership of, 62

Imperial palace: shrine, 70; the
  acreage of, 62
Inoue, Yasushi, 110
Inside/Outside. *See* Boundary(ies);
  Space; Space/Time; *Uchi/Soto*
Interior/Exterior, 12. *See* Space/Time;
  Uchi/Soto
Internationalists, 136, 155, 157
Internationalization/multinationaliza-
  tion, 8, 14, 135–136, 139, 158;
  "internal," 155; and personal net-
  works, 161
Inukai, Tomoko, 56
Itami, Hiroyuki, 163n.10

Jige, 63
Jikohihan, 199
Jinrikisha, 58
Jirei, 147, 152, 154
Johnson, Erwin, 17
Josei(-teki), 167, 187n.6
Joyū, 170, 187n.10
Jūtaku, 79

Kabuki, 11, 170, 172, 187n.7
Kaigai: -*bu,* 155; -*jigyō-bu,* 158; -*kikoku-*
  shijo, 137
Kaigai-kogaisha. See Overseas invest-
  ment
Kaigai-shukkō, 136, 146, 155, 159, 162.
  See also Personnel transfer(s)
Kakusa, 208, 210, 214, 215: back-
  ground of, 196; consciousness-
  raising technique with, 198; feminist
  position/women's liberation in, 196,
  198, 202; purge victims in, 221;
  sexual concerns of, 202. See also
  Kyōsanshugika; Nagata, Hiroko;
  Rengō Sekigun (United Red Army)
Kami/Shimo, 63, 64. *See also* Bounda-
  ry(ies); *Omote/Ura;* Space; *Uchi/Soto;*
  Vertical opposition
Kamura, K., 181, 182
Kanpai, 154
Kanto Earthquake (of 1923), 13, 25,
  54, 55
Kasahara, M., 175–176
Katai, 120

Kawahara, Y., 174, 178
Kawashima, Takeyoshi, 16
Kazoku (the family), 113. *See also*
 Family(ies)
Kazoku (the nobility), 6, 7; the crea-
 tion of, 51; households, 53; *kunkō-,*
 51; in the national hierarchy, 51; the
 number of, 52; privileges and duties
 of, 52; term for, 50
Keesing, Roger, 3
Keiretsu, 8, 11, 17, 135, 139–141, 144,
 158; hierarchical order of, 161; types
 of, 140
Keith, Jennie, 115
Kekkon, 79. *See also* Marriage
Kessler, S., 166
Kido, Kōichi, 76n.13
Kinship: fictive, 113; terms/terminol-
 ogy of, 114–115, 119, 170–171, 172–
 176. *See also* Family(ies)
Kitano, Seiichi, 17
Kitaoji, Hironobu, 16
Kōbata, Yoshiko, 56
Kobayashi, Ichizō, 165, 169, 175, 180,
 183; and choice of nomenclature,
 170–172; and creation of Takara-
 zuka, 169–170; and denaturalization
 of *otokoyaku,* 181; and gender con-
 struction, 172–173. *See also* Takara-
 zuka (Music) Academy
Kobayashi, Tetsuya, 163n
Kodama, Kōta, 62
Kogai-no buka, 152
Kogaisha, 135, 139, 160; and relation
 with parent company, 135, 136,160,
 162
Kōhai, 169
Koike, Kazuo, 85, 141
Kojiki: ancestor gods in, 53
Kojima, Kiyoshi, 163n.3
Komazaka, Y., 175
Kondo, Dorinne, 6
Kosei, 167–168
Kōzoku, 51. *See also* Royalty
Ku, 6; redrawing the boundaries of,
 55. *See also* Ward
Kuge, 51; *-kazoku,* 51; pauperized, 53.
 See also Court nobles

Kumagai, Fumie, 99, 101, 110
Kumichō/fukukumichō, 168
Kumin Matsuri, 31, 32, 33. *See also*
 Festival(s); *Matsuri*
Kure, H., 188n.13
Kurō, 157
Kyōiku, 79. *See also* Education
Kyōsanshugika: ambiguity of, 201–202;
 beatings as method in, 205; con-
 sciousness-raising/group criticism
 in, 200, 201, 204; fighting spirit in,
 201, 208, 219; introduction of, 198–
 199; moral discipline/self-improve-
 ment in, 203–206; no-exit rule in,
 202–203, 209, 216–217; participa-
 tory violence in, 206–207, 208, 215–
 216, 219; and sexuality, 202. *See also*
 Kakusa; Mori, Tsuneo; Nagata,
 Hiroko; Rengō Sekigun (United
 Red Army); *Sōkatsu;* Victims

Labor market: and gender, 91–93,
 100; internal 85, 91–92, 100; (ir)re-
 versibility of participation in, 92–93,
 100; recruitment in, 91. *See also*
 Education; Employment; Gender
Lakoff, George, 112
Land ownership: of the hereditary
 elite, 60–62; the postwar loss in, 62
Lanham, Betty, 110
Lateral opposition, 63
Lebra, Takie, x, 50, 52, 54, 64, 72, 93,
 99, 115
Legitimacy: bestowed by tradition, 44;
 of the community, 24; competition
 for, 24
Lesbian(ism): *butch-femme,* 175, 176,
 184; girls' schools and, 176; subcultural styles of, 184; and Takarazuka *otokoyaku,* 178–180; term in
 Japan, 176; types of, 176–178. See
 also *Otokoyaku;* Takarasiennes;
 Takarazuka (Music) Academy
Life course: age-(in)congruity and, 83,
 90, 93, 97–99, 100; of American
 women, 84–85, 101; changes in, 84,
 101–102; individual(ism) and, 82,
 85, 96; institutions and, 80, 100–

102; (ir)reversibility and, 83, 90, 92–93, 96–98, 100; men's, 81; variance and, 83, 100; woman's, 10–11. *See also* Age; Education; Employment; Labor market; Marriage; Stakeholder(s)

Linhart, Sepp, 5

Lofland, John, 202, 212

Luhrmann, T. M., 76n.13

Machi-zukuri, 29

McLaughlin, Steven, 84, 87, 90

McLendon, James, 93

Maeda, Daisaku, 110

Maid(s): escorted by, 56; head, 70; kitchen, 67, 74n.7; lower, 63; upper, 63. *See also* Servant(s)

Male/Female, 10; in power relationship, 74; as servants, 66. *See also* Gender; Sex/Sexuality

Marginality: in class, 25; spatial, 66, 67. *See also* Anomaly

Marriage: age-congruity and, 97–99; age variance in, 97; and (hetero)sexuality, 185; married students, 14; and motherhood in female adulthood, 173–174; the nobility and, 54, 59; reversibility of, 96–97; of Takarasiennes, 172, 173. *See also* Elderly; Labor market; *Mukoyōshi*

Marxism/Marxists, 3

Master family: as *kami,* 63

Matsuri: aki-, 31; as a dramatic symbol of communal identity, 32; Kumin, 32. *See also* Festival(s); *Mikoshi*

Maturation: sexual, 11; and adulthood, 11. *See also* Career; Life course

Meiji: Civil Code and gender/sex norms in, 171, 175, 177, 185; government and education in, 188n; leaders in, 51; period of, 14

Meiji Restoration, 13, 51, 74n.2; contributions to, 52

Meiwaku, 123

Meyer, John, 83

Mikoshi, 32; children's, 33; in competition, 36, 39; conflict with laborers over, 42–43; construction in local campaign, 39–41; financial cost for

constructing, 40; the metaphorical "carrier of the," 76n.13; in procession, 34, 35; as symbol, 34. *See also* Festival(s); *Matsuri;* Shintō; Shrine

Minoura, Yasuko, 163n.2

Minyō, 116

Miya, 6, 50. *See also* Shrine

Miyahara, Kojiro, 91

Miyake, Y., 181

Miyamoto-chō, 6, 7, 8, 14, 23; composition of, 26–29; external and internal relations of, 24–25, 29–31, 36–44; history of, 25–26; traditions/traditionalism of, 24. See also *Chō; Chōkai;* Community; *Matsuri; Mikoshi;* Neighborhood(s)

Mizukawa, Y., 176

Mochizuki, M., 175

Modell, John, 83, 101

Modernization: and life course, 81–82

Moga, 174, 179; hair symbolism of, 179–180

Monarchy, 72, 73

Monzeki: for illegitimate children, 75

Moore, S., 173

Morgan, S. Philip, 81–82, 99

Mori, Tsuneo: arrest of, 222; ideological interpretations of, 197, 203, 205–206, 207, 208, 211, 212, 213, 215, 216, 219, 220; *(Rengō) Sekigun* leader, 196, 197, 198, 199, 200, 201, 202, 207, 210, 221

Mukō sangen, ryō donari, 118. *See also* Elderly: social networks among

Mukoyōshi, 37

Murakami, Yasusuke, 1979

Musumeyaku, 165, 169, 170, 172, 176, 183; postwar changes in, 182. *See also* Takarazuka (Music) Academy: actors

Muteikōshugi, 177

Nagata, Hiroko: arrest of, 222; as kakusa leader, 196, 197, 198, 200, 206, 207, 208, 210, 213, 214, 216, 221

Nakamura, Hachirō, 29

Nakane, Chie, 5, 16

Nakano, Takashi, 17

Nakata, Yoshifumi, 86
Neighborhood(s): associations of, 6, 29, 57; dispute in, 31; hallways as, 117–118; insignificance of, 57; merger of, 30; as a recent administrative creation, 25; Tokyo, 23; urban, 26. See also *Chō; Chōkai;* Community; Elderly; Festival(s); *Mikoshi*
Nihonjinron, 4, 18n.2
Nimaime, 168, 187n.2
Nishiyama, Misako, 102
Niwa, Fumio, 110
Nobility: the abolished, 50; the cultural survival of, 73; five ranks of, 52. See also Aristocracy; Elite; *Kazoku* (the nobility)
Noguchi, Paul, 11, 141
Nolte, S., 171, 181, 188n.12
Norbeck, Edward, 115, 132, 175

Obasuteyama, 7, 112, 131. See also Elderly
Occupations: self-employed merchants and artisans, 25–26
Ochūgen, 148
Oharasan. See Concubine(s)
Ohikizuri garment, 53, 57
Okama, 176
Ome (no kankei), 176, 177–178. See also Lesbian(ism)
Omote/Oku, 63
Omote/Ura, 5, 64
On, 1, 110
Onabe, 176
Onēsan, 172
Onna(-rashii), 167
Onnagata, 170, 172, 187n.9
Onnayaku, 182
Opposition: to leader/group, 212; in Rengō Sekigun committees, 213–215
Oseibo, 148
Osenbetsu, 148
Oshiroi, 179
Otoko(-rashii), 167
Otokoyaku, 165, 169, 170, 172, 176, 181; as exemplary female, 185; and hair, 179–180; in lesbian relations,

178, 179; and male gender, 182, 183. See also Takarazuka (Music) Academy
Otōsan, 171
Otsugi, 63; the meaning of, 74n.6
Outcaste, 51
Overseas assignment. See *Kaigai;* Personnel transfer(s)
Overseas investment: in developed countries, 138; in developing countries, 137; history of, 137–138; joint ventures in, 137; in manufacturing, 137–138, 155, 158
Oyabun-kobun, 172
Ozawa, II., 175, 188n.11

Paternalism, 170, 171
Peerage, 52. See also *Kazoku* (the nobility); Nobility
Peers' clubhouse, 60
Pelzel, John, 16
Perrot, Roy, 74n.4
Personnel management, 135, 139; human resources development in, 154–155. See also Personnel transfer(s)
Personnel transfer(s): centrality and hierarchy of, 159–160; dilemmas of, 147; and life course, 144; and personal connections, 150–151, 152, 153–154, 158; as rationalization measure, 145; reasons for, 142; *Shukkō* system in, 135, 141, 143–144, 158, 159, 161; suddenness of, 152; *Tenzoku* system in, 135, 141, 142–143, 159
Pflugfelder, G., 188n.13
Plath, David, 11, 82, 112, 116, 141
Power, 3; at institution for the elderly, 123–125; in local politics, 36, 37; political, 24; of subordinates, 76. See also Authority
Privacy, the lack of, 59
Promotion: competition for, 149–151; seniority wages and, 150

Racism, 8
Ranking, of gates and doors, 68. See also Hierarchy(ies); Stratification

Red Army, The. *See* Rengō Sekigun;
Sekigun
Reischauer, Haru, 61
Religion, separation of the state and,
15, 32. *See also* Ancestors; Buddhism; Shintō; Shrine; State
Rengō Sekigun (United Red Army),
195, 100, 201, 209; beating/torture
in, 195, 204, 205, 207; central
committee(s) of, 210, 213–215; as
closed system, 216–217; commit-
ment/responsibility to, 217; followers' acquiescence to purge in, 212–
213; hierarchy in, 197; leadership
in, 210; merger in, 196, 197–198,
199; purge in, 195, 203, 209, 222;
newcomers, socialization in, 215–
216; and police, 221–222; rivalry
between groups/leaders in, 205;
sexual behavior/confessions in, 204,
205; unification ritual of, 197–198.
See also Kakusa; *Kyōsanshugika;* Mori,
Tsuneo; Nagata, Hiroko; Sekigun;
Victim(s)
Residence: of the elite, 55
Resident(s), 7, 26, 30; newcomers and,
33. *See also* Boundary(ies); *Uchi/Soto*
Rice, class difference in the weight of,
74–75n.7
Robben, Antonius, 73n.1
Robertson, Jennifer, 11, 12, 13, 176,
185
Rohlen, Thomas, 91, 110, 115, 116,
132
Rōjin mondai, 110
Rosenbaum, James, 91
Rosuke, 127
Royalty: as a lineage group, 51; the
British, 70
Russo-Japanese War (1904–5): as a
turning-point of the kazoku lifestyle,
53
Ryōsai, kenbo. See "Good wife, wise
mother"

Sakai, Miiko, 61
Samurai, 51; ethic of, 213. *See also*
Vassal(s)

Sanmaime, 168
Sarariiman, 28
Schneider, David, 17n.1
Schwartz, Barry, 49, 69
Segregation, vertical, 66. *See also* Sex/
Sexuality
Seidensticker, Edward, 6, 55, 58
Seito, 173
Sekigun, 13; background of, 195–196;
purge victims in, 221. *See also*
Kakusa; Mori, Tsuneo; Rengō
Sekigun (United Red Army)
Senpai, 169
Servant(s): a pool of, 58; ambivalence
toward, 71; as escort, 59; manage-
rial male, 64; as *shimo,* 63
Sex/Sexuality: distinction between,
166; and harassment of maids, 75;
and heterosexuality versus homosex-
uality, 18; Japanese female and, 165,
185; lesbian alliances and, 12;
modes of, 184; segregation and,
11–12, 66. *See also* Gender; Lesbian-
(ism)
Shataku, 153
Shida, A., 185
Shikitari, 120
Shimada, Haruo, 85
Shima-nagashi, 151. *See also* Personnel
transfer(s)
Shimo, 63. See also *Kami/Shimo*
Shinjū, 174
Shinkeishitsu, 177, 188n.16
Shintō: rites, 15, 32; god hidden in the
shrine and, 76. *See also* Shrine
Shitamachi, 6, 26, 28; Asakusa in, 56;
and neighborliness, 58; and
yamanote, 6, 55, 74. *See also* Tokyo
Shizoku, 51
Shōjo, 11, 173–175, 180–181, 185,
188n.11; inversion of, 175. *See also*
Gender; Maturation; Sex/Sexuality;
Takarasiennes
Shōwa (the period), 14
Shrine, 6, 25, 26; parish in, 25, 32, 36;
tutelary deity in, 34, 35
Shūdan Seikatsu, 123
Shukkō. See Personnel transfer(s)

Shūshin Koyō, 93
Silverberg, M., 188n.12
Silverman, K., 166
Skinner, Kenneth, 141
Smith, Robert, 16
Sōgō-sōsha, 155
Sōkatsu, 199, 201, 204, 205, 209, 215, 218, 219. See also *Kyōsanshugika; Rengō Sekigun* (United Red Army); Victim(s)
Sokkin, 76n.13
Solidarity, communal, 34
Sorensen, Aage, 103n.2
Soto. See *Uchi/Soto*
Space: legendary, 7; demarcations of, 7; design in, 54; domestic, 12, 50; hierarchy of, 7, 33; private/public, 7, 50; residential, 54; seclusion by, 13; terminology of, 6, 49–50; as tropes, 6
Space/Time: boundaries 5–14, 16; zones and, 5, 8, 9
Stakeholder(s), 80, 100, 103n.2; American family as, 84–85; educators as, 100; employers as, 92, 100; Japanese family/parents as, 85, 86; social institutions and, 82–83; state as, 85; women's living arrangements and, 93, 96. See also Life course
Stanislavski System, 172
State, the, 186n.2: and the family system, 165; and female gender/sexuality, 171, 174, 181, 182, 185; and hair symbolism, 179–180; and idealized heterosexual relations, 176; and religion, 15
Steiner, Kurt, 45
Steinhoff, Patricia, 12, 13, 199
Stereotype(s), 4; and stereotyping, 17n.2
Stranger(s), 8
Stratification: within the neighborhood, 33. See also Class(es); Hierarchy(ies)
Subsidiary(ies): overseas, 8, 135, 137, 138. See also *Keiretsu; Kogaisha*
Subversion: without destroying the order, 72; of filial symbolism, by

Takarasiennes and fans, 171; and inversion of shōjo image, 175; and secondary gender, by Takarasiennes, 173; subversive potential of Takarazuka, 186. *See also* Lesbian-(ism); Takarasiennes; Takarazuka (Music) Academy
Sugita, M., 176
Surrogacy: institutionalized, 70; in conducting religious rites, 70–71; by subordinates, 72
Symbol(s): manipulation of, 7; *matsuri* as, 32, 44; *mikoshi* as, 35; neighborhood hall as, 30; processing, 3; and social reality, 2–3; and status distinctions, 33–34; and symbolic expression of community, 23; and symbolism of Takarazuka, 165; of traditionalism, 27. *See also* Community; Festival(s); Hair, symbolism of; Kinship; *Matsuri; Mikoshi*

Tachi(yaku), 176
Tachibanaki, Toshiaki, 142
Taihō Kaisha/America, 135, 144. See also *Keiretsu;* Overseas investment; Personnel transfer(s); Subsidiary(ies)
Taishō (the period), 14
Taishū engeki, 165
Takano, M., 188n.11
Takarasiennes, 165, 179, 182; and assignment of secondary genders, 167, 171, 183–184; and inversion of *shōjo* image, 175; and marriage, 172; and rejection of gender roles, 171, 173. *See also* Gender; Lesbian(ism); *Musumeyaku; Otokoyaku*; Sex/Sexuality
Takarazuka (Music) Academy, 11, 167, 168–169, 170, 180, 181; applicants to, 168; creation of, 169–170; fans of, 174, 179, 181; and lesbian relations, 178, 184; modern and erotic phase in, 179; postwar revival of, 182; Revue, 11, 165, 168, 170, 174, 180, 181, 182; senpai-kōhai relations, 169; troupes, 168–169. *See*

also Gender; *Musumeyaku; Otokoyaku;*
Sex/Sexuality
Tamura, T., 176, 177
Tanabe, S., 175
Tanaka, Kazuko, 87
Tanin, 115
Tanshin funin, 10, 152, 158; numbers
of, 136–137. *See also* Personnel
transfer(s)
Tarai-mawashi, 151
Tenugui, 32,40
Tenzoku. See Personnel transfer(s)
Theater, all-female. *See* Takarazuka
(Music) Academy
Time schedule, 9. *See also* Space/Time
Titus, David, 76n.13
Tobin, Joseph, 116
Togawa, S., 176
Tokugawa: regime, 56; ruler in, 72–
73; Shogunate, 170
Tokyo, 23, 24, 51; the central mer-
chant quarter in, 26; kazoku concen-
tration in, 54; the 1945 air raid in,
55
Tomioka, M., 188n.14
Tonosama, 50
Torture. See *Kyōsanshugika;* Rengō
Sekigun (United Red Army); Vic-
tim(s)
Tradition: the continuity of, 14; "dis-
tinct," 30; and modernity, 23; as a
usable past, 24
Traditionalism, 14; meaning of, 24;
and traditionalistic activities, 31
Transportation, private, 58, 59
Tsukiai, 57; class-bound, 58
Tsurumi, Yoshi, 163n.3
Tsuya, Noriko, 103n.6

Uchi/Soto, 5, 16, 64; boundary in, 8. *See
also* Boundary(ies); *Kami/Shimo;
Omote/Ura;* Space; Space/Time
Ueda, Y., 169, 173
Uegaki, Yasuhiro, 211, 216
Uhlenberg, Peter, 99
Upham, Frank, 91
Ushijima, Y., 176
Ushiogi, Morikazu, 91

Vance, C., 166
Vassal(s), 51; lower ranking, 69
Vernon, Raymond, 163n.5
Vertical opposition, 49, 62, 64, 67. *See
also* Hierarchy(ies)
Victim(s): blaming the, 208–209, 219–
220, 222; and perpetrators, polariza-
tion of, 218–221; and process of
victimization, 220–221; of Rengō
Sekigun purge, 209, 210; separa-
tion/rejection of, 218–219
Vincinus, M., 188n.13
Violence. See *Kyōsanshugika;* Rengō Se-
kigun (United Red Army); Victim(s)

Wada, T., 175
Wagatsuma, Hiroshi, 6
Wakiyaku, 169
Ward, 6; assembly in, 30; office of, 31.
See also Government(s); *Ku*
Watanabe, Y., 99
Watsuji, Tetsuro, 9
Westernization of the elite, 53
White, Merry, 155, 163n.2
Women: confinement of, 56–57; Japa-
nese and American, 10, 14; mar-
ried, 59; in matsuri as a dancing
troupe, 33; and power, 75. *See also*
Gender; Life course; Male/Female;
Sex/Sexuality
World War II, 26, 54, 59: postwar
property taxes in, 71; prewar (sen-
zen) -postwar (sengo), 13, 15

Yamamoto, George K., x
Yamanote, 7, 28, 55; the heart of, 56;
lifestyle in, 57; taste for, 60. See also
Shitamachi
Yano, Christine, 18
Yasuda, T., 177
Yōgo Rōjin Hōmu, 111
Yoshihara, Hideki, 163n.3
Yoshitake, T., 175
Yoshiwara, R., 178
Yuasa, Yasuo, 9

Zachō, 168
Zaibatsu, 140, 163n.6